Praise for *Tension: The Energy of Innovation*

"The authors clearly understand the balance between Six Sigma perfection and the uncertainty and confusion inherent at the beginning of any new creative project. Using the word 'tension' is a great way of describing this dynamic balance, for we have to hold contradictory and competing ideas simultaneously while moving through the lifecycle of any product. *Tension* is set apart not only for the deep insight of Chris and Mitch, but also for their personal recounting of the failures and successes they encounter on their own journeys. Tension contains very practical wisdom to guide leaders to move towards, and embrace, creative tension."

— **ED CATMULL**
Co-founder of Pixar Animation Studios,
President, Walt Disney and Pixar Animation Studios and
New York Times bestselling author of *Creativity, Inc.*

"Innovation is the key to long-term organizational survival. In this well-researched book, the Wasden brothers create the map of where innovation comes from (tension); how it works in our brains, lives and organizations; and, most importantly, how to unleash it both in ourselves and in our organizations. *Tension* is an important read and a great confidence builder for both entrepreneurs just starting their journey and leaders of established companies."

— **NEAL PATTERSON**
Co-founder, Chairman and Chief Executive Officer, Cerner,
Ranked #8 Most Innovative Company in America by *Forbes*

"The accelerating pace of change in healthcare challenges us to continue to build our managerial and leadership toolkits—to be more agile, to use more gears of mindfulness so that we can lead successfully, and to tap innovation throughout our organizations. *Tension* provides a succinct, highly readable and engaging ride through the innovation cycle with lessons for all!"

— **VIVIAN LEE**
Chief Executive Officer, University of Utah Healthcare,
Dean of the School of Medicine

"This book is amazing. Truly amazing. I read constantly but especially books that are relevant to my personal or business life. This book is both. I'm able to read most books relatively quickly because a lot of the content is repetitive or just filler. Not so with *Tension*. After reading the first few chapters I started over and underlined the parts I wanted to refer to again later. There is hardly a page that doesn't have my marks.

At the beginning I thought that I'm glad I'm reading this book even though I've started hundreds of businesses and should intuitively already know what you're writing about. After a few chapters I then thought I need to make it mandatory reading for all my direct reports. After having read the entire book I'm convinced it's not only a must read for any startup, new company or entrepreneur but it's a must read for EVERYONE in business who wants to remain viable and grow. ESPECIALLY those who are in industries undergoing significant change. I'll also make sure all of my nine children read this book. I just wish I could get everyone of influence around them to read it too.

I am particularly impressed with how Chris and Mitch make *Tension* implementable. I could go on and on about the figures, the summary points and questions at the end of each chapters. It's truly a HOW TO on innovation."

— **DAN TASSET**
Founder, Chairman and Chief Executive Officer, Nueterra, innovative healthcare company with over 100+ facilities worldwide and an industry leader in the patient-to-consumer revolution

"Chris Wasden is a leader in healthcare innovation and this book is a must read for anyone looking to advance innovation and harness tension to fuel their creative genius."

— **JOE RANDOLPH,**
President and Chief Executive Officer, The Innovation Institute

"*Tension* is a masterpiece. . . . *Tension* provides an approach that can be used by organizations both big and small to increase their innovative capabilities and capacities."

— **MATTEO RIZZI**
General Partner, SBT Venture Capital

"*Tension* provides the road map of how to release the genius in you that is innovative."

— **CHESTER ELTON**
New York Times bestselling author of *The Carrot Principle, All In* and *What Motivates Me*

"*Tension* clarifies the way to balance efficiency and innovation in an approach that is actionable. In the digital economy it is critical for executives to find that balance."
— **JOHN GEYER**
Senior Vice President and Head of Innovation, MetLife

"The Wasden brothers provide the path for personal and organizational success; how to truly think, use tension creatively and balance the need for routine with the need for meaningful change. . . . This book is a good ride and a great read!"
— **PATRICK QUINLAN, MD**
Chief Executive Officer, Ochsner International and
Chief Executive Officer-Emeritus, Ochsner Health System.

"*Tension* provides well thought through and clear mental models and frameworks to harness the available energy in my organisation to bring more value to customers."
— **CHRISTOPHER MCGOWAN**
Chief Executive Officer, Silver Chain Group (Australia)

"Reading *Tension* will be the catalyst that launches you on your journey from a mindless organization to one that unleashes employee's personal creativity . . . a path to tap into the individual creativity inside you and transform your company along the way."
— **FRANCIS GOUILLART**
Co-author of *The Power of Co-Creation*

"*Tension* provides a useful and actionable framework for getting disparate groups on the same page to realize what they can achieve if they can harness these tensions to create the impossible."
— **WILLIAM D. PAIVA, PhD**
Executive Director, Center for Health Systems Innovation,
Oklahoma State University

"Full of practical advice and wisdom for organizations wanting to drive innovation. . . . how to balance the demands of the everyday business with creating tomorrow's blockbusters and new sources of value."
— **NAOMI FRIED, PhD**
Vice President, Medical Information and Innovation, Biogen and
former Chief Innovation Officer, Boston Children's Hospital

"In *Tension* Chris and Mitch Wasden describe this paradox of encouraging creative solutions to advance their companies while continuing to invest in strategies that discourage innovative power. "
— **ALIDA MOOSE**
Senior Vice President and Chief Human Resources Officer, Penn Mutual

"*Tension: The Energy of Innovation* should be required reading for the growing number of venture incubators and accelerators that will continue to be a key source of innovation for generations to come."
— **MIKE LOWE**
Chief Executive Officer, OrthoAccel

"*Tension* shows how companies can unleash their creative genius by applying the Innovation Life Cycle. This is a must read for any organization struggling to innovate!"
— **DR. MICHAEL MARQUARDT**
President, World Institute for Action Learning, Author of 25 books including *Leading with Questions* and Professor and Director of Executive Leadership Program, George Washington University

"The Wasden brothers bring a wealth of experience and perspective to this important topic. *Tension* itself is a gem, chocked full of insights around the challenges of innovating while tending to the day-to-day aspects of a scaling business . . . a must-read for those interested in refining the innovation process in their businesses."
— **JOSEPH KVEDAR, MD**
Executive Director, Center for Connected Health, Partners HealthCare

"*Tension* provides outstanding direction for how we can engage our employees to liberate their creative genius and drive our innovative efforts forward."
— **KHOSROW R. SHOTORBANI, MBA**
President and Chief Executive Officer, TriCore Reference Laboratories

"In *Tension*, the Wasdens and their Innovation Lifecycle have achieved a 'Tour de Force.' Both executives and managers will benefit from reading this conceptually sound and practically based book and so would anyone contemplating organizational change through innovation."
— **DR. DAVID SCHWANDT**
Professor and Director of Executive Leadership Program, George Washington University

"Each has the best intentions to be innovative and collaborative, but struggle to overcome internal tensions between running the big machine of the day-to-day operations and adjusting to the fast pace required to support an innovative startup."
— **ERIC ROCK**
Chief Executive Officer, Vivify

"Successful, dynamic companies can't afford not to innovate. The Innovation Life Cycle can help companies and leaders leverage the tension that accompanies creativity and innovation."
— **LESLIE BRUNNER**
Senior Vice President of People and Process, Athena Health

"In *Tension*, the Wasden brothers address the dilemma: we all believe in lean strategies, but most of us have a nagging concern about the effect of standardization on innovation."
— **HAROLD WILLIAMSON**
Executive Vice Chancellor of The University of Missouri Health Sciences

"*Tension* provides a guide that companies in this industry could follow to increase their innovative capabilities and capacity and provide greater value to the benefits of patients."
— **PETER MAAG**
President and Chief Executive Officer, CareDx, Inc

"*Tension* is the definitive guide for how to harness the power and energy of the inherently difficult process of innovation. A must-read book for any CEO looking to create new customer value through innovative products."
— **RYAN BECKLAND**
Co-founder and Chief Executive Officer, Validic

"A relevant and thoroughly researched effort. *Tension* is the manual for the work I've been doing at Qualcomm . . . as my team and I try to create a new business within the confines of a very large company."
— **RICK VALENCIA**
Chief Executive Officer, QualcommLife

"*Tension* outlines how companies can unleash the hidden creative genius of its people. . . . a must read for companies struggling to innovate and for new startup companies needing help bringing innovations to market."
— **TIMOTHY T. PEHRSON**
Chief Executive Officer, Intermountain Healthcare—North Region

"*Tension* is the ONE book that you should read. . . . a how-to-guide to maximizing your ability to innovate in a productive and realistic manner. . . . it will help me become a better manager/leader and I highly recommend it."
— **KAREN LIGHTMAN**
Executive Director, MEMS Industry Group

Anyone who has never made a mistake
has never tried anything new.

– ALBERT EINSTEIN

TENSION
THE ENERGY OF INNOVATION

Mike,

Thanks for the support.

Chris

TENSION

THE ENERGY OF INNOVATION

HOW HARNESSING TENSION ACCELERATES INNOVATION
AND FUELS YOUR CREATIVE GENIUS

Chris Wasden, EdD ✿ Mitch Wasden, EdD

SCIPIO
P R E S S
Midway, Utah

Tension: The Energy of Innovation

Copyright © 2014, 2015
Chris Wasden, EdD and Mitch Wasden, EdD

Published by Scipio Press
Midway, Utah

ISBN: 978-1-944465-01-8 (hardcover)
978-1-944465-02-5 (Kindle ebook)
978-1-944465-03-2 (iBook)

Publisher's Cataloging-In-Publication Data
(Prepared by The Donohue Group, Inc.)

Wasden, Chris.
    Tension : the energy of innovation : how harnessing tension accelerates innovation and fuels your creative genius / Chris Wasden, EdD + Mitch Wasden, EdD.

        pages : illustrations ; cm

        Issued also as an ebook.
        Includes bibliographical references and index.
        ISBN: 978-1-944465-01-8

        1. Creative ability in business.   2. Executive ability.
    3. Organizational change.   4. Mindfulness (Psychology)
    I. Wasden, Mitch.   II. Title.   III. Title: Energy of
    innovation
    HD53 .W37   2015
                                                    658.4063

Printed in Canada

*We dedicate this book to our wives, Leslie and Sonja,
who have helped nurture the rediscovery of our creative genius
and supported our harnessing of creative tensions.*

Contents

CHAPTER ONE

You Are a Creative Genius

Be honest: you think of yourself as a creative person. Why wouldn't you? When you think about things you've done or thought of doing, your heart beats a little faster. You crave to be in a business situation where you can share your innovations without fear, but that kind of environment seems beyond your reach. There is a reason you become frustrated at work, on teams, and in organizations. You have great ideas and you want an outlet to express and develop them, but you don't know how to do so within your current structures and processes.

We understand, because we've run up against the same kind of professional obstacles you've encountered, and we've always thought of ourselves as creative.

Gramp—our granddad, our master teacher, and resident creative genius—may have had something to do with our outlook. He only finished the ninth grade and was, at five foot nine and 140 pounds, a slight man. Yet he seemed to be able to repair or build anything and to solve most any problem we encountered. If we ever came back from the field early because we had a problem with the tractor, baler, windrower, wagon, or truck, he would ask why we had returned when the work wasn't done. We would tell him we had to because we couldn't fix the problem. He would tell us that *can't* isn't a word. Then, he would take us back to the field, help us figure out a way to do what seemed to be impossible, and finish the job.

The training on the farm has stuck with us throughout our lives and caused us to believe that we inherited Gramp's creative genius. It's something we had to remind ourselves of, because long before we went to work, we, like you, went to school.

We Are All Creative Geniuses

Very few teachers are like Gramp. Too few encouraged, enabled, or empowered us to discover, much less reinforce, the creative genius within. When we encountered problems and failures that drove us to discover or invent imaginative solutions, we were often discouraged from developing them.

That's not so surprising since our society has modeled its school structures and processes on mass production systems. The objective of our education system is to apply a standard operating procedure by all teachers to turn out a uniform product, namely, educated students. This mindless approach assumes that all teachers will follow the same process to transform all students into the same end product. We have found through our experiences, and science now supports this, that most of us are creative geniuses stifled by mindless organizations, processes, and structures.

Psychologist E. Paul Torrance is considered one of the founders of the *psychology of creativity*. Torrance worked for sixty years, researching creativity and also developing tests to measure ingenuity in children (called the Torrance Tests of Creative Thinking). Torrance noticed that children began to lose their spontaneity, took fewer risks, and were less playful as they aged. As a result, their creativity dropped off rapidly.

In a 1968 study, educators George Land and Beth Jarman confirmed Torrance's observations by using an assessment tool created by NASA to measure creativity, or, as they termed it, *divergent thinking,* in engineers and scientists on a group of sixteen hundred kids. Divergent thinking broadens possibilities when one is faced with a question. If asked what are multiple uses for a brick, a divergent thinker might describe it as a keyless vehicle entry system, the world's most powerful nutcracker, or a low-cost barbell.

These same children were tested at various intervals in their lives. The intervals were three to five years old, eight to ten years old, thirteen to fifteen years old, and then a final time after they were over the age of twenty-five. After the results were calculated, the following data was reported to determine what percentage of children in the age groups tested at the "creative genius" level. Of the three- to five-year-olds, 98 percent tested as creative geniuses. In the eight- to ten-year-olds, only 32 percent tested at that level. Once they reached adolescence, only 10 percent of the thirteen- to fifteen-year-olds met that standard. And finally, by age twenty-five, a paltry 2 percent of these same children tested as creative geniuses.

What happened to the inspired brilliance of these children over the years? Where did it go? It can be argued that the structure of schools and the emphasis on convergent thinking makes divergent thinking an unacceptable pastime. As children, we conform or face social consequences based on grading systems that reward *convergent thinking.* Convergent thinking is typically thinking in which there is one answer, such as 2+2 = 4 or the state capital of Missouri is Jefferson City.

But there is another factor in play. As enjoyable as it is for children to express their creativity, there are two things they enjoy even more, and they will give up anything to get them. Those things are love and acceptance. If your social group views your creativity as abnormal or bizarre, 98 percent of us will mask it and conform to what our immediate social group sees as normal. In this way, society is the ultimate groupthink. Imagine what would be possible if schools, families, and organizations were structured in a way to allow all 98 percent of individuals to retain their creative genius? A country that could pull this off would lead the world in technology, education, government, manufacturing, and every other category of endeavor.

If 98 percent of all employees had the internal wiring from birth to be creative geniuses, every company in the world could boast the following corporate identity: "**We are** creative geniuses!"

So what happened?

Often companies inadvertently foster identity shifts in employees away from "**I am** an innovator" because they lack the systems and processes to manage a workforce where so many innovators would be unleashed. Instead, companies have predominately operated with the mindlessness we experience when exercising on a stationary bike.

Let's take a look at what happened to that inborn creative genius in each of us.

In organizations, this conformist dynamic often reveals itself in an over-reliance on Lean Six Sigma policies and processes that drown out the innovative potential of employees. In organizations this conformist dynamic often reveals itself in an over-reliance on Lean Six Sigma policies, which we will discuss in greater detail later in the book and focus on removing all unnecessary waste and inefficiency within organization, and similar other processes that drown out the innovation potential of employees.

In previous decades, this was less noticeable because the pace of change was slower, making the status quo acceptable over longer periods of time. We can see this in the shortening life span of innovations such as the steam engine, electric power, computers, and smartphones. Consider that it took a hundred years for the steam engine to become mainstream and fifty years for electric power to replace the steam engine. It took twenty years for computers to become the dominant productivity tool of modern society, but the smartphone rose to ubiquity in less than five years. Social, mobile, analytic, and cloud technologies (which we call SMAC) are now further accelerating this change. With each new paradigm, the half life has fallen by half, meaning that there are much shorter periods of stability and equilibrium, which in turn generate more pressure, stress, and tension to drive more change more often.

Given the present pace of accelerated change and the corresponding technology revolutions, companies are more aware that innovation is necessary for survival. But while executives have much more experience with Lean Six Sigma as a discipline, the art and discipline of structuring a company for innovation is less understood and poorly applied. Often executives even confuse the two and believe that Lean Six Sigma is innovation. They are quick to point out that Lean Six Sigma has a defined and structured process for continual improvement, but they have to be reminded that improvement is not innovation and that Lean Six Sigma is the epitome of mindlessness, whereas innovation is practically the definition of mindfulness.

What we mean by this is that Lean Six Sigma is designed to get the same outcomes every time, regardless of who is operating the process. We don't want differentiation that occurs through mindful divergent thinking; we want mindlessness by following established and proven practices in rigid structures. Innovation, on the other hand, only emerges through mindfulness, by not accepting the status quo, rejecting current processes, and creating new structures and practices to do things differently.

The challenge that today's organizations face is to craft a culture that can balance Lean Six Sigma's intolerance for waste and variation with one that encourages innovation's messy, divergent, and sometimes wasteful processes.

The Organizational World

Your employer has established policies and procedures to ensure a standardized and uniform product and service. You are expected to do, not to think. The employer knows from experience that if any employee follows the prescribed formula and discipline, then outcomes will be a standardized product and service of uniform quality and price. The approach, though mindless, does produce tremendous results. Our society has emerged from the application of these mindless processes to provide greater productivity and higher standards of living around the world. But to sustain this standard of living requires us to come up with new creative solutions that can eventually be scaled.

In our experience, we often found that our bosses determined our creative efforts distracted us from doing the job we were hired to do. If we continued to focus on developing innovative solutions, we inevitably created tension between our leaders and ourselves, because we seemed more focused on thinking of new answers to problems than using the toolbox of solutions already in place.

But as we all know, no process is perfect and nothing lasts forever. The world always changes. These changes inevitably break all mindless processes and produce a powerful tension between running the businesses of today and building the businesses of tomorrow. These tensions force us to become more creative in order to adapt. Only those people and organizations that adapt to these tensions will survive.

So how do we break out of the mindlessness that delivers consistent but temporary results and enable mindfulness that will differentiate us and ensure our long-term success and survival? How do we free ourselves and others to draw upon the creative genius within to keep pace with the relentless and rapid changes buffeting us daily? In short, how do we simultaneously explore innovative new horizons to ensure future survival while also exploiting existing opportunities to fund that exploration?

> Being mindless means doing an activity over and over again without thinking about it. In business, being mindless means following established standard operating procedures. You are not investing anything new or experimenting, much less being creative.
>
> Being mindful is the opposite. When you are mindful, you are aware of what you are doing with a goal in mind.

This book will show you how. Before we do, we'll illustrate how mindlessness restricts our abilities to create, invent, innovate, and change, because creativity and inconsistency are replaced with predictable and reliable processes and structures. Doing so ensures that no matter who is the cog in the machine that does the work, the organization will get the same outcome.

For any organization to survive and thrive, it must tap into our mindful and creative energies. This is the source of differentiation, novelty, new value creation, and innovation. The problem is that most leaders and organizations don't know how to do this. They're great at applying things like Six Sigma and Lean discipline to achieve mindlessness, but what is the equivalent approach for mindfulness? Can you complete the following comparison?

Six Sigma is to mindlessness as *(insert word)* is to mindfulness.

What well-established process like Six Sigma would you use? The ready analog doesn't seem to exist.

This book will share our insights from personal experience and research as to how individuals and organizations can become more mindful, creative, and inventive within mindless organizations.

Since we pull heavily from personal experience, let us begin by telling you about ourselves.

First, Chris

My two college degrees from Brigham Young University, one in accounting and another in Asian studies, gave me the yin and yang that provide the foundation for my ideas of mindlessness and mindfulness. Accounting was mindless. There was always a right answer, and everyone should be able to come to the same conclusions. Asian studies, on the other hand, provided a creative outlet. The study of calligraphy, art, history, and languages required mindful engagement and creativity.

After earning my undergraduate degrees, I decided that international investment banking would be a great way to combine creativity with structured market discipline. I went to UCLA's Anderson Graduate School of Management to get my MBA. During the summer I worked for J. P. Morgan in its global banking business, and I had a great time, but I came home thinking I wanted to do something more entrepreneurial where I could make something with my hands. But having grown up in small rural towns in California and Utah, I didn't have any good ideas to start a company. All the businesses I had seen were general stores, bakeries, dental practices, etc. I didn't understand the problems that businesses faced or that I could solve through innovation as an entrepreneur.

During my second year at UCLA I took an entrepreneurship course to see if I had what it took to be one. For the class, I had to come up with a good idea to solve a problem and create a business plan for a new venture. I discovered a new embalming technology applied to plants that preserved their color and lifelike look and feel. I thought this would be a great technology to transform the

office and home live-plant business. It would eliminate maintenance costs and the need to replace dead plants without sacrificing
the look and feel of live plants. Well, my professor wasn't impressed
with either the technology or the plan. He gave me a B, and I finished the class believing I could never be a technology entrepreneur
because I didn't have a degree in the hard sciences or engineering.

So I went to Wall Street to become an investment banker at
J. P. Morgan. I did deals across Europe, Asia, Latin America, and
the United States, but I always felt a pull toward something more
creative and inventive that would lead to entrepreneurship. After
eight years in high finance, I decided to try my hand at two new
businesses simultaneously. I left J.P. Morgan to join Union Bank
of Switzerland (UBS) and start their newest business, which was
Latin American equity research. At the same time, my wife, Leslie,
and I started a retail kosher Jewish bakery in South Orange, New
Jersey.

Both of these two start-ups demanded more creativity and
innovation than I imagined. They were exciting *and* stressful. The
tensions that emerged from these businesses powered an amazing education and provided the foundation necessary for the many
new businesses I would later launch.

Both the bakery and the UBS business were great successes. In
our first year, the bakery hit $1 million in revenues and broke even.
My work at UBS became so well recognized in the market that
Goldman Sachs offered me a job to do the same thing for them.

Amazingly, the job offer from Goldman set off a series of events
that took us to Wichita, Kansas. When a friend of mine at Koch
Industries heard that I was exploring a position at Goldman, he
called me and had me interview for the position of the chief financial
officer of Koch Refining and Chemicals in Wichita. The opportunity
to work for the second largest private company in America—and
with its founder, Charles Koch, one of the most successful entrepreneurs in the world—sounded too exciting to pass up.

Prior to my arrival, Mr. Koch had become frustrated with the lackluster performance of his businesses. During the previous five years, revenues and profits were flat and very disappointing when compared to the 25 percent compound growth rate he had enjoyed the previous twenty years. Mr. Koch decided he needed to shake things up and create some tension in his organization, so he brought in some young Turks like me from Wall Street and others from management-consulting firms like McKinsey.

During my tenure, Mr. Koch completely restructured his senior leadership team several times and launched many new businesses that were either de novo or acquired. The tumultuous environment at Koch led most of my young Turk friends to leave Koch within two years. At that same time I got a call from a headhunter who told me that Enron, a company that had been voted the most innovative in the world for seven years running, had just launched a new business in the water industry in Houston, Texas, and was looking for someone to lead their strategy-businesses development and mergers and acquisitions activities.

So I left Koch and moved to Houston, but I actually never worked for Enron but rather for its most recent start-up, a water company called Azurix. Our goal at Azurix was to bring to the water industry the kind of creative thinking, products, and services that Koch and Enron had brought to the oil, gas, power, and energy businesses. While I was there we created an Internet marketplace at the height of the dotcom boom to trade water and water-related products and services. We bought an underground aquifer in the Central Valley of California so we could do water derivatives trading to help farmers and water utilities manage their drought risk. We bought run-down water utilities in Mexico and Argentina to turn them around. But as exciting as all this was, the water industry wasn't interested in the type and magnitude of change that we thought it needed. At the same time, Enron was beginning to have its own troubles that have now become notorious. After eighteen months I left Azurix and joined an innovation-consulting boutique, GEN3 Partners.

For a year after the dotcom bust I traveled the country with Michael Treacy, the cofounder of GEN3 Partners and author of the *New York Times* bestselling business strategy book *The Discipline of Market Leaders*, working with Fortune 500 companies to help them be more innovative in creating new business models using the Internet. While the dotcom boom had ended in a bust, large companies were still anxious and concerned about their inability to rapidly innovate with this new technology and sought outside help. We worked for banks, technology businesses, and chemical companies.

During this time I regularly spoke at venture capital conferences on innovation. At one conference in New York City, I was asked if I would look at a new start-up in the medical field and tell the founders what I thought of their business plan. After a quick read, I told Dr. Michael Glasscock, one of the most prominent otologists in the world and who was heading the start-up, that the attempt to do a roll up of small audiology shops was a dumb idea and would never work. The new venture they proposed provided no new sources of value, lacked any differentiation in the market, and had the wrong team. I expected them to be offended and to hang up the phone. To my surprise, he agreed on all three points and then asked, "So what should we do if we want to shake up the ears, nose, and throat (ENT) medical market?" I told him I had no idea, but the next time I was in Austin, Texas, I would stop by and we could explore this further.

Within a month we talked about the ENT market, its structure, pain points, technologies, workflow, etc. After a couple of hours Dr. Glasscock asked, "So what do we do?"

I said the market needed to transform the diagnostic process through automation to eliminate the need for an audiologist at every step of the process, which would decrease costs, increase convenience, and provide greater confidence and reliability that would then allow a new business model.

He said, "Great. How do we start?"

After working with Dr. Glasscock and some others for about a year (and convincing Mitch he should leave his cushy job in health-care administration), we decided to found Tympany, an automated diagnostic-hearing testing technology company. (I will share more of this story in a later chapter.)

This experience launched me into technology innovation. Through it I found I didn't need to be an engineer or scientist to become a named inventor on eleven issued patents; I could hire those kinds of people to work with me. Over the course of four years, we took our invention, the Otogram, through the FDA process, raised angel and venture capital, and steered our business to $5 million in revenues and a successful sale of the company to a larger publicly traded medical device company that saw our company as a disruptive force in the industry.

After we sold Tympany, I convinced Mitch that we should both start a doctoral program in human and organizational learning at George Washington University. This became one of the most trans-formational adventures of our lives and sharpened our innovation insights. Eventually we would each complete our dissertations on different aspects of innovation. Mitch focused on innovation from the inside out, that is, the role that mindfulness and mindlessness play in creativity. I focused on innovation from the outside in by exploring how structures and practices create social tensions that disrupt mindless processes and provide the energy that forces organizations to innovate through mindfulness to survive.

The doctoral program also became a critical time for Mitch and me to continue to collaborate. After the sale of Tympany, he returned to executive leadership within healthcare administration in Louisiana. At the same time, I decided to stay in Houston and try my hand at creating a new medical technology incubator called SimplexityMD.

SimplexityMD stretched me further, forcing me to evaluate over one hundred technologies that eventually led me to license two and raise venture financing to launch them as medical technology companies. The first, MC Nanotissues, used a biomaterial called microbial cellulose to create artificial blood vessels, surgical implants, and wound management products. The second, Ortho-Accel, uses acoustic energy to double the rate at which the jawbone remodels itself and thereby cut orthodontic treatment times in half.

Despite success with SimplexityMD, I wanted to take my ideas on innovation to a larger platform than the next start-up so I could help others become more innovative. Though I had become very active in the Houston entrepreneurial community, helping other entrepreneurs raise money and start and advance their businesses, I didn't want to limit what I did to my or someone else's new venture. Instead, I wanted to use my dissertation and experience to provide innovation-consulting services to others on a bigger scale. It was at this time that a friend approached me about the possibility of working for PwC (formerly known as PricewaterhouseCoopers).

I was looking for a larger platform to provide innovation services, and PwC was committed to re-creating the management consulting business they had sold to IBM five years earlier. Since joining PwC, I have written dozens of articles and reports on innovation, leveraging heavily on my and Mitch's dissertations and previous experience in nine start-ups. I have helped clients create new products, services, technologies, and business models to expand and enter new markets. I continue to work with PwC as a consultant, but I am now the executive director of the Sorenson Center for Discovery and Innovation at the University of Utah, where I am a professor at the business school, and also the associate executive director of the Center for Medical Innovation at the medical school.

In this book, I will share my insights and experiences as an innovator, educator, and consultant in helping my clients become more mindful in mindless organizations and to excel at innovation.

Next Mitch

Of the six children in my family, I was by far the least serious about academics. For most of my elementary schooling, I attended a one-hundred-year-old little red schoolhouse in Solvang, California. There was only one other boy in my grade, and he was even less interested in academics than I was. My scholastic objectives were not to get good grades but to get slightly better grades than the other boy. I remember in the fourth grade getting a D+ in science on my report card. When questioned by my dad about it, I told him, with some relief, that my fellow classmate had gotten a D-. So, in some ways, I set the curve for the boys in my class.

There was an internal logic to my odd academic strategy: why expend more energy on a goal than the goal requires? In many ways I was a model of academic efficiency. A minimalist. I was mindfully Zen without knowing it.

When I was a junior in high school, this all changed as I embarked on the two years that I knew colleges cared about. My American history teacher had a unique grading proposition for the class. Students were required to sign a contract for the grade we wanted in his course. An A required more reading, papers, presentations, and higher grades on tests. A B required a moderate amount of work, and a C required that students pass only two exams. Failure to meet the terms of the contract meant the student received a failing grade.

Since I needed A's and B's to get into college, I announced to my parents that I was going to sign a contract for a B. My dad disapproved and told me that I should be contracting for an A. While I was a bit surprised in his confidence in my academic abilities (given past performance), I nonetheless contracted for an A.

As the year wore on, I was pushed more than I had been in any class before, and in many ways it was surprisingly rewarding. I made an A by two points by the time the year was over.

Based on that experience, I decided to become a history major in college. While I loved the stories and principles taught by history studies, I was awful with the linearity of dates, places, and names. I cared more about the overall conceptual teachings of history, not the name, rank, and birthplace of historical figures.

While at Brigham Young University, I worked as a research assistant at the National Archives in Washington on a project that looked at the causes of human longevity by abstracting data from Civil War veterans' pension records. Dr. Robert Fogel of the University of Chicago, who won the 1993 Nobel Prize in Economics, headed the work. It was during that project that I realized my true interest was not history but rather epidemiology, the study of diseases and health on populations.

Upon returning from Washington, I applied to the University of Michigan's School of Public Health. I was called out for an interview but couldn't afford the plane ticket, so I took a two-day train ride from Provo to Ann Arbor. I remember being quite embarrassed when the admissions director seemed startled by my transportation choice. My final interview was with the department chair, who was interested in my work at the National Archives. When he shook my hand, his eyes lit up and he said, "Wow! So you're the guy who took the train!" I later learned that when you are called for an interview, you've already passed the test that shows you can handle graduate-level work. What they want to see at the interview is who really wants to be at Michigan the most. My taking the train sent a strong message that I truly wanted to be there. Apparently being too poor to fly actually helped me.

After my studies at Michigan, I was accepted for a postgraduate fellowship at the Lovelace Clinic in Albuquerque, New Mexico. (This was the same clinic where, in 1959, NASA sent thirty-one prospective astronauts for several days of medical testing before the final seven were selected.) The Lovelace Clinic has a history of integrated medicine, namely, the full continuum of healthcare—physicians, hospital, and insurance products—are organized under one roof for better quality and coordination. During my time at Lovelace, I was paired with a new physician leader, Dr. Patrick Quinlan, who, a decade later, was named by *Modern Healthcare* magazine as the number-one most powerful healthcare leader in the nation. Our task as new leaders with little experience was to turn around a regional clinic operation that was losing millions of dollars each year.

The turnaround of these practices from money-losers to money-makers required basic management principles. Like many businesses, it was losing money for dozens of reasons. The doctors lacked transparency regarding their productivity or expenses. To fix that problem, we instituted a set of monthly reports that compared doctors to their physician peers. Physicians are accustomed to getting A's, and so showing up on a report at the bottom of the list motivated many, but not all, to increase their patient visits. Each physician received a flat salary, and the productive ones began to complain that the work-and-reward ratio was out of balance. This led to a production-based compensation system, where pay was tied to work effort. These efforts, and dozens of others we implemented, were not innovative in the sense that we invented them. Each of our management strategies was widely known and could be found in numerous publications as effective ways to manage a group of physician clinics. While, as an industry, these tactics were not considered innovative, to the physicians undergoing the transformation in their practice, these changes felt extremely innovative as well as turbulent and painful. This was a great lesson for me in that I understood that innovation is not only context dependent but there are different kinds of innovation.

After two years, the regional clinics were breaking even, and Dr. Quinlan was recruited to the Ochsner Clinic in New Orleans, where he would later serve as CEO for over a decade. Dr. Quinlan recruited me to Ochsner to run the regional clinic operation. The world-renowned Ochsner Clinic was named after Alton Ochsner, one of the first physicians to discover the link between smoking and lung cancer.

As a person who craves simplicity, I was at first driven crazy by the complexity of healthcare. Healthcare as an industry defies traditional economic models due in part to its reliance on third-party insurance as its primary funding source. (Renowned management expert Peter Drucker said that healthcare organizations are the most complex form of organization we've attempted to manage in human history.) The simplest and most effective analogy I can use is to compare healthcare to the grocery business. Imagine that we paid for food items by purchasing grocery insurance. Anytime you wanted food, you simply went to the grocery store, paid a twenty-dollar co-pay, and filled your cart with whatever you needed. The result would be a grocery store filled with price-insensitive consumers who may come in for peanut butter and bread but left with a cart full of steaks, wines, and chocolates. With this model, in less than a year, there would be a grocery insurance crisis, and people would be complaining that their grocery insurance premiums were skyrocketing.

During Chris's and my doctoral studies at George Washington University, I studied the science of mindfulness as it relates to the functioning of complex adaptive systems, such as those found in nature with flocking birds, ant colonies, and human systems. I learned that complexity couldn't be managed by more complexity, but it can be controlled by a focus on mindful simplicity.

Consider one of the tasks I helped simplify through innovation: scheduling a physician appointment in a large multispecialty group. Within Ochsner, we had 800 physicians with over 150 appointment types. When patients called for an appointment, their calls were taken by an entry-level employee who had to deal with this staggering level of complexity. The result was frustrated patients, staff, and physicians when the wrong appointment types were used, which complicated all their lives. To simplify this complexity, I launched a program where patients could schedule their own appointments through an Internet portal or on a mobile health (mHealth) app. Through this same portal or mHealth app, patients could receive lab results and messages from their doctor.

At first, providers responded with huge resistance. How could patients navigate 150 appointment types? What if the patients made mistakes and booked too much time? The solution was to innovate by mindfully simplifying. We reduced the number of appointment types from 150 to just 2: fifteen-minute and thirty-minute appointment types. Within a few months of launching the portal, we saw huge patient adoption, with over a thousand new patient portal accounts created each month, and we saw patient no-show rates cut in half. Innovating by simplifying complexity, what Chris calls *simplexity,* proved to be a powerful growth strategy, but I later saw that this strategy could improve operations as well.

In the 2006 aftermath of Hurricane Katrina, Ochsner purchased a struggling for-profit hospital in Baton Rouge and asked me to serve as CEO of this two-hundred-million-dollar business and turn it around. Our employee turnover was 40 percent, which meant that we were overrun with temporary agency nurses. We had the distinction of having the worst quality, worst patient satisfaction, and worst employee engagement in the entire eight-hospital system. This experience proved to be a great laboratory for applying mindful innovation to reduce complexity. Within four years of the application of mindful innovation, our hospital led the system in patient satisfaction, quality, and employee engagement. Our employee turnover dropped to just 14 percent, the same as that in our other hospitals, and we had gone two years without a single temporary agency employee.

My academic interest in the mind's internal innovative processes continued after my doctoral studies. I became involved in the NeuroLeadership Institute in Australia, where I served as a member of the governing brain trust and at the same time became a frequent lecturer nationally on the mind's role in innovating and transforming organizations. NeuroLeadership, a term coined by Dr. David Rock, is a new branch of leadership studies that uses advances in neuroscience and functional magnetic resonance imaging (fMRI) technology to understand the inner workings of the human brain. These findings give objective evidence and insight into the best ways for leaders to innovate and manage complex organizations.

Using these concepts, our medical center was transformed from an organization with poor patient satisfaction and quality to one that consistently ranked in the ninetieth percentile nationally. Our turnaround garnered national attention at conferences and was featured in Frances X. Frei and Anne Morriss's *Uncommon Service: How to Win by Putting Customers at the Core of Your Business* (Harvard University Press, 2012). The concepts resonated with other organizations at national conferences, and I was often asked to speak to local leadership teams about innovating with the brain in mind. These talks led to interviews with local and national news outlets such as ABC News to discuss how the study of neuroscience could benefit people on an individual and organizational basis.

At about this time, I was certified as an executive coach at the NeuroLeadership Institute and introduced my staff to these the principles. I was selected to be the executive sponsor of the Ochsner Leadership Institute, which was responsible for the professional development of over one thousand leaders annually. I decided to begin introducing some of the concepts of mindful innovation to our leaders and share some of the concepts that had made our medical center successful. At first, I was cautious about discussing the concepts of mindfulness publicly with leadership, as I was concerned they wouldn't see it as a mainstream concept. But after several seminars and presentations within the leadership institute, I found that leaders were not only open to this kind of content but hungry for it. A new model that could explain how to lead in complex situations—by balancing the tensions of mindfulness and mindlessness—resonated deeply with leadership and was exactly what they were looking for. It took less than twelve months for these concepts to become mainstream ideas within the organization.

After my experience at Ochsner, I was recruited to be the COO of University of Missouri Health Care, a $1.2-billion-dollar health system in Columbia with seven hospitals and over fifty-five hundred employees. Two months after arriving, the CEO announced his retirement, and I was selected as the CEO/COO, a dual role where I continue to apply the principles of both mindlessness to achieve improved efficiency and mindfulness to innovate and transform our organization.

It's Time for You to Innovate

In the pages that follow, we will reveal the emergence of mindlessness in organizations, the false myths that perpetuate it, what it takes to become creative, innovative, and mindful, and how you can be ambidextrous enough to operate mindfully among mindlessness. This will enable you to ride the Innovation Cycle along its lifecycle path. We will take you on a journey of believing in your creative genius, knowing what you need to do to innovate, and doing what is required to realize your innovative potential.

Never forget that you are a creative genius. You just need to learn, as we did, how to ride the Innovation Cycle.

REMEMBER

✔ Tension and the pain it causes drives change. Without them, there is no progress.

✔ Tensions are neither good nor bad. They are energy sources that can be harnessed for either creative or destructive ends.

✔ Effective leaders create tensions and enable their organizations to harness them to drive creativity and innovation.

✔ Being mindless means doing an activity over and over again without thinking about it. In business, being mindless means following established standard operating procedures to eliminate failure, decrease risk, and improve efficiency. It is the signature of Lean Six Sigma discipline. Although mindlessness's primary virtue is that it is very efficient, it does not lead to new innovations that sustain organizations into the future.

✔ Being mindful is the opposite of mindlessness. When you are mindful, you are aware of what you are doing and have a creative goal in mind.

✔ Research shows that 98 percent of us possess the hardwiring to be creative geniuses, but over time that number can fall to only 2 percent if we stay in mindless thought routines without practicing mindfulness.

CHAPTER TWO

Riding the Innovation Cycle

Why should you be innovative? Only 10 percent of issued patents yield commercial revenues. One in ten venture-backed start-ups provide nearly all the returns on a venture capital portfolio, while most of the other nine are partial if not total losers. Of one thousand good ideas, only one hundred will be refined into proof-of-concepts (POC), and a mere ten of those will become prototypes and pilots, and just one will become a commercially successful offering. The sad fact is that 90 percent or more of our creative and innovative efforts result in failure.

If failure rates are so high, why keep trying?

You keep at it because the successes you experience continue to support your passion to create and give you the optimistic energy to propel yourself through a cycle of innovation.

But the reality is that standard operating procedures, processes, practices, and structures in most functions in most organizations are based upon Lean Six Sigma business models designed to ensure success 99.999 percent of the time. This means that you only fail three times out of every one million attempts. Many organizations attempt to decrease their innovation-related failure rates and improve creative productivity and efficiency by applying mindless efficiency-oriented business models to innovation. The irony is that this further increases failures and decreases innovation.

Mindlessness so rules our daily business lives with virtually no freedom to start riding the Innovation Cycle, which must include failure. The fact is that failure is the spark that ignites the Innovation Cycle, whose fuel is the pain and maladaptive tensions it causes. But pain is not enough to continue to power the cycle. The cycle requires harnessing tensions and passions in a mindful way. Doing so transforms these maladaptive tensions into creative and adaptive ones that lead you to innovate in ways that eliminate the cause of failure and pain. The Innovation Cycle is mindful because it requires a break from the mindless status quo and produces new models, structures, and practices that will lead to innovative solutions.

Figure 1

THE INNOVATION CYCLE

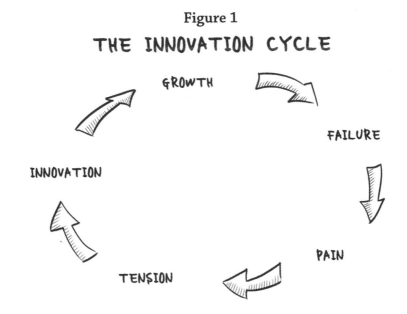

So how can you
- Ride this mindful Innovation Cycle while operating in mindless organizations?
- Mine failure to start the cycle?
- Set up jobs for failure?
- Encourage and reward failure?
- Innovate individually or in groups or organizations if mindless business models are built for success and not failure?

Failure Succeeds

To begin the cycle, you must accept that 90 percent of your creative attempts will fail. To innovate, you need mindful business models built for failure. You must seek out, accelerate, and increase the frequency of failure and do so on a frugal budget. You need a fast, frequent, frugal operating model that powers the Innovation Cycle.

There are two cycles related to innovation:
- The Innovation Cycle, encompassing failure, pain, tension, innovation, and growth and describes innovation emergence.
- The Innovation Lifecycle describes how you ride this cycle from mindfulness to mindlessness and take a discovered idea to a scaled commercial success.

Four Kinds of Bikes to Ride the Innovation Cycle

Why do we use bikes as an innovation metaphor?

Innovation follows a lifecycle with four distinct phases: discovery, incubation, acceleration, and scaling. There is a simple way to illustrate these phases, namely, as easy as riding a bike. What you need to know as you move through these cycles is that the symbolic type of bike you ride changes from one kind to another. You start with a *mountain bike* in discovery, move to a *hybrid* in incubation, then to a *road bike* in acceleration, and finally to a *stationary bike* in scaling.

Figure 2

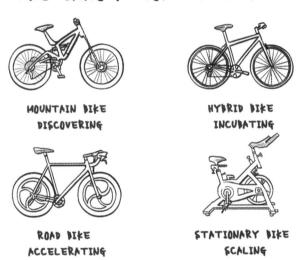

FOUR BIKES FOR RIDING
THE INNOVATION LIFECYCLE

MOUNTAIN BIKE
DISCOVERING

HYBRID BIKE
INCUBATING

ROAD BIKE
ACCELERATING

STATIONARY BIKE
SCALING

Organizations tend to exploit existing opportunities and explore for new prospects. But the way you need to go about it radically differs, just as road bikes differ from mountain bikes. Opportunities that are merely incremental and adjacent to your current focus can be reached with a road bike or at most a hybrid model. The more exploratory and radical the opportunity, the more you need a bike built for failure in order to overcome the dangers associated with sudden turns, unexpected hazards, and difficult and rapid climbs and descents.

The biggest challenge we see in most organizations is that they use the wrong bikes to explore and exploit their opportunities. In the worst of all cases, people may be kept on a stationary bike in the name of mindless efficiency, thereby eliminating any opportunity to explore even the most modest of opportunities. Mindful biking is mountain biking; mindless biking is stationary. You transform maladaptive tensions into creative, adaptive ones by using the right bike for the right terrain, where as maladaptive tensions occur when the bike and the terrain do not match.

Another biking metaphor that helps explain the difference among these three tensions is shown in the following figure. Look at the three different bike drive train systems below. You experience a maladaptive tension when your bike chain is too loose and therefore easily and frequently falls off; alternatively, a chain that is too tight would also be maladaptive since you can't pedal with it either. When the chain is either too loose or too tight you have the wrong type of tension which then leads to failure – you can't pedal the innovation cycle. Alternatively, when you have a rear derailleur, as in the middle example, it ensures that you optimize the chain tension so that it adapts to your energy needs based upon the gears you select for the type of terrain you are facing. An important principle regarding adaptive tension is that you can realize your energy needs within the existing structure, you merely have to shift to the right gear. Creative tension is different, it requires an entirely new physical structure that then leads to new ways to practice and can't be achieved with the existing drive chain. In the far right example, to achieve creative tension you would need to actually replace your large traditional round chain ring with an innovative new oval one that transforms the way you create energy from each stroke of the pedal.

Figure 3

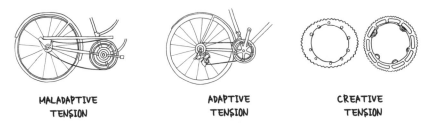

These are the three tensions that power the innovation cycle. Maladaptive tensions are those we must overcome through innovation because they are leading to failure and pain. Adaptive tensions enable us to incrementally innovate and sometimes achieve breakthrough innovations by adapting our current organizational and personal structures and practices to changes in real-world conditions. But to achieve radical and disruptive innovations requires creative tensions, which means that we have to change both the physical structures and associated practices in meaningful ways.

Get to Know Your Innovation Bicycles

The Mountain Bike

Mountain bikes are built for failure, not speed, and require constant mindfulness on the task at hand. To mitigate danger and risk from failure, they feature big shocks on the forks and powerful shocks on the back to protect riders from unexpected and rapid descents and turns that could cause crashes. The wheels and tires are three times as wide as those of a street bike, with large treads and knobby tires to maximize gripping of unstable terrain, such as dirt, sand, gravel, and mud. The heavy and sturdy frame is built to endure the punishment of mountain terrains. Their disk brakes are better at dealing with the constant, powerful braking necessary for steep and treacherous slopes.

Mountain biking is highly technical, requiring constant vigilance with more gearing, allowing a much wider range of tension management with lower gears that almost allow riders to pedal in place when going up steep hills and higher gearing that allows rapid descents. Taking your mind off the course, the required shifting and braking, or steering for even a second can lead to disaster. When mountain biking, mindlessness is never an option, failure is a constant companion, and anticipating dangers ahead is key as every next yard of terrain differs from the last.

The Road Bike

Sleek, lightweight, and aerodynamic, road bikes are built for speed. The wheels have a large diameter with few spokes in order to eliminate wind resistance. The tires are very narrow to decrease contact and friction with the ground. There are virtually no treads and very high air pressure so that only the narrowest portion of the tire ever contacts the ground. The gearing allows you to adjust to the road tension to go up steep hills with 5–10 percent grades in low, slow gears and to race down those same hills at 40 mph or faster to gain momentum to go up the next hill. The handlebars allow many different hand positions to avoid fatigue while on long, monotonous rides of many miles.

Part of the beauty of these long rides is that all riders really need to do is focus on the white line of the smooth, paved road, occasionally miss potholes and debris, and make a few infrequent turns on well-known and remembered routes. This mindless physical activity allows the rider's brain time for mindful thinking about other things, such as problems at work, challenges with kids, or introspection while observing nature.

The Hybrid Bike

Hybrids combine elements of both of these bikes and seem like a good compromise when riders aren't sure where they may be going and how they will need to respond. If, however, they asked us to classify a hybrid into one of two categories of road or mountain bike, we would definitely call them a road bike. The tires are narrow with high pressure, and the frame is more aggressive and lighter with no shocks or disk brakes. While the gearing and handlebars look very much like those of a mountain bike, these bikes are suitable for gentle trails. If someone used these on a real mountain trail, they would quickly crash and injure themselves. On such a bike, riders generally are on gentle trails that have more hazards than roads but fewer than mountain terrains. Therefore they require more mindfulness of the rider than road bikes do, but not quite the vigilance required for a mountain bike.

The Stationary Bike

This is the ultimate mindless machine. The biggest challenge when sitting on this bike is to find something (magazines, newspapers, audio books, music) to engage your mind. (At some gyms, bikes with monitors show a computerized scene from a well-known segment of the Tour de France.) If you take a spin class, your focus will be on the instructor's directions to lead the class through some unexpected routines that decrease the monotony of mindless stationary cycling.

Since these bikes don't actually take you anywhere, the wheels are replaced with metal disks in the front. In place of gears, they have knobs to increase tension to simulate steep climbs or fast sprints. Despite the difference between stationary bikes and real bikes, the former is the most efficient and effective of all bikes in burning calories. By stripping away all the parts of the bike needed for the real world, it enables you to focus mindlessly on one thing: efficient exercise. It may not be fun, but it works with Six Sigma precision and results. With this bike, there is no risk of crashing from road or mountain hazards. It's stable and reliable. It works the same for everyone. It has very few moving parts and requires virtually no maintenance.

The Organizational Bike

Traditionally, organizations employ symbolic bikes on a functional basis. Mountain bikes go to the R&D department, hybrids to business development, road bikes to commercial development, and stationary bikes to operations. But what if someone in operations has a great idea that requires a mountain bike to explore? In the real world, there are multiple bikes available, based on the terrain you want to explore. While some people prefer mountain biking to road biking, and others just want to use the stationary bike at the gym, the key to having a good time biking is to allow people the opportunity to choose their terrain and the bike they need to navigate it. Without this choice in the workplace, it's not possible to demonstrate and develop creative genius. Being locked into one model and one terrain forces you into mindless compliance with standard operating procedures, which keeps you a part of the 98 percent who lost their creative genius after entering school and becoming adults.

So how do you leave the 98 percent, mount the cycle of your choice, and pedal to innovation?

On the Road to Innovation

This book will answer that question in three parts. The first is called "Becoming." Here, we describe why you are a creative genius and an innovative being. We explain why mindlessness dominates the organizations you operate in, the myths you erroneously believe that perpetuate those beliefs, and how your brain prefers mindlessness for most of what you do. We'll illustrate how the latter perpetuates the organizational desire for mindless structures and practices. We will show you that you can *become* a creative genius if you understand the structural, practice, social, and physiological barriers to innovation.

Our experience is that people on organizational stationary bikes—which seem to be the vast majority in our experience—yearn to change it up and ride different kinds of bikes, sometimes on the same day. They want to be able to explore radical, breakthrough, or incremental ideas. They may not all want to use a mountain bike but rather a hybrid or a road bike to move them toward discovering new, valuable opportunities. The problem we find is that most organizations consign their people to only one type of bike, day in and day out, and the most common is a mindless stationary bike.

In chapter 3 we will chronicle the history of mindlessness in organizations, why it dominates most processes, and why people, in order to be creative, need to be enabled to be both mindless and mindful.

The dominant nature of mindless organizational systems, structures, and processes has led to the creation of and belief in a dozen innovation myths that lead individuals to believe not only that they are not creative geniuses but that they can never be one. The purpose of chapter 4 is to dispel those myths and convince you that you possess the abilities to be mindful and to innovate. It will show you that you need to get off your stationary bike from time to time and explore different terrains in order to develop your ideas, engage your passions, and realize your dreams.

The paradox of mindfulness and mindlessness is that you need both to be a creative genius. No one has the physical and mental capacity to be just mindful. This is how Mother Nature designed our brains. The brain uses mindlessness to both generate and conserve energy. For instance, visualize a clown attempting to juggle some chainsaws. This is a difficult feat requiring intense focus and attention, a truly mindful activity. But imagine how much more difficult it would be if the clown were also standing on a teeter-totter. This would require more mindfulness than the clown could muster and would lead to disaster. To do something as intensely mindful as juggling chainsaws, the clown needs stability; his feet need to be mindless. Only by standing on a foundation of mindlessness can he be mindful enough to juggle.

Or imagine you had to figure out a new route to work every morning. What a waste of mental resources. Our brains use mindlessness to hardwire routines that work, such as the shortest route to the office. Mindless organizations do a masterful job of replicating the mindless process of the brain but, unfortunately, fall very short where mindful processes are concerned. Chapter 5 will describe how the brain and mind operate to synergistically use both mindfulness and mindlessness to enable your creative genius. To prove this is true, we will use a case study from the most mindless of all organizations to reveal how creative genius rests within us all.

The second part of the book we titled "Knowing." These chapters explain how existing mental maps enable mindless efficiency. They also explain how to draw new maps through mindful creativity, thus allowing you to explore new opportunities that demand innovation. We will then describe the innovative cycle with its fast, frequent, frugal failure approach to learning, exploring, creating, and innovating. Finally, we will explain how to combine, refine, synthesize, and improve innovative ideas to drive the process and yield compelling value propositions.

Just as a bike rider starts by selecting a route and a map that determines the type of bike needed for the terrain, the brain uses and creates mental maps to engage your creative genius. Existing mental maps support mindless efficiency by enabling you to follow an established, predictable, and reliable process to get something done. Exploring new routes requires the formation of new maps through a mindful process that is full of failure, setbacks, and challenges. You were designed to embrace this tension between mindfulness and mindlessness. We will explore the role, use, and development of mental maps in chapter 6.

As a mindful process, innovation doesn't occur in a linear fashion like the mindless Six Sigma processes in most organizations. Instead, it operates as a cycle that starts with a point of failure in a process or system. What is crucial to recognize is that failure is the genesis of innovation. You identify, quantify, and measure the pain the failure generates and then engage your passions to envision the world without this failure and pain. You then harness the tensions that emerge from the gap between the pain and passion to generate an innovation that solves a problem in a novel way to provide a new source of value. Finally, you take the innovation to the market to experiment with it through a (1) fast, (2) frequent, (3), frugal, and (4) failure process to improve it. Then the cycle begins again. The Innovation Cycle is the focus of chapter 7.

All ideas from creative geniuses have the potential to become innovative. The trick is to develop, refine, and improve ideas and then select and further develop the best ones and turn them into innovations. Chapter 8 provides our value creation framework for evaluating new ideas and turning them into value propositions that remove failure, pain, and waste in original ways. This evaluation process is key to moving an innovation through its lifecycle.

The final part of the Innovation Cycle is called "Doing." Here we describe three phases of the Innovation Lifecycle and how organizations harness the tensions that emerge from within as well as how to bring your innovative ideas to the marketplace. We provide case studies of organizations that have employed Innovation Lifecycle management to improve their discovery, incubation, acceleration, and scaling of new ideas. We will also discuss the various ways to measure, benchmark, and scorecard innovation to support and improve management along the lifecycle.

In chapter 9 we will outline the eight stage process for ensuring that all three elements that drive innovation (variation, interaction, and selection) operate in your innovation challenges and campaigns. Chapter 10 will provide tools and methods to select and improve ideas by eliminating technical uncertainty to create prototypes and pilots. This chapter will also provide the structures and practices necessary to successfully operate an incubator.

Most organizations are not comfortable changing bikes and routes, especially at the worker's discretion. Bosses complain that you weren't hired to be innovative but rather hired to do a specific job. They find your efforts to be creative distracting and disruptive to the status quo. They don't believe that people trained on stationary bikes can use road bikes, let alone mountain bikes.

Of 1000 ideas, only 100 may be good enough to combine and create 10 viable proof of concepts that could advance to incubation. Of these, only about three will move to the next phase of acceleration. Chapter 11 focuses on accelerating those good ideas that have been prototyped, piloted, and commercially launched and then figuring out how to iteratively modify the business model in order for it to move towards a scaled, successful, commercial business.

Organizations are masters at measuring mindless processes, as evidenced by Lean Six Sigma. But what about innovation? What are the measures that should be used here? How do you assess a process that is prone to frequent failure and uncertainty? The challenge with innovation is that you have to consider different things. Chapter 12 will lay out our approach to measuring innovation that we have used with several different types of organizations.

In the epilogue we reinforce the pivotal power of mental models in creating the identity of an innovator. We were all born creative geniuses, we just need to rediscover this identity and then act upon it by applying the right structures and practices that support innovation. We need to hop off our stationary cycles and start riding mountain, hybrid and road bikes to explore, discover, create and invent. To start your bicycling journey, let's first understand the value and limitations of mindlessness. By itself, there can be no innovation, but without it there can be no mindfulness.

REMEMBER

✔ The Innovation Cycle—encompassing failure, pain, tension, innovation, and growth—describes the emergent process of innovation.

✔ The tension energy in the Innovation Cycle powers innovation across the entire lifecycle. The Innovation Lifecycle has four phases: discovery, incubation, acceleration, and scaling.

✔ The four bikes that symbolize the Innovation Lifecycle are mountain (discovery), hybrid (incubation), road (acceleration), and stationary (scaling).

✔ Mindful biking is mountain biking; mindless biking is stationary. The edge of chaos can be found in mountainous terrain; equilibrium is found in the gym. Creative and adaptive tension is achieved by applying the right bike to the right terrain, whereas maladaptive tensions occur when these things are misaligned.

✔ Most of the failures to create and innovate as individuals, groups, and organizations arise because we don't match the bike to the terrain.

✔ Growth only occurs as we solve problems through creativity and innovation by following the Innovation Lifecycle.

———————————— QUESTIONS ————————————

> How often do you take time to ride more than one bike to be innovative?

> How well does your organization allow and ideally encourage its people to ride more than one bike?

> How much does your organization value having all of its people engaged in the Innovation Cycle?

> How willing is your organization to allow people to spend roughly 10 percent of their time riding mountain bikes to explore new ideas and opportunities?

Becoming

The test of a first-rate intelligence is the ability to hold two opposed ideas in the mind at the same time, and still retain the ability to function.

—F. SCOTT FITZGERALD

CHAPTER THREE

In Defense of Mindlessness

Is mindlessness a virtue or a vice?

Isn't mindfulness the more virtuous path to take?

Shouldn't you prefer mountain bikes to stationary cycles for exploring the world?

So often, when we refer to organizational processes and structures as mindless, people assume we're being critical or negative. They assume that mindlessness is a value judgment, like being perceived as dumb or ugly. This couldn't be further from the truth. We see mindlessness as a virtue and symbiotic with mindfulness. Without mindlessness there could be no mindfulness. Mindlessness provides the resources, time, and money for mindfulness.

The problem with mindlessness is that our human physiological, emotional, and social preferences for efficiency and economy lead us to allow mindlessness to dominate our activities and crowd out mindfulness. We generally see the byproducts of mindful behaviors, such as experimentation, trial and error, waste, failure, inefficiency, and pain as greater vices.

It's a paradox that while all innovation is born of mindfulness, it can only become great through mindlessness. To create value in a social system, such as a society or an organization, you must find ways to improve productivity, decrease waste, and increase efficiency. You have to systematize those activities that lend themselves to standard operating procedures and provide more rigid structures that ensure you get the same quality and quantity of outcomes regardless of who does a task. This is what Henry Ford did when he created the assembly line. This is what Frederick Taylor did through his time and motion studies. Organizational structures and practices can turn what was once a mindful activity into a mindless one. By doing so, you conserve energy and resources that can be used to scale a big opportunity based on mindfulness.

But carried to an extreme, mindlessness will kill innovation. In this chapter, we will discuss 3M's imbalance when it let both mindfulness and mindlessness run amuck. We will then provide a brief history of organizational mindlessness over the past century. We will end the chapter by providing evidence to support our call for greater mindfulness to enable the magnitude and rate of innovation our world demands.

The Birth of an Innovator

In 1902, five investors formed Minnesota Mining and Manufacturing (3M) to excavate and process abrasive material on the banks of Lake Superior. They believed the substance was as hard as diamonds and would be the future of the abrasive industry. After pooling their funds to create their new enterprise, they tested their magical material and found instead that the matter was low-grade sand and worthless.

So the team turned to another segment in the abrasives market—sandpaper—with similar initial euphoria and disastrous results. This time, however, they let others do the mining and imported a special type of sand from Spain. But when they attempted to adhere the sand to paper, it refused to stick. The 3M team, along with their investors, experienced some real pain and tension after the second failure. But this disappointment drove some very innovative research to understand what had gone wrong.

A technician in the nascent group, in what would eventually become 3M's R&D group, analyzed the sand and found it was covered with olive oil, which was why it couldn't stick to the paper. Further research revealed that during a stormy crossing of the Atlantic, some barrels of olive oil had spilled onto the sand by accident. They cleaned off the oil, made their sandpaper, and they were in business.

These two experiences at the genesis of the company revealed key elements in the Innovation Cycle to this inexperienced 3M team of would-be innovators. They found that not only is necessity the mother of innovation but that necessity is born of failures that create pain, with the most painful being that associated with survival. They also saw how this pain then led to tensions between the near demise of their fledgling enterprise and the desired state of success they eventually realized through R&D. 3M's early brush with mortality firmly established R&D and innovation as the core of 3M's capabilities and discipline.

Masking tape is another iconic example of a 3M innovation that emerged through the Innovation Cycle. In 1920s, Richard Drew, a 3M lab assistant, was visiting an auto body shop to learn firsthand about a customer's failure, pain, and tensions around his use of 3M's abrasive products. During the visit he heard a blast of cursing and screaming from the paint room. When he went to see what had happened, he found that newspaper glued on the car as a mask for a two-toned effect had failed to come off during cleaning, and this ruined the result of hours of work. The pain that emerged from this failure was emotional and costly.

This encounter with the body shop painters had nothing to do with the abrasives 3M sold, but it was serendipitous, because it led Drew back to the lab to invent what became known as masking tape. The process he developed became the standard for how to innovate within 3M for the next several decades. This process required employees to explore unexpected experiences in order to identify failure and pain points that needed to be overcome through innovation. It then empowered the 3M would-be inventors to harness their passions to drive the creative process, even when it created organizational tension, which it generally did.

Driven by his passion to create the best customer solution, Drew ignored his boss's demands (an internal tension) to focus on only incremental improvements of existing abrasive products. He stole time from existing incremental R&D activities in abrasives and worked long hours each day and weekends (harnessing creative tension) to perfect his ideas about masking tape, which required inventing a new weaker type of adhesive. His success led to two important leadership principles that would support 3M's innovation engine and establish its 15 percent free-time rule, which says that employees have the right to use 15% of their time in any way they would like to explore, create and invent new things. The first is that employees should harness the tension between their day-to-day jobs and their passion around innovation by seeking forgiveness rather than permission in order to follow their gut instincts about new ideas. Second, leadership should allow this creative tension to enable passion-driven innovation by getting out of the way and allowing innovative people to be protected from their bosses. These two principles drove and enabled the three processes that drive innovation: *variation, interaction,* and *selection.*

The Innovation Trio

By employing *variation, interaction,* and *selection,* employees were empowered to serendipitously seek out failure and pain, which, they found, generated maladaptive tensions in the marketplace. Maladaptive tensions are those that perpetuate failure and pain. They would then take the initiative to transform these maladaptive tensions into adaptive and creative tensions that would lead to innovative solutions. Initial failure in the market was seen as the source of innovation, and trial-and-error experimentation was expected to feed the innovative process and therefore was not punished as in other companies. Employees were encouraged to think and act differently. The result was an innovation bonanza unseen at other large organizations.

To support individual creativity, employees could spend 15 percent of their time to pursue their passionate instincts. Additionally, the company provided several separate and diverse pools of capital that employees could access to fund their ideas. This ensured that the three primary processes that drive serendipity and innovation operated throughout the organization.

Variation

The process of variation gave employees license to think and act differently. They sought out problems to solve and established novel solutions to address them. They knew that, when it came to innovation, being different was more valuable than being the same. Seeking out variation is something that can be seen among all great innovators. Steve Jobs, for example, was quick to point out that the genesis of most of his ideas came from outside Apple, like Xerox PARC, the MP3, or the cell phone market. Google acquired most of its new innovations, like Android and YouTube, and then expanded them.

Interaction

3M institutionalized the process of interaction by ensuring that all innovative endeavors had small cross-functional teams representing several different operating perspectives, as well as the input and perspective of different customers. This interaction among diverse groups further enhanced and supported the variation process and generated greater serendipity by having people with different backgrounds look at the same problem from opposing perspectives. 3M found that the value of interaction is inversely proportional to the size of the team; a large diverse innovation team will yield to groupthink rather than variety. Therefore teams must be kept small. (For this reason, Amazon limits the size of its innovation teams to three people.)

Selection

By providing significant autonomy to small cross-disciplinary teams, allowing them to select how they used their 15 percent free time to innovate, protecting them from their bosses who generally wouldn't have chosen the same things for their employees to spend their time on, and providing multiple capital pools they could access to fund their ideas, innovative companies enabled several different selection processes to drive innovation. When people can choose where and how they spend their time, they work harder, longer, and more effectively to become the creative geniuses they need to be to passionately solve tough problems.

The application of these two principles (forgiveness trumps permission and protecting people from their bosses) and three processes (variation, interaction, and selection) enabled Drew to invent Scotch Tape and other 3M inventors to formulate, among other things, Thinsulate, which transformed the insulation market, and Post-it Notes. Through similar chance encounters, 3M found that the culture and processes they shaped enabled a very mindful, imaginative, and inventive organization. 3M found that they could increase the *volume, velocity,* and *value* of serendipity and thereby accelerate innovation by providing the right structures and practices.

3M and its employees also found that, to the people they were liberating, the very acts of creation and invention were their own rewards. For example, 3M employees didn't require royalties or bonuses for their innovations. What leadership found was that freedom to use their own time to be inventive, recognition of their efforts—both failures and successes, and not punishing failure but rewarding it as a source of learning for future success were the primary compensations people sought. Instituting this kind of innovative culture provided rewards that would attract and retain inventive minds.

3M's leaders seemed to understand what science is just now beginning to reveal: when people are allowed to create, they are in a state of "flow" or "being in the zone" that generates a mental high. Scientists refer to this as an autotelic reward. Flow exists when a person is deeply immersed in a task and when the job provides feedback to its creator that gives a feeling of oneness with the task. Such emotional rewards override all others, making them the key to attracting and retaining the most ingenious people.

The Innovation Lifecycle

To enable this type of perpetual innovation, 3M's leadership found they couldn't run the company like a traditional hierarchical manufacturing organization. Rather than as a global conglomerate with rigid bureaucracies, 3M had to be run like a portfolio of start-ups with flexible and agile organizational structures and practices. As innovations advanced through the four phases of the Innovation

Lifecycle—*discovering, incubating, accelerating,* and *scaling*—structures and practices to support innovation had to change for each phase of innovation. Doing so enabled 3M to adapt to new information and market demands that required changes in products, services, processes, business models, and distribution.

To enable innovation teams the freedom to grow through all four of these Innovation Lifecycle phases, 3M's leadership facilitated the development of decentralized groups for each new technology family. In the 1920s, there were only two: abrasives and adhesives. But by the 1990s there were over thirty. As such, 3M looked more like a holding company of independent businesses in various phases of the Innovation Lifecycle, where each enjoyed significant autonomy but also created substantial excessive overhead, administrative, operating, and production costs and redundancy. From the outside, the company looked bloated and inefficient.

By the 1990s, these excess costs created waste and inefficiency, which made it difficult for 3M to continue to realize its key financial objectives of generating 30 percent of its revenues from products that were less than four years old, realizing over 10 percent annual earnings per share growth, and delivering a 20–25 percent annual return on equity. Increased spending on R&D seemed to be responsible for diminishing returns to shareholders. The innovation discipline that had governed the company for nearly a century seemed to be missing the operating discipline so much in vogue among the global Fortune 500.

3M's Fall from Innovation Grace

After nearly a century as one of America's most iconic innovators, 3M began to falter. In the late 1990s, 3M's businesses and leaders seemed to have lost their way and were in disarray. Sales growth and profitability had steadily declined, and the stock price hadn't budged in a decade. Shareholders demanded change at the top, forcing the board to look outside the company for a new CEO for the first time in nearly a century. The 3M board felt that innovation disciplines that resulted in tremendous waste, duplication, and inefficiency had ruled too long. It seemed that 3M operations needed to become more efficient, like those of the streamlined General Electric Corporation (GE). That organization demonstrated relentless incremental improvements driven by the application of Lean Six Sigma.

At the same time, GE's board was making its final selection of a new CEO to replace Jack Welch, who believed in and implemented Lean Six Sigma. Three men were in the running, and the board gave the final nod to Jeff Imelt, a young GE lifer who had been a longtime disciple of Welch. This meant that the other two candidates were free agents to look for CEO posts at other firms. Robert Nardelli left to run Home Depot. The other was Jim McNerney.

A Lean Six Sigma Black Belt like McNerney, who could impose mindlessness on 3M's overly mindful organization, seemed to be just what the 3M board was looking for.

When the board announced on December 5, 2000, that McNerney had accepted their offer to lead 3M in the new millennium, the stock price increased by 20 percent over the next several days.

McNerney put together a classic GE playbook for turning around 3M, with the stated intent that he was going to change the DNA of 3M through the application of Lean Six Sigma discipline. He fired eight thousand employees (11 percent of the workforce), eliminated nearly a quarter of capital expenditures, cut a third of the R&D budget, intensified the performance review process, and eliminated most of the discretionary spending and freedom that business units had enjoyed for decades.

To drive these changes into the DNA of the organization, he launched Lean Six Sigma processes he had helped develop and lead while at GE to decrease product default rates and increase operating efficiency. These processes replaced individual choice, freedom, autonomy, and discretion with mindless standardized approaches and operating procedures to ensure that 3M delivered the same outcome from every process, regardless of who was doing the work. In manufacturing terms, this meant that there would be fewer than 3.4 defects for every million items produced, which, from a statistical perspective, represented six standard deviations from the mean, hence the name *six sigma*. Costs would be continuously and relentlessly driven lower and lower over time, hence the adjective *lean*. Under McNerney's leadership, 3M trained thousands of employees as Lean Six Sigma Black Belts who became masters at the new discipline in manufacturing and could train others. 3M also put nearly every one of its employees through several days of Lean Six Sigma Green Belt training to ensure they knew and could apply the basic operating principles in supporting and administrative functions. The initial results were impressive and seemed to justify the large jump in stock price that heralded McNerney's reign.

Black Belts found ways to eliminate 40 percent of manufacturing costs by abolishing variation and establishing efficiency in the production process. Green Belt projects found similar opportunities to remove inefficiencies from other administration and operating processes. McNerney's Lean Six Sigma playbook yielded stellar results, with operating profit margins increasing from 17 percent to 23 percent between 2001 and 2005.

But the same investors that demanded greater Lean operating discipline and efficiency that McNerney delivered began to see the early warning signs that 3M's iconic innovation engine was misfiring. New products less than four years old began to decline from 30 percent to less than 25 percent of total sales. The innovation pipeline looked full of uninspiring incremental innovations and me-too novelties, not the breakthrough and radical innovations of the past that generated larger profit margins and stronger growth prospects than those seen in incremental innovations.

McNerney next had 3M apply the same Lean Six Sigma process to R&D and innovation that was applied to other production and operating areas. This approach violated 3M's key innovation principles and processes. Steven Boyd, a PhD researcher at 3M, said that 3M employees "found the constant analysis stifling." Part of the Lean process was to complete a "red book" that required an employee to record scores of pages of charts and tables of information regarding market size, market potential, and production issues. The outcome of this approach, according to Boyd, was to drive the process toward lower risk incremental innovations. He said, "You're supposed to be having something that was going to be producing a profit, if not next quarter, it better be the quarter after that." There was no longer any focus on blue-sky opportunities. Lean Six Sigma had eliminated the first two growth phases (discovery and incubating) of the Innovation Lifecycle. By doing so, 3M lost its innovation pipeline.

The Lean Six Sigma focus on the short-term meant that 3M could no longer spend years developing new products. Art Fry, one of the 3M scientists who had invented Post-it Notes, and several other 3M employees familiar with this innovation, discussed how the new Lean process would have impacted Post-it Note development. He said, "We all came to the conclusion that there was no way in the world that anything like a Post-it Note would ever emerge from this new system."

Ultimately, the innovation DNA of 3M began to reject the Lean Six Sigma DNA transplant by McNerney. Employees found that rigid processes stifled ingenuity, because they no longer allowed variation, interaction, and selection. Of course the processes did, since the objective of Lean Six Sigma is to eliminate variation and make everything and everyone the same. Eliminating interaction and keeping people isolated in their own functional departments, rather than in cross-functional teams, accomplished this. Freedom of choice in selecting new projects and ideas to pursue was eliminated. Passionate people could no longer follow their intuition, gut, and excitement and obtain forgiveness rather than permission. Failure was frowned upon and discouraged. Leaders were not allowed to stand by idly and allow and enable people to take charge. Instead, they were charged with stopping variation and limiting both choice and wasteful interactions that violated standard operating procedures.

Balancing Lean and Innovation

Perhaps McNerney was prescient enough to see the limits of his Lean Six Sigma approach to 3M's revival. After a few years of impressive efficiency gains, he began to see that future gains could be earned only through top-line growth that would emerge from innovation. Yet the methods he had used to eliminate waste were killing innovation. Investors and employees were also seeing this and realizing that something had to change. The change was to swap out McNerney for a more ambidextrous CEO who could apply both mindless Lean and mindful Innovation Disciplines simultaneously.

On June 30, 2005, less than five years after arriving, McNerney abruptly announced he was leaving 3M to take the helm of Boeing. (BCG, BusinessWeeks' annual most innovative company rankings showed that 3M had fallen from number one the year he arrived to number seven the year after his departure.* This time the 3M board sought someone who seemed to understand how to apply both mindful innovation and mindless Lean Discipline. They turned to George Buckley, a British businessman with a PhD in electrical engineering who was a scientist at heart with several patents to his name.

---

* Jena McGregor, "The World's Most Innovative Companies," businessweek.com, April 23, 2006, accessed May 23, 2014, http://www.businessweek.com/stories/2006-04-23/the-worlds-most-innovative-companies.

Buckley immediately began dialing back McNerney's Lean Six Sigma initiatives.[†] He said, "Perhaps one of the mistakes that we made as a company—it's one of the dangers of Six Sigma—is that when you value sameness more than you value creativity, I think you potentially undermine the heart and soul of a company like 3M." In explaining the limits of Lean Six Sigma in innovation, Buckley said, "You can't put a Six Sigma process into that area and say, well, I'm getting behind on invention, so I'm going to schedule myself for three good ideas on Wednesday and two on Friday. That's not how creativity works." Craig Oster, a thirty-year 3M innovation veteran, agreed, saying, "It's really tough to schedule innovation."[‡]

Buckley applied the mindless Lean Discipline to the production of 3M's fifty-five thousand products, but he removed it from its more mindful R&D and innovation efforts. By restoring an innovation discipline after McNerney left, 3M has seen its revenues from products less than three years old bounce back from 20 percent to over 30 percent. This is critical to 3M's identity, because, according to Larry Wendling, the head of R&D at 3M, "Our business model is literally new-product innovation."[§]

Buckley found that the key to balancing the tension between mindfulness and mindlessness is to have a general bias for mindfulness to dominate discovery and incubation while allowing a gradual, but not exclusive, hand off to mindlessness for accelerating and scaling. When companies fail, it is because they do not understand this balancing act.

Ambidextrous leaders like Buckley are rare. Most tend to be good at one discipline or the other, which is why we generally see

---

[†] Stefan H. Thomke and Ashok Nimgade, "Innovation at 3M Corporation (A)," Harvard Business School Case 699-012, August 1998 (revised July 2012).

[‡] Marc Gunther, "3M's innovation revival," money.cnn.com, September 24, 2010, accessed May 23, 2014, http://money.cnn.com/2010/09/23/news/companies/3m_innovation_revival.fortune/index.htm.

[§] Brian Hindo, "At 3M a struggle between efficiency and creativity," businessweek.com, June 10, 2007, accessed May 23, 2014, http://www.businessweek.com/stories/2007-06-10/at-3m-a-struggle-between-efficiency-and-creativity.

organizations cycle back and forth from a more Lean orientation to a more innovative one. Leaders see themselves as only being able to support one identity at a time within the organization. More often than not, to the detriment of mindful innovation, that identity is based upon a mindless Lean Discipline. It is generally the Lean way or the highway.

The Emergence of Scientific Management and Ford Motors

Today, two-thirds of the Fortune 500 claim to follow Lean Six Sigma disciplines, and we would argue that all companies of meaningful size follow this discipline in some form or other, even if they don't officially classify it as such.

Why is this?

When leaders are forced to choose between running the business of today and creating the business of tomorrow, most choose the former. If the priority is on running an existing business, then leaders will employ mindless processes and structures to ensure efficiency, productivity, and near-term profitability.

Where did this mindless Lean Discipline come from?

The genesis of Lean Discipline occurred in the 1880 and 1890s with Frederick Winslow Taylor and the scientific management breakthrough. The objective was to apply science and engineering to business and management processes to improve productivity and efficiency. Through time and motion studies, Taylor identified best practices that would increase productivity by standardizing activities in a way that decreased time and resources for the same quality and quantity of output. Taylor didn't want variation or creativity in the work process. He valued labor, but in a mindless way, where standardized and scientific processes could replace any worker and maintain the same output and outcomes.

Scientific management hit its zenith in the 1910s and 1920s. Perhaps no better example of the application of these principles exists than Henry Ford's Model-T assembly line. Ford launched the Model-T in 1908 with a standardized production process that replaced the handmade and mindful custom assembly methods of the day. Through this approach, Ford decreased production time from twelve and a half hours to just ninety-three minutes, which allowed him to sell the car for less than half of what other manufacturers charged. By 1914, Ford had a 50 percent market share and was producing more cars than all other car manufacturers combined. Mindless mass production could achieve what mindful custom assembly could never envision.

Deming Helps the Japanese Destroy the U.S. Auto Industry and Then Redeems Himself

These principles continued to drive production processes throughout the Second World War with amazing effect. To improve production quality and quantity, the U.S. government brought five scholars of statistical process control (SPC) together to form the Emergency Technical Committee. W. Edward Deming was a leader among these five production process luminaries who taught manufacturers across the country how to apply SPC in the production of planes, tanks, jeeps, trucks, guns, and other equipment. The results were astounding. Whereas at the beginning of the war the United States was only producing seven thousand airplanes per year, by the end of the war, the country was producing nearly that many per month.

After World War II, the SPC discipline began to fade since the United States easily dominated global manufacturing as one of the only nations whose domestic industries had not been destroyed during the war. Japan, on the other hand, was eager to find ways to build a competitive advantage for its domestic companies. So when Deming was assigned by the government to assist Gen. Douglas MacArthur in rebuilding Japan, the Japanese were eager to learn and apply Deming's SPC principles to restart their industries. Although Deming went to Japan as a statistician to assist in a postwar census of the country, he frequently lectured and consulted with Japanese industry leaders regarding how SPC could improve quality while reducing expenses and increasing productivity and market share. Among those attending Deming's lectures were Akio Morita, the cofounder of Sony, and Genichi Taguchi, a statistician who later developed the Toyota manufacturing process.

By the 1970s, U.S. car manufacturers were experiencing significant declines in revenues and profits due to poor quality. Japanese automakers, however, following Lean Deming disciplines, grabbed larger and larger shares of the U.S. market while U.S. firms failed to understand how they should respond to this competition. For example, Ford simultaneously manufactured transmissions for one car in both Japan and the United States. American customers found the performance and quality of the Japanese transmission superior, so they did not purchase the U.S. version but rather waited weeks and months for the Japanese units to arrive.

When Ford's engineers tore the two transmissions apart, they found that the one produced domestically was within manufacturing specifications and tolerances, which was plus-or-minus one-eighth of an inch. But the Japanese transmission had more precise tolerances that measured within one-sixteenth of an inch. Ford engineers had thought this level of precision was not possible to achieve, but it made a huge difference to transmission performance and consumer satisfaction. This discovery triggered Ford to approach Deming to help it achieve the quality levels he had helped the Japanese realize.

Between 1979 and 1982, Ford lost over three billion dollars. John Manoogian, Ford's head of quality, recruited Deming to help jump-start the quality program at Ford. To his and Ford's leadership surprise, Deming diagnosed that the company had a leadership, management, and culture problem, not a quality problem. And the latter, he noted, couldn't be addressed without the former being transformed. Deming claimed that 85 percent of the quality issues arose from bad management practices and a culture that didn't value quality.

Deming worked with Ford to change its culture by altering the management and leadership philosophy, values, structures, policies, and procedures, not just in quality, but across the board. Within four years, Ford launched one of its most successful products of all time: the Taurus/Sable line. Doing so allowed Ford, in 1986, and for the first time since 1920, to earn more than General Motors and Chrysler. When asked about its transformation, Ford CEO Donald Peterson said, "We are moving forward, building a quality culture at Ford, and the many changes that have been taking place here have their roots directly in Dr. Deming's teaching."

The United States Learns Lean Lessons from Japan

Shortly after the Taurus and Sable models started rolling off the production lines, an article titled "Triumph of Lean Production System" by John Krafcik appeared in the Fall 1988 issue of *Sloan Management Review*. The article was based on Krafcik's master's thesis, which chronicled his experience as a quality engineer at the GM/Toyota joint venture New United Motor Manufacturing (NUMMI) plant in Fremont, California. The production processes he experienced emerged from the work done by Taguchi at Toyota in the 1950s and 1960s. While many Japanese manufacturers followed the same Deming principles under the Lean Discipline, Toyota's version epitomized the discipline.

In Lean processes, the objective is the elimination of non-value-added work (*muda*), which improves quality and reduces time and production costs. This type of waste adds additional features to a product to differentiate it in ways consumers don't value. (This happened in the toothpaste marketplace when the proliferation of different types actually destroyed value by confusing customers. See page 80.) Elimination of *muda* enables a smooth flow of production by eliminating unevenness (*mura*), which, in turn, enables just-in-time (JIT) inventory management. This allows a stable, predictable, and reliable process without interruptions. Once *muda* and *mura* are in place, unnecessary burdens on the production system (*muri*) are eliminated, and the right resources can be matched with the right task to achieve balance. For Toyota, the focus on Lean is to eliminate all three forms of waste (*muda, muri,* and *mura*) to achieve Deming's promise of "highest quality, lowest costs, and largest market share."

Deming's teachings initially emerged from SPC, but as organizations refined them, they were rebranded as Total Quality Management (TQM), an integrated management philosophy for continually improving the quality of products and processes. As a management philosophy, it focuses on establishing the values and beliefs that form the foundation for a culture of quality characterized by Toyota and Ford. TQM capitalized on the engagement of all stakeholders, including management, workforce, suppliers, and customers. The five key elements that emerged from TQM are (1) continuous improvement, (2) Six Sigma statistical applications, (3) employee empowerment, (4) benchmarking, and (5) JIT inventory management.

Lean Emerges as the Dominant
Discipline in the United States

In the 1980s, as GM adopted the Lean production methods of Toyota and Ford after losing its profit leadership to these two Deming disciples and his SPC principles. Simultaneously, Motorola began addressing its own quality and productivity issues. In 1986, Bill Smith, a senior engineer and scientist at Motorola, under the direction of Bob Galvin, son of Motorola founder Paul Galvin, introduced the Six Sigma quality system, which would eventually become a global standard for quality and productivity.

Since its founding in 1928 as Galvin Manufacturing Corporation in Chicago, Motorola had become one of the most innovative companies in the world. It pioneered most of the technologies that are the foundation for today's mobile phone industry, which is why Google found Motorola's intellectual property portfolio so attractive and decided to acquire it in 2012. It also became a leader in the development and commercialization of transistors and microprocessors, providing the digital brains for most of the earliest and most successful computers, including Commodore, Apple I and II, and Apple's Macintosh.

However, by the mid-1970s, Motorola's heavily weighted Innovation Discipline had led the company to experience unacceptable levels of production error rates that were hurting quality, productivity, and profits. These failures and the associated pain came to a head when Art Sundry, a senior Motorola executive , severely criticized the company's poor quality and demanded improvement. Its quality failures and pain associated with poor operating performance caused significant tension in the organization once Sundry demanded improvement.

As we have already pointed out, the key in balancing the tension of mindfulness and mindlessness is to have a general bias for mindfulness to dominate discovery and incubation while allowing a gradual, but not exclusive, hand off to mindlessness for accelerating and scaling. When companies fail, it is because they do not understand this balancing act.

Up to this point, Motorola, like most other U.S. corporations, operated under the paradigm that quality isn't free and therefore costs extra, and a company like Motorola that was struggling to achieve operating performance targets couldn't afford better quality. What it found, however, through the application of SPC systems, was that quality actually lowered costs by decreasing defects and improving productivity. Once this dawned on the leadership, Motorola, under Smith's leadership, spent the next decade more formally developing this management system and christened it Six Sigma. It is now a registered trademark of Motorola and has been responsible for generating over twenty billion dollars in savings at Motorola over the past quarter of a century.

GE Merges Lean and Six Sigma

While developed and refined by Motorola, perhaps no organization has had a greater influence on its adoption on a massive scale than General Electric. When Jack Welch assumed the leadership mantle at GE in 1981, he inherited a sprawling but poorly disciplined conglomerate that lacked adequate core and standardized processes, procedures, and structures. He saw Six Sigma as the discipline he could drive throughout all management and operating activities across the organization to improve quality and profits. By adopting Six Sigma, GE experienced dramatic improvements across its business and then began to add the Lean principles developed and applied by Toyota to Six Sigma to establish what is now labeled Lean Six Sigma. Other corporations, large and small, began to see the Lean Discipline, as did Welch, as a way to impose discipline across complex organizations that could standardize best practices in a scientific, measurable, and quantitative way.

Through a decade of operational refinement and improvements, organizations such as Motorola and GE took the basic principles of SPC and expanded them. The three primary principles of SPC, which provided the foundation for Six Sigma, are*

- **Eliminate variation**—Continuous efforts to achieve stable and predictable process results (i.e., reduce process variation) are of vital importance to business success.
- **Control outcomes**—Manufacturing and business processes have characteristics that can be measured, analyzed, improved, and controlled.
- **Organization support**—Achieving sustained quality improvement requires commitment from the entire organization, particularly from top-level management.

To these, the Six Sigma movement added the following elements:†

- **Economic outcomes**—A clear focus on achieving measurable and quantifiable financial returns from any Six Sigma project.
- **Leadership engagement**—An increased emphasis on strong and passionate management leadership and support.
- **Specialization of roles**—A special infrastructure of "Champions," "Master Black Belts," "Black Belts," "Green Belts," etc. to lead and implement the Six Sigma approach.
- **Fact-based choice**—A clear commitment to making decisions on the basis of verifiable data rather than assumptions and guesswork.

---

* "Statistical process control," wikipedia.com, n.p., accessed May 23, 2014, http://en.wikipedia.org/wiki/Statistical_process_control.

† "Lean Six Sigma," wikipedia.com, April 2014, accessed May 23, 2014, http://en.wikipedia.org/wiki/Lean_Six_Sigma.

No leader should question the need for Lean Discipline because mindlessness is essential to survival. It has become the dominant management system for nearly all organizations. It has even become the discipline applied to incremental innovation, with the stated purpose to drive sustainable innovation that reduces frequent failures. But the paradox is that sustainable and incremental innovations don't actually enable organizations to survive over the long run. In fact, they tend to create barriers to sustainability. This is because several of the Six Sigma principles above run counter to those complexity-based principles and processes necessary to drive innovation, namely, variation, interaction, and selection.

Command Cannot Control Innovation

In PwC's *2011 Annual CEO Survey,* innovation shot to the top of the list of issues that concern CEOs. As the rate of change has accelerated across all industries and geographies, CEOs and their leadership teams are finding their organizations struggling to adapt to increasingly turbulent markets. These leaders have discovered that unlike the command and control they experience in Lean Discipline, they need to develop a new tool kit to become innovators. In stable markets, Lean Discipline enables companies to lock into optimal standardized processes to deliver high-quality products with declining costs, rising profits, and high productivity. But in chaotic and rapidly evolving markets, Lean Discipline fails to enable the *variation, interaction,* and *selection* necessary for long-term survival.

To succeed, organizations and their leadership must realize that equilibrium doesn't really exist and never will. This means that the application of Lean Discipline will always be ephemeral and that management processes that presuppose and require equilibrium won't experience long-term survival. Breakthrough, radical, and disruptive innovation can't emerge from mindless practices and structures. This means the methods you apply to exploit efficiency won't enable exploration of innovation since each requires very different management practices. This also explains why organizations that have followed a growth strategy of fast followership—like Dell in PDAs or Hewlett Packard (HP) in tablets—are rarely leaders and why such an approach often leads to failure. This is increasingly the case as the rate of change accelerates because success in the digital age generally benefits from network effects that lead to nonproportional success. As Microsoft learned, being a fast follower of Google has only led to perpetual failure. To understand the basic theory and principles of today's change, it helps to understand some complex adaptive systems theory.

Operating at the Edge of Chaos

All systems we interact with—whether social, economic, political, biological, environmental, or legal—are complex adaptive systems. None of these operate in a stable state of equilibrium, at least not for very long, and they rarely enter a true state of chaos, again not for very long. They tend to operate between the edges of the two states of equilibrium and chaos.

A characteristic of a complex adaptive system, therefore, is that it is always changing and moving between the edges of these two states. Individual agents that operate within the systems, such as people or organizations, must adapt to these changes in order to survive. Those that adapt quickly and effectively thrive; those that don't will die. Adaptation occurs as a result of the three primary processes we discussed earlier: *interaction, variation,* and *selection.* To adapt, an agent must interact with other agents, and through this interaction they must create and/or identify new variations that will be more successful in adapting to a new environment.

Then these agents must have the freedom to select those variations and modify them in ways that will increase utility and value within the system to ensure survival. As the magnitude and amplitude of change increases in a complex system, the levels of *interaction, variation,* and *selection* must also increase to accelerate adaptation and thereby ensure survival.

When operating at the edge of chaos, the underlying turbulence of the system requires rapid and radical innovations to ensure survival. The smartphone market, for example, operates near the edge of chaos. Leading organizations that developed and dominated the smartphone market (e.g., Motorola, Nokia, Microsoft, Palm, and Research in Motion [RIM]) are failing to adapt to the changing paradigm created by new entrants. As a result, many of these players have failed because they haven't been able to keep pace with the changes brought to market by Apple, Google, and Samsung. As a market operates at the edge of chaos, product lifecycles are short, having collapsed to less than a year. Successful new products emerge and scale rapidly to dominance, while most of the rest, like the Palm and RIM tablets, fail within weeks.

But not all industries and markets operate at the edge of chaos. Many have more modest rates and magnitudes of change. The numerous parts of the energy and transportation industry represent examples that operate at the edge of equilibrium. The internal combustion engine has dominated transportation for over a century and will likely not be replaced in a major way by electric cars or any other alternative for decades, if at all. This is why we have seen so many failures of electric car engine and battery companies that expected market dynamics similar to smartphones at the edge of chaos but found they were operating nearer the edge of equilibrium. The outcome is a fairly stable demand for gasoline, which is the primary output of oil refining. While this market also experiences meaningful innovation, it occurs over longer time frames and requires greater resources.

One of the most radical innovations to emerge in the past several decades has been horizontal drilling and fracking oil shale thousands of feet beneath the surface of the earth. The consequence is the release of enormous volumes of hydrocarbons. These innovations have changed the energy industry structure and dynamics in ways unimaginable five years ago. New entrants have become very successful, but the overall scope, magnitude, and rate of market turbulence pales in comparison to what we have seen in the media or telecommunications industry.

Most businesses and industries operate somewhere between these two edge states and rarely at the edge of either chaos or equilibrium. In most cases, industries will move to an edge state and remain there for a period of time and then shift more toward the center. Internet media, for example, is an innovation that pushed the news media to the edge of chaos over the past decade and has led to massive failures among the largest news companies. However, many, such as the *Wall Street Journal* and *New York Times,* have since learned how to innovate their business and revenue models to adapt, and they have moved from the edge of chaos toward the center between chaos and equilibrium.

The trouble with all industries and markets, and the difficulties for leaders, is that information technology innovations such as social, mobile, analytics, and the cloud (SMAC) have caused nearly all industries and market dynamics to heat up and become more turbulent. This has moved nearly all industries toward the edge of chaos. It is also why continual and sustainable Innovation discipline has become so critical to survival.

The Creative Genius Imperative

Nowhere is the impact of the accelerating rates of innovation more powerfully felt than on the mortality of companies. Organizations that fail to innovate fail to survive. For this reason, the average life span of a company in the S&P 500 has continued to decline as innovation has accelerated. In 1957, when the S&P 500 was first created, the expected life-span of a company was sixty-one years. By 2012 it had fallen by nearly two-thirds to only eighteen years.* For this reason, most of the companies in today's S&P 500 will not survive long enough to employ people during even half of their working careers.

This also means that organizations generally don't have the time to be fast followers. By the time they decide to come to market with a me-too solution, the market has moved forward to the next generation or two. HP experienced this in just one year with its failed attempt to compete in the tablet and smartphone markets by buying Palm. By the time HP resuscitated Palm's business and brought its first products to market, Apple had launched the second generation iPad, and HP's tablets couldn't even be given away at a 50+ percent discount. Cisco ran afoul in the video market within just eighteen months of buying Flip as the market moved rapidly to smartphones as the mini-digital video recorder of choice. Within a span of just three years, Johnson & Johnson found that, by not keeping pace with the cardiovascular stent market innovations of other market leaders like Medtronic and Boston Scientific—a market the company had initially pioneered—became out of reach. Johnson & Johnson could not keep up with the new innovations and had to shut the business down because there were no buyers for an also-ran in a dynamic industry.

A failure to innovate led these businesses to worthlessness in a very short time. They couldn't even be sold for scrap value despite the fact that they had been worth hundreds of millions or even

---

* "Creative destruction whips through corporate America," innosight.com, n.p., accessed May 23, 2014, http://www.innosight.com/innovation-resources/strategy-innovation/upload/creative-destruction-whips-through-corporate-america_final2012.pdf.

billions of dollars just a year or two before. The companies had to shut these businesses down completely and write them off.

What happened to these companies has three important implications:

1. You must develop your creative genius to keep pace with a rapidly and radically changing world.

2. Leaders must tap in to everyone's creative genius to keep pace with industry dynamics.

3. The type of leadership required in organizations today is radically different than that required in the past. Leadership must now promote mindlessness while at the same time ensuring and enabling ever-greater mindfulness. But to do this, leaders must first put aside the innovation myths that keep them in a mindless world and limit their creative genius.

REMEMBER

- ✔ In organizations, mindlessness, which provides resources, time, and money, is viewed as a positive, given it is so efficient.

- ✔ Mindfulness, including experimentation, trial and error, waste, failure, inefficiency, and pain, is often viewed as negative by organizations.

- ✔ All innovation derives from mindfulness but can only become of value by scaling it through the processes of mindlessness outlined in the Innovation Lifecycle.

- ✔ The Innovation Trio consists of variation, interaction, and selection. Without all three, you can't innovate.
  - › Variation gives employees license to think and act differently.
  - › Interaction allows cross-functional and cross-organizational teams to communicate and share their variety.
  - › Selection gives individuals and teams free time to innovate while protecting them from their boss.

- ✔ All organizations operate on a seesaw between equilibrium and chaos. Lean Six Sigma is an effective operating model near equilibrium, but the Innovation operating model is necessary when operating near the edge of chaos.

- ✔ Individual creative genius must be developed in order to keep pace in a rapidly and radically changing world (a.k.a. near the edge of chaos).

✔ Leaders must tap into everyone's creative genius to keep pace with industry dynamics. The greater the turbulence, the more innovation required.

✔ Leadership must promote mindlessness for Lean efficiency while simultaneously ensuring and enabling ever-greater mindfulness to enable innovation and growth.

QUESTIONS

> How well does your organization see the benefits and limits of Lean Six Sigma as its primary operating discipline?

> How often do you, at a personal level, allow such mindlessness to dominate most of what you do?

> How often do you take time to be mindful and ensure you create and apply the structures and practices necessary to support mindful creativity?

CHAPTER FOUR

A Dozen Mindless Myths

We live in a world filled with mindless organizations, structures, and processes. Forget about hybrid or mountain bikes; it's a struggle to find the time and freedom to ride anything other than a stationary cycle or an occasional road bike. As a result, we have come to believe in many myths that maintain our beliefs and overdependence on mindlessness. A real problem for innovators is that false beliefs create mental models that obstruct innovation because they lead to overreliance on Lean processes.

The greatest barrier to being an innovator is a lack of belief that you are or can become one. Without an identity as an innovator, you can never become one. Groundbreaking actions flow from original thoughts that have their genesis in innovative beliefs. Therefore, if you want to become more innovative, you must first change your beliefs and overcome the twelve myths that are holding you back.

Myth 1: Any New Idea or Product Is an Innovation

After discussing the challenges in medical technology with the executive team of one of the world's largest orthopedic device companies, several people from R&D came to me. A spokesperson asked if I could help get the organization and leadership to understand that most of what was thought of as innovation wasn't innovation at all. Their Lean R&D process guided them to create a steady flow of new features to meet the competition, but these too often lacked focus on developing new sources of value. They found that this mindless, Lean R&D process resulted in a significant waste of time and resources. The person asked, "Isn't innovation more than just matching competitors in a never-ending arms race of new features?"

When we meet with people in any organization and ask them to define innovation, we seem to get as many definitions as there are bodies in the room. Most people correctly think that innovation must be novel, new, and unique in some way. But when this is the only measure of innovation, organizations and consumers can drown in a sea of meaningless choices that overwhelm, confuse, and bewilder. We call this *novelty fatigue*.

Perhaps no market has experienced as much excess novelty as toothpaste. In the fifty-five years since Crest hit the market, the number of toothpaste choices exploded from one to over four hundred, with a hundred new product introductions per year. Yet the two leading toothpaste companies, Procter & Gamble and Colgate, which controlled 70 percent of the market, readily admit there isn't much difference among them. A backlash from retailers and consumers has caused these companies to recently decrease their variety of choice by 25 percent.*

---

* Ellen Byron, "Whiteness brightens and confuses," wsj.com, February 23, 2011, accessed May 23, 2014, http://online.wsj.com/news/articles/SB10001 424052748703373404576148363319407354?mg=reno64-wsj.

We have seen novelty fatigue in the cell phone, smartphone, and tablet markets. It is interesting to note that the organizations we often regard as the most innovative in personal electronics seem to provide the fewest choices and options. Less successful competitors rush to market with a torrent of half-baked products that overwhelm would-be customers with a variety of low-value or no-value offers. And the results are disastrous: HP writing off the $1.2 billion purchase of Palm within a month of its tablet launch; RIM taking a $600 million hit to earnings due to their failed tablet introduction; and Microsoft pulling its Kin smartphone within three months of launch.

Novelty does not create value.

We often find organizations that begin to focus on innovation open the floodgates to all employees to come up with new ideas, and then they drown in novelty and suffer from novelty fatigue. Hundreds and thousands of new ideas rush forward, overwhelming the capacity of the organization's innovation support teams to evaluate them. When they assess these novelties, they find that most are half-baked and are not focused on creating new sources of value.

The role of value is often overlooked and yet critical in classifying something new as an innovation. Former P&G CEO A. G. Lafley makes this point: "You need creativity and invention, but until you can connect that creativity to the customer in the form of a product or a service that meaningfully changes their lives, I would argue you don't yet have innovation."[†]

Ideas must be new and novel, but until they create value, they are not innovations. Organizations that apply this standard don't suffer themselves, nor do they cause their customers to suffer from novelty fatigue.

---

† A. J. Lafley, "How Procter & Gamble plans to clean up," businessweek.com, April 1, 2009, accessed May 23, 2014, http://www.businessweek.com/stories/2009-04-01/how-procter-and-gamble-plans-to-clean-up.

We define innovation as value-creating novelty.

Myth 2: Innovation Can Be Delegated

Many innovation teams within organizations have asked us how we can help them get their leadership to believe in and support innovation. Recently, a global cardiovascular medical device company's leadership selected a dozen executives to lead an innovation team. Yet the team was not given any resources or budget to support these efforts and had to continue to do their day jobs without any new backing. They were expected to use their alleged free time to diagnose the company's innovation failings and fix them without distracting or engaging senior leadership. Consequently, this team correctly identified that their first priority was convincing their C-suite to be personally engaged. These executives approached us about building a burning platform to get their senior leadership's attention and commitment to create an innovation culture at the company.

This doesn't mean that the CEO is the primary creative genius and innovator. The names of Jeff Bezos and Steve Jobs appear on very few patents. But great leaders ensure that their organizations have the necessary innovation operating model to instill the culture, values, beliefs, and identity to propagate innovation throughout their organization so their people believe they are or can become creative geniuses.

The CEO of a Fortune 25 insurance company approached us recently for some help. He said that while innovation was one of the five stated values of his organization, recent employee engagement surveys and customer satisfaction studies revealed that both groups thought this was a farce. He was preparing to retire within the next eighteen months and felt like he needed to personally address the innovation failing of the organization before he left and "get innovation into the DNA of every associate within our organization." He took the lead to define the identity of innovation at the company and provided the resources and support for structural reform to do so.

Senior leadership is essential because innovations are fragile when they are born and need protection, support, and resources to help them grow into successful solutions. But they also need varying types of discipline, just as with real people progressing from infancy through childhood and into their teenage years. This is not a mindless discipline applied to mature, lean, and scaled parts of the rest of the organization, but rather a mindful one necessary for fragile new initiatives. When the leadership team doesn't provide the right conditions and encouragements, innovations are stillborn or spend years in the innovation NICU, where they fail to thrive and eventually die.

This is why a failure to innovate is a failure of leadership. When innovation doesn't occur, there is no one to fault but the CEO and the leadership team. Moreover, because innovation by its nature cannot be controlled, CEOs must attend to what can be enabled, that is, structures and practices to support a culture that nourishes and rewards fresh thinking.

Southwest Airlines and Internet shoe retailer Zappos offer well-known case studies of effective innovation to improve customer service, particularly customer loyalty. Both outpaced established rivals in very competitive industries. They did so by building the right culture. Zappos CEO Tony Hsieh said, "When they get the culture right, other elements such as the customer service or innovation all fall into place."*

CEOs must help their organization to value fast, frequent, frugal failure and use it effectively to learn and thereby improve

---

* Jeremy Twitchell, "From upstart to $1 billion behemoth, Zappos marks 10 years," lasvegassun. com, June 16, 2009, accessed May 23, 2014, http://www.lasvegassun.com/news/2009/jun/16/ upstart-1-billion-behemoth-zappos-marks-10-year-an/.

their company's innovation processes, capabilities, and culture. "Management's job is not to prevent risk but to build the capability to recover when failures occur," observed Ed Catmull, president of Pixar and Disney Animation Studios in the *Harvard Business Review*. "We must constantly challenge all of our assumptions and search for the flaws that could destroy our culture."*

The goal for the entire leadership team in an innovation environment is to celebrate failure, enable it to happen fast, and to learn from the failures to explore other options that improve the quantity and quality of ideas that can lead to innovation. You just can't stand on the sidelines and instruct others to take the lead.

You must not just delegate but lead and take personal responsibility for the innovation agenda, because a failure to innovate is a failure of leadership.

Myth 3: Innovation Means Technology and New Products

When asked to identify an innovation, we probably think of the newest and coolest widget: a phone, television, car, etc. Yet innovations can occur in a number of areas beyond technology and products, because any type of novelty that creates value is an innovation. This means that a new service, process, distribution model, marketing approach, branding, or business model can all be innovative.

Indeed, when you look at studies on the probability of success and the value produced by innovations, you see that product development is the riskiest of all types. You also see that business-model innovation generates the most value and is generally the result

---

* Ed Catmull, "How Pixar Fosters Collective Creativity," Harvard Business Review, hbr.org, September 2008, accessed May 23, 2014, http://hbr. org/2008/09/how-pixar-fosters-collective-creativity/ar/1#.

of combining several original ideas together in a novel approach across a system or solution set.

The emergence of the mobile app market provides a great example of going beyond product innovation. The mobile device, whether a phone or tablet, provides an innovation platform. But without the addition of new processes and business models, it wouldn't be very successful. By leveraging a new technology platform combined with an effective marketplace for distributing apps and simple development tools (like software development kits [SDKs]) to enable and empower millions of programmers, an entirely new market and ecosystem has emerged. The biggest failing of RIM, Nokia, and Microsoft was too much focus on traditional technology innovation and too little on these other ways of generating new value through business models.

When you succeed in getting innovation into your DNA, then you will engage the creative genius of everyone in the organization to invent all types of innovation in all business activities.

Myth 4: Innovation Is Only About Transformational or Radical Ideas

We have been asked by the leadership of several pharmaceutical companies to help them identify the most disruptive new technologies that will enable them to provide value beyond pills. They often ask us to limit our views to those things that will transform the market in the next twenty-four to thirty-six months. When we share findings that our clients see as commonsensical or a variation on a known theme, they often ask, "Is that all you've got? I've read about all these in the paper. I want to see something I've never heard of before."

At the same time, those things we share with our clients are things that they aren't currently doing and have no immediate plans to do anything about, even though they've already heard about them. They then further explain that their organization is struggling to figure out how to think about innovating in the areas we've identified.

How often have you had a similar experience? Have you worked on some innovation initiatives and come up with some new ideas, just to hear other leaders or team members complain that they aren't big enough or they aren't billion-dollar ideas? If these are not ideas that are going to put a dent in the universe, are they still not worthwhile pursuing?

Be honest. Do you think it likely that something you've never heard of will transform the market in the next two years?

Very few ideas are transformational or radical. Even those that are didn't start out that way, and they were nearly always composed of many incremental ideas fashioned over time into a new, big idea that eventually became disruptive.

When it comes to ideas, it appears that you are often damned if you do and damned if you don't. If you don't come up with big ideas, then no one cares. If you come up with big ideas that you project could transform the marketplace, then your organization doesn't believe they will be successful. As a result, you are asked to temper your aspirations in such a way that they look more realistic, that is, adding to what is already there.

An interesting observation of radical ideas, however, is that if you take an exponential growth curve that looks like the traditional hockey stick graph from your projections of adoption of your radical new innovation, and you then select any small segment of time along the graph, each segment is a straight line. It is only when you look at radical change over a long enough time frame that things look exponential. So change in short time periods is always linear and only becomes nonlinear as time increases.

The same is true for radical and disruptive innovations. Smartphones are a case in point. If you disassemble and deconstruct one, you find that they have been built by combining many incremental innovations in novel ways. Figuring out how to combine incremental innovations in ways to build radical ones with transformational power is the job of a creative genius.

Most innovation is not radical. Leadership should not disparage smaller-scale innovations. The nonstop discussion of disruptive, transformative, and radical innovation within the business community and academia tends to establish the impression that if it isn't radical, it isn't an innovation. The outcome is unrealistic expectations with regards to the volume and nature of innovations that organizations will bring to the marketplace. As Unilever CEO Paul Polman said, "People tend to see innovation strictly in terms of revolutionary, breakthrough products—technologies to sequester carbon emissions or microchips that can process data 600 times faster. That's fine. But most innovations are the result of steady, continuous improvement."[*]

Radical, transformational and disruptive innovations are the by-products of reconfiguring many incremental innovations in novel ways.

Myth 5: Formal Structures and Process Stifle Innovation

People generally think that since innovation is serendipitous in nature and can't be controlled, it can't be disciplined. They reference Post-it Notes or Viagra as examples of how innovations occurred through chance encounters. Others talk about the

---

[*] "Demystifying innovation," pwc.com, 2011, http://www.pwc.com/gx/en/corporate-strategy-services/assets/ceosurvey-innovation.pdf.

innovation process like dreaming and suggest that organizations need a nonstructured, nonstressful, unencumbered environment to enable innovation to randomly occur. Too often we tend to think of innovation as a mystical process with magical elements, where any process or structure applied to improve innovation would be like bottling lightning. Is this really the case?

When we look at people whom we consider the greatest innovators of all time, people like Leonardo da Vinci, Thomas Edison, Henry Ford, and Steve Jobs, a common characteristic among them all is that they were highly disciplined in applying structure and process to their pioneering endeavors. They developed an innovation operating model that allowed them to systematically employ and enable serendipity to promote innovation.

The research that explores how intuitive innovators think and how their thinking patterns can be incorporated in the problem-solving steps that lead to discoveries find that they apply a disciplined approach to drive their creative genius. This is usually referred to as *structured problem solving,* and it reveals three broad themes:*

Problem solving is the core of innovation: Problems often emerge from failure and pain, for example, loss of market share, decline in profitability, dissatisfied customers, etc. Setbacks produce social tensions that become maladaptive and perpetuate a cycle of failure and pain. These tensions then engage passions and promote an innate creative genius to find answers and develop solutions. Innovators ask both why and why not.

Natural innovators are good at defining problems; they often see factors that others do not: They also tend to believe that (1)

---

* Christopher Wasden, Bo Parker, and Vinod Baya, "Decoding innovation's DNA," pwc.com, 2011, http://www.pwc.com/us/en/technology-forecast/2011/issue2/.

the first solutions most people provide to a problem are generally too simple because they are based upon existing mental models and (2) that the second solution is almost always too complicated because it arises by mashing up several existing mental models. Innovation comes about only by improving the understanding of the root cause of the problem and then designing a simple and elegant solution that becomes a new mental model for success.

Almost all innovation involves the application of a known solution to a problem, or part of a problem from one domain, to a new problem in a different domain: For example, the recent focus on automated automobiles is applying what has been done in aeronautics for the last twenty years to improve roadway safety and efficiency. As leaders engage the creative genius of everyone in an organization, they open collaboration to increase the source of ideas that address design problems and expose the design challenge to a large number of people from different knowledge domains. This increases the likelihood that someone will intuit what the problem has in common with a similar problem and thereby provide the solution from somewhere else. This is the application of variation, interaction, and selection.

Combining these themes, it becomes clear how organizations can recast invention challenges into problem-solving tasks that solicit creativity from all concerned. Thinking about the invention challenge as problem solving and using patterns and principles that already exist greatly simplifies the invention task. The result is a transformation into a knowledge search, pattern recognition, engagement, and growth process.

This doesn't mean that the need for serendipity should be eliminated; however, it does suggest that you can develop structures and practices that discipline serendipity in ways that will enable you to increase its frequency and focus.

Myth 6: Innovation Results from Lucky Accidents That Can't Be Planned

If only this were so. It's a fact that innovative people and companies spend most of their time running up blind alleys and taking wrong turns. Yet, crucially, they are also disciplining the creative process, increasing the chance that some ideas will score. What they do differently is work in structures and apply practices that are designed specifically to deliver innovations successfully and quickly. A mindful innovation-operating model increases serendipity, or to use a baseball term, more at bats increase the odds of success.

With companies counting on innovations to open new revenue opportunities and improve productivity, this is the time to shape a process designed to filter ideas quickly and advance the best ones to execution. The most successful organizations marry creativity and disciplined execution systems in a way that enables them to flex their focus, depending on the opportunity they are addressing.

To do so, you must see innovation as occurring along a lifecycle. To make that possible, we've broken down the innovative process into four lifecycle phases: *discovery, incubation, acceleration,* and *scaling.* Market discipline through feedback and testing, also known as *design thinking,* are incorporated into each to reduce the impact of internal thinking and consensus on the innovations. Moreover, the process structurally and operationally separates early stage innovations to give them freedom and flexibility to adapt, iterate, and morph into commercially viable solutions before bringing them into the mainstream once they achieve established milestones.

Information technology is now becoming an important tool that can increase serendipity in a disciplined manner. Applications are becoming available that help manage the complexity and learning challenges associated with structured problem solving. They do this by addressing the two biggest mental challenges facing anyone trying to adopt structured problem solving.

Applications that support structured problem solving can also be understood as *digital interfaces* in a business process that today is mostly either analog or human-based. As problems are encountered and solved by an enterprise, the flow of knowledge is added to the possible digital potential solutions available to the enterprise in an organic and spontaneous manner. No one needs to assess, classify, or otherwise intervene.

Social media, which is often incorporated into these applications, is yet another discipline that increases serendipity. It enables inventors to experience chance encounters with individuals they would never be able to meet physically due to time and location constraints and to partner with people who are otherwise unavailable.

By harnessing new technologies and the appropriate innovation operating model, you can increase the volume, velocity, and value of serendipitous encounters.

Myth 7: The More Open the Innovation Process, the Less Disciplined It Is

Many organizations keen to adopt more open approaches to innovation are reaching outside their companies to customers, suppliers, and partners in new ways. Close to 40 percent of CEOs around the world expect their company's innovations will be codeveloped.* In part, these business leaders are tapping into an established tradition behind a more open approach—for example, the automotive supply chain. What's changing is that more businesses in varied sectors are moving in this direction. The attractions are manifold and are based on a growing acceptance that the rate of change and

---

* "Demystifying innovation," http://www.pwc.com/gx/en/corporate-strategy-services/assets/ceosurvey-innovation.pdf.

the complexity it generates means that no one organization has enough of the right people and resources to innovate on its own.

P&G, for example, has set a target for 50 percent of revenues should come from innovations that have their genesis from outside sources. "Today, nearly every new item we bring out was produced with at least one partner somewhere in the world. So, for example, we co-locate scientists from partner organizations and from our organization in the same laboratory. It's amazing what you can do when you knock down the barriers in an organization or the barriers between organizations," said Bob McDonald, P&G chairman of the board, president, and CEO.*

Many are looking across the supply chain to boost new development with customers and even competitors. Former HP CEO Mark Hurd described plans for a new online applications store where some would be sourced internally while others would come from outside the company, adding, "We can't create all of this innovation by ourselves."†

There is no doubt organizations are struggling to determine how to best discipline and exploit greater customer access and input with minimum disruption to current production processes. Some companies are adding incentives to outsiders to submit ideas. GE launched an Ecomagination Challenge in 2010, backed with two hundred million dollars in seed capital for the best ideas or start-ups for the power grid. As a result, GE said it formed a dozen new partnerships.‡

---

* "Demystifying innovation," http://www.pwc.com/gx/en/corporate-strategy-services/assets/ceosurvey-innovation.pdf.

† Ben Worthen and Ian Sherr, "H-P CEO takes the stage," wsj.com, March 15, 2011, accessed May 23, 2014, http://online.wsj.com/news/articles/SB10001424052748703363904576200992379192546.

‡ "GE launches Ecoimagination," businesswire.com, May 9, 2005, accessed May 23, 2014, http://www.businesswire.com/news/home/20050509005663/en/GE-Launches-Ecomagination-Develop-Environmental-Technologies-Company-Wide.

Advances in collaboration tools, like social networking, are accelerating open innovation. Within their organizations, companies can deploy internal social networks along with collaborative tools that provide added discipline to develop interactions that go far beyond just a network of specialists. Social tools connect people who are loosely tied to the problem-solving challenge. When the open collaboration process works, these loosely connected people successfully translate the problem into their own context and suggest solutions to others with similar problems.

Nonetheless, significant variations to the open model exist. Businesses are seeking to adopt the models that shelter where they think they can extract value from their innovation without shutting out external contributors or supply partners. Some are open in the discovery phase but try to be very closed in the scaling phase. Medical device makers, among others, use that model. In a truly open model, companies not only take things in but they also spin things out they don't believe they can turn into value. Sometimes it may make sense to bring an innovation back at a later date.

By introducing an operating model based upon the Innovation Lifecycle, you can provide discipline across all four phases while still applying an open innovation paradigm.

Transitioning to a more open approach to innovation can be difficult, however. Companies are very concerned about giving away their intellectual properties (IP). Unfortunately, lawyers tend to get involved to help protect and secure IP, and they tend to overcomplicate the process. (One client company spent over eighteen months working with attorneys at two companies to agree on the terms for an open innovation approach to specific innovation challenges. While they successfully agreed on the terms, taking a year and a half before you launch each collaborative effort doesn't make sense.) Still, controls are often in place even in the most open systems.

Google, for example, is committed to an open-source platform for its Android mobile operating system, and device makers are welcome to customize features. At the same time, the company also noted that it has long required device makers to conform to certain requirements to prevent fragmentation.

P&G also has streamlined and simplified its approach to IP management. Doing so allows them to reach the target of acquiring from outside the organization nearly half of all its innovations.

Some of the barriers to fast-frequent-frugal innovation are related to this instinctive need to safeguard potentially valuable knowledge from walking out the door. Many leading innovators have begun to realize that much of what they and their lawyers are trying to protect wasn't really proprietary to them in the first place. The information was already in the public domain, either because they or someone else had published the discoveries. Others have finally begun to realize that **valuable information never shared is worthless.**

Open innovation processes can be disciplined to share valuable information as well as control and commercialize the IP that originates from it.

Myth 8: Innovative Talent Are Mercenaries That Just Work for Money

The more work we have done regarding this myth, and the more research and real-life evidence we have seen focused on what incentivizes and motivates innovators, the more we find that money is not the primary or even the secondary motivator of creative geniuses. At best, it is tertiary. For example, we were asked to evaluate what motivates academic researchers by an academic medical center that earned hundreds of millions of dollars annually from licensing its innovations to pharmaceutical companies. To answer this question we compared the center to fifteen others to see how the level of innovation in their institution could be increased. The feeling among this organization's board was that the medical center had billions in unrealized innovations because their inventors lacked the necessary rewards and incentives to motivate them. And we found that rewards weren't the problem.

Don't get us wrong. We found that inventors want to be rewarded fairly, and uncertainty about how royalties would be shared with them, or a lack of a fair-sharing model, could be a barrier to innovation. Yet money was rarely and almost never mentioned as a motivator for the inventors' innovative efforts.

Why was this?

We found several reasons. First, these inventors knew that most innovative efforts lead to failure. If only one in a thousand ideas actually advances from discovery to incubation, and then only a third of those advance to acceleration, and then only a third of those to scaling, the odds of their ever making any money, let alone enough to change their lifestyle, was remote at best. These long odds meant that money could never be a primary motivator.

Second, their passion for the creative process and their joy of learning kept them plugging along, undaunted by continual failure. They realized that failure is the most constant and valuable teacher and that few organizations pay for failure. Therefore, the only source of motivation to enable them to overcome failure was their passion for creation and learning.

Third, what these inventors valued more than money was freedom and the autonomy to pursue their passion-inspired and driven dreams. This is not to say they didn't care about money. They wanted to be paid fairly and at market rates, but changing the formula for sharing royalties beyond what was the standard practice among leading institutions had no motivational impact on their innovative efforts.

Finally, public and private recognition for their efforts came after freedom and passion but before money in providing a valuable reward for their innovative efforts. The recognition they sought came from peers, colleagues, supervisors, and leadership.

When we interviewed the chief innovation officer of PwC on this topic, he made an interesting point.* He said that when they were designing and rolling out the PwC innovation operating model, they debated whether or not they should provide some type of monetary reward for submitting ideas and participating in the innovation program. They decided against doing so for the reasons already stated. Then he said, "While our financial resources are limited, our ability to recognize and praise our people for their innovative contribution is almost infinite. And since this is what people really value more than money to motivate and drive their innovative behaviors, we realized we really needed to invest heavily in praise and recognition of our people's participation in our program."

Measures to motivate all of us to be more innovative must include many nonmonetary rewards, such as acknowledgment and a high degree of autonomy in imaginative pursuits. These are important components of a culture that fosters innovative thinking at the outset. For example, 3M embraces approaches that allow individuals and groups to choose to spend some of their time harnessing their passions.

We all want to work for companies with reputations (as well as rewards) for innovation that also enable us to regain our creative genius. So building that reputation for innovation helps an organization become an employer of choice.

Leadership must tap into the creative genius of us all, not just a few hired guns, and provide incentives, more important than money, that engage the passion to innovate.

---

* Sheldon Laube, April 2011, interview with Christopher Wasden

Myth 9: Senior and Midlevel Managers Are Natural Allies of Innovation

While senior and midlevel managers may not be the enemies of innovation, they're not cheerleaders either. Their focus on improving profits through ever-greater mindless operating efficiency encourages them to reject new ideas that detract from perpetual Lean improvements. Companies tend to promote executives who successfully conform to norms and operate, often under a tight cost discipline. Innovation, however, is idiosyncratic and generally occurs at the periphery and close to the pain points where changing customer demands are first experienced.

While at PwC, Chris surveyed five thousand employees across all organizational functions, levels, geographies, and divisions of a global insurance company. One of the most surprising findings was that the people most interested in being innovative were the executive leadership group and those at lower and entry-level positions. Both senior and middle management were the least interested in, the most resistant to, and in many cases even hostile to innovation.

The reason was that these professionals found innovation disruptive to their mindless daily activities. Innovation got in the way of their running an efficient operation, which was what they are paid to do. Therefore, when their employees identified new and potentially innovative ways to address customer needs or remove operational pain points that differed from the standard operating procedures, their managers told them to forget it. They pointed out that there were no processes, no resources, and no time to be mindful and do anything with the ideas. They were all being paid to run the business of today, not daydream about the business of tomorrow. They were all supposed to focus on maximizing profits through tried and true methods. Additionally, none of them had the time or luxury to chase innovative ideas, nor would executive leadership forgive any shortfall in daily performance that resulted from such efforts.

Innovation requires protecting people from their bosses. It means empowering people to use some of their own time for mindful creativity. People need the license to focus on addressing failures and pain points in novel ways to originate new sources of value without their bosses getting in the way.

The values and culture of the organization must enable employees to get forgiveness rather than permission from bosses to pursue creative passions.

Myth 10: Innovation Is the Responsibility of Creative Geniuses, Often in Isolation

Edison's incandescent light bulb, Google Search, and Apple's iPod: many people would describe these hallmark inventions as examples of rare talent in action or the products of uniquely innovative companies.* But to attribute them to some magical genius not available to others lets everyone else off the hook with an easy excuse not to be innovative: "How can we possibly expect this type of rare talent or unique capability in our company and among the rank and file of our organization?"

Is rare insight only the domain of the few extremely brilliant? Is radical innovation conceived in a single, stunning act of invention and delivered as an entirely new offering?

No.

Innovation is a process, one that taps into the minds of many. It is not the accidental province of the madly talented. Rather, it is a mindful process that liberates the creative genius within us all.

---

* Wasden, Parker, and Baya, "Decoding innovation's DNA," http://www.pwc.com/us/en/technology-forecast/2011/issue2/.

Even some of the most celebrated inventions don't quite fit the "Eureka!" stereotype. Consider these:

Edison's incandescent bulb: Thomas Edison didn't arrive at tungsten filaments in a vacuum through a once-in-a-lifetime insight. The basics of making a light bulb were known: pass electricity through a filament in a vacuum. The *problem* was the filament. Those Edison had tried did not last long. His genius was in dedicating scores of engineers to systematically test thousands of materials. Eventually, they discovered tungsten lasted the longest. Edison brought the idea to cash through a *disciplined process to solving a problem.*

Google's Web search algorithm: Larry Page, cofounder of Google, was using the Alta Vista search engine to find ecommerce websites and encountered the *problem* of search results being plentiful but of limited value because they were not ranked by relevance. He *connected two patterns*: the importance of the web of links among Internet sites and the way academics use journal citation counts to measure the importance of articles. Then, using the number of links among pages to determine which are seen first, he transformed Internet searching. Page did it intuitively, but *connecting two patterns from dissimilar domains can be used as a formal disciplined and repeatable process to accelerate invention.*

The iPod: Despite its inspired combination of many smaller inventions resulting in an elegant portable music player, Apple released the iPod in 2000 to middling success. The *problem*: the digital music ecosystem was in chaos—illegally posted songs on the Internet often mixed with malware, there was no single place to buy music legally, and there were complex challenges in moving music between multiple sources and the iPod. Apple soon made *two additional, incremental inventions to unlock the vast commercial success* latent in MP3 players: (1) they made the iTunes Store a safe, legal, and user-friendly way to get music to the device and (2) they expanded the iTunes ecosystem to include the Windows operating system. Neither iPods nor iTunes by themselves was a radical innovation, but together, and expanding into Windows, they changed the game.

It's time to discard the stereotypes of innovation, radical or otherwise, and treat innovation for what it is: an enterprise business process that we all can and must contribute to through a better understood, redesigned, improved, and measured operating model.

Mountain bikes can't be restricted for those in R&D. We must all be free to ride them from time to time to explore, create, and invent.

Myth 11: Innovation Can't Be Measured

One of the hallmarks of mindless processes, structures, and practices is the precision with which almost everything can be measured. Nearly all decisions are based upon a careful calculation of the return on deployed capital. Predictions on the net present value, the discounted cash flows, and the internal rate of return over a five- to ten-year forecast period are calculated to the second decimal point. Variance between actual and planned outcomes is analyzed and then used to further improve efficiency. However, when it comes to innovation, most organizations struggle to find similar simple and precise measures.

The challenge is that the mindless running of business today lends itself to highly predictable outcomes as well-established and proven processes are employed to meet highly reliable expectations. Innovative success, on the other hand, is not predictable but merely plausible. Failure results nearly as reliably as Six Sigma success from Lean processes.

Despite its difficulty and lack of precision, you can measure innovation and those things that lead you to it. You just need to know what to measure and how to do it.

We have helped many organizations apply the same measurement rigor as it is applied in other areas. It is necessary to apply discipline to our innovative efforts. Doing so enables you to manage those efforts like any other portfolio of investments: allocate resources, set out the milestones, and measure both leading and lagging indicators of activity as well as employing a results-oriented measure of the impact and outcomes of innovation.

Because of the lack of certainty and predictability in innovation, we advocate measures in multiple dimensions to understand the numerous dimensions of the innovation landscape. More robust and broad measurement allows an organization and its leadership to see how it can better manage and discipline the innovation operating model. This type of measurement identifies gaps in performance that can be closed by applying leading practices to drive improvement.

Through work with over a dozen clients and their leadership teams, we developed an Innovation Scorecard to help leaders better manage innovation. This framework looks at innovation in four different dimensions: *input, process, culture,* and *impact* (see page 309).

Performance in each of the dimensions is based on the application of best innovation practices. Gaps in measured performance are closed by the application of best practices. In total, the scorecard may measure around forty metrics to quantify an organization's capabilities and capacities to innovate.

Just as precision measurement enables Lean Six Sigma processes for mindlessness production, innovative measures ensure that you understand your commitment to and outcome from mindfulness at all levels and in all parts of your organization.

Myth 12: Organizations Know How Much Innovation They Need

We recently had a client interested in entering the healthcare industry by applying some innovative new business models and solutions from other industries. After two years of working with this client, the leadership began questioning how much innovation they really needed to provide in the newly emergent mHealth (mobile health) marketplace. They had launched solutions around remote patient monitoring for chronic disease patients, mobile emergency response systems, and mobile medical records and imaging solutions, to name a few. With all they had already done, how fast and far did they really need to push these efforts? After all, the client seemed to be outpacing its largest competitor already. How much farther ahead did it really need to be? Within nine months of expressing this concern, the competitor entered the market with a shockingly robust solution set that included multiple external partners and a level of senior leadership support and sponsorship that our client hadn't yet been able to muster within their organization. As such, the two-year lead the client thought it had disappeared almost overnight.

The reality is that you can't pace your innovation efforts based on some preconceived notion about where you are versus the competition. In our fast-paced world, any lead you think you have can be overcome in just a few years or even months. Look at what happened in the smartphone market. Not one incumbent has survived a change in the technology paradigm. Each market leader failed to make the next great leap. Palm, Sony Ericson, Motorola, Research in Motion, and Nokia were all smartphone industry leaders at one time, yet they all lost ground to new entrants as the paradigm shifted. What are the odds that Apple, Samsung, and Google can remain at the top? What will be the new paradigm? Who will be the new disruptors?

So business leaders need to ask themselves, how much growth does the firm need from innovation? This involves considering how much growth will be driven by existing products and services and how much is required from new offerings, business models, processes, distribution, and marketing strategies. Furthermore, leaders must calculate how much inorganic growth their company needs through mergers and acquisitions, business development, partnerships, and alliances. The gap between your desired growth objects and these traditional sources must be filled through innovation. And keep in mind that competitors are innovating in all these other dimensions as well, meaning that you must innovate just to maintain your current standing.

Of course, the marketplace—not just firms—dictates the pace of change. If innovation in the outside world is advancing more quickly than innovation in the company, the company will fail in the long term. We call this phenomenon meeting the demands of the *Law of Requisite Variety and Complexity*. In order to survive, you need the same variety within your organization that you observe in the outside world.

Firms in industries where new technologies are seeing substantially changing business models require disruptive innovation to survive—think media, retail, healthcare, or telecommunications. John Sviokla, a colleague at PwC, calls this process of disruptive change "de-maturity" because mature industries are becoming more vibrant again through innovation. Some previously stable industries are in the process of de-maturing now. Others will follow in five or ten years. Think of the effects of the sixty-seven-dollar Chotukool fridge, launched in India by Godrej and Boyce, the white goods business, whereas a fridge in the United States currently costs around eight hundred dollars. GE Healthcare sees the same phenomenon in ultrasound technology, where new products costing ten thousand dollars made for India and China can replace those made for the United States previously costing one hundred thousand dollars. Sviokla finds that a stable industry is de-maturing when at least two of the following four situations arise:*

1. **Core customer behavior changes.** The accelerating uptake on electronic book formats offers a dramatic example from the book printing industry. E-book sales, as a percentage of the book market, had reached 13 percent by 2013.†

2. **Core technologies that produce the product or service change.** Video on-demand, video-sharing sites like YouTube, Netflix, and peer-to-peer file sharing are among the technology-driven disruptions under way on traditional models of content distribution and advertising revenue for broadcasters and music companies.

3. **The number of large competitors interested in the same market is on the rise.** The rising interests among automakers to grow their footholds in China offer an example. In the United States, consider the number of IT companies like Cisco, Intel, Microsoft, and Google, to name a few, that are interested in getting into healthcare.

4. **Significant change in government regulation is under way.** Clearly, regulatory change is impacting financial services and healthcare providers in many countries around the world.

De-maturing industries are more likely to be disrupted by innovation because customer needs, along with the competitive landscape, are in flux. They are moving from the edge of equilibrium to the edge of chaos. As we've mentioned, the level and rate

---

* John Sviokla, "Is your industry in danger of being disrupted?" sviokla.com, accessed May 23, 2014, http://www.sviokla.com/innovation/is-your-industry-in-danger-of-being-disrupted/.

† Jim Milliot, "E-book sales growth slows in 2013," publishersweekly.com, September 20, 2013, accessed May 23, 2014, http://www.publishersweekly.com/pw/by-topic/digital/retailing/article/59194-signs-of-stability.html.

of innovation needs to be set by CEOs and leadership teams, but to realize it they must enable all of the creative genius to emerge and allow passion to drive innovative efforts. For example, if the CEO seeks to build five new billion-dollar businesses in the next five years, that puts in motion a completely different set of organizational moves than if the CEO were to say that the company's approach should be "steady eddy" with only 5 percent incremental growth during that time frame. The former enables creative tensions that provide the energy to drive the transformational change associated with empowering and disruptive innovations, while the latter merely requires adaptive tensions for incremental and sustaining innovation.

Most industries are experiencing these de-maturing forces, so most leaders can't predict and schedule the innovation they think they need. They must innovate to cannibalize their current businesses before their competitors do.

Let Go of the Myths

In order to liberate the creative genius within yourself and your organization, you have to abandon these mindless myths. Instead, you must harness your passions to solve problems, overcome failure, and remove the pain points encountered every day. Leaders must develop an innovation operating model that enables more mindfulness within the mindless organization. They must allow all those who are willing to ride the Innovation Cycle to hop on a mountain bike and explore.

REMEMBER

- ✔ New ideas or products should not be automatically classified as innovative unless they create value.

- ✔ Innovation cannot be delegated.

- ✔ Innovation doesn't mean technology and new products.

- ✔ Innovation is not only about transformational or radical ideas.

- ✔ Formal structures and processes do not always stifle innovation.

- ✔ Innovation does not always result from lucky accidents that can't be planned.

- ✔ The more open the innovation process doesn't mean that discipline disappears.

- ✔ Innovators are not mercenaries who just work for money.

- ✔ Senior and midlevel managers are not the natural allies of innovation.

- ✔ Innovation is not only the responsibility of creative geniuses.

- ✔ Innovation can be measured.

- ✔ Organizations struggle in not knowing much innovation they need

---
QUESTIONS

> How many of these mindless myths do you or your organization believe?

> How do these beliefs restrict your ability to change your identity and think of yourself or your organization as having greater creative capabilities?

> Which myths do you find to be the most damaging to your creative genius?

CHAPTER FIVE

Discovering the Innovator Within You

Simplifying What Motivates Us to Innovate

The balance between running the company of today and innovating to form the inventive company of tomorrow is not a trivial problem. With the exponential rate of change in business and in life, innovation has moved from buzzword to vital organizational staple. Yet what is really known about how to structure innovation in companies? You often read stories about innovative companies or people who inspire others to want to be pioneers, but you aren't quite sure how to go about it. You also may study the traits of innovative people in hopes that their genius can be copied. Last year alone, over one thousand business books were written on topics such as innovation, leadership, performance management, and a host of other related topics.*

---

* "Aiming high," economist.com, January 30, 2011, accessed May 23, 2014, http://www.economist.com/node/18894875.

If the knowledge about what makes people or companies innovative is available, why can't every person or company replicate it? Is the problem really that organizations don't know enough? Or is there so much to know that the resulting blizzard of information feels like white noise which causes employees to tune out? As the pace of change has increased, many executives worry that even the most current publications are at best predictors of the past.

Is there a more elegant way to look at the problems facing us in organizations?

Does a simple framework exist that allows employees to shift between the reliable spinning of a stationary bike that doesn't require mental agility—and, in fact, eliminates it—to the mental agility required of a mountain bike that improves your employees' performance?

The answer is "yes," and the best place to start on your journey is to understand that a simpler framework begins with the idea of personal and collective *identity*. Identity is the core of our being and in large part drives our actions. If we are seeking different and more innovative action, then we must uncover the identity driving the desired actions. While identity is key to understanding human action, its importance is often missed because we are too close to it. The following example, called the *narcissist test,* helps illustrate how deeply connected we are to our own identity and how failing to appreciate the inseparable bond with that identity can lead to blind spots that undermine our success as innovators.

The Narcissist Test

Imagine your best friend from childhood has just invited you to his wedding. You couldn't be more thrilled; you also know the bride and you are confident they will be a very happy couple for years to come. You go shopping to get them the right gift, and after weeks of searching you find it: a modern-looking lead crystal sculpture for their dining room table. Although it was quite expensive, you thought it was worth every penny since you know they will find the gift very thoughtful. You've even helped plan aspects of the wedding and honeymoon since you know the two had so much on their plate. When the wedding day comes, it's perfect. The weather is beautiful, the chapel is packed, and the reception is a mixture of joyful tears, laughter, and dancing.

A month later, when the couple is back from their honeymoon, they invite you over to look at the wedding pictures. As they pull out the album, the first picture they show you is a group photo of the bride, groom, yourself, and thirty of their closest family and friends. As you glance at the picture, who is the first person you look for?

Having asked this question in countless seminars, the answer we almost universally get is "me." This is an interesting finding, since the wedding was about the bride and groom and not you. As the best friend, shouldn't you be looking at how the pictures turned out for the happy couple?

Even when dealing with our friends and family, we can't help but focus first on ourselves. Others have made this observation in similar ways. Oscar Wilde said, "To love oneself is the beginning of a lifelong romance." There is a reason for this seemingly selfish response. The brain powers identity, which, in turn, drives action. This can work to your advantage if you have the right identity, as it can dictate a kind of behavioral autopilot. It can also work to your detriment if you have a problematic identity that limits your success.

Identity Drives Action

The term *identity* is often used as if each individual or organization carries only one. Identity theft is typically a case in which a single identity has been stolen. On the other hand, an individual with multiple identities is typically referred to as someone with serious psychiatric pathologies.

For the purposes of this discussion, we will define an identity as any statement that can be phrased as "I am" or "We are." Each of these statements is a conjugated version of the verb "to be" and imply an inner state of *being* that may be unseen but drives current and future behavior. If you examined every action you took each day, you would find that behind it is an unseen identity moving you to action. The potentially unsettling thing to some may be that every one of us carries countless numbers of identities around with us at any given time. A stimulus in the environment can cause one of these identities to be recruited from deep inside the brain, and after this recruitment occurs, actions follow.

For instance, imagine you are at football game on a beautiful Saturday afternoon, cheering and screaming for your alma matter. Suddenly you receive a text from your spouse that you need to leave the game early to attend a Catholic mass that you earlier committed to but forgot. Reluctantly, you run home and change. You make it to mass an hour later and proceed to sit quietly and listen to the service. Only one hour earlier you had been cheering at the top of your lungs based on the identity "**I am** a football fan," but as you walked into the church, the environment provided a new stimulus that recruited a new identity, namely, "**I am** Catholic." This newly recruited identity provides your brain with its own set of rules on what behaviors should follow, namely, sitting quietly. Notice in this example that your spouse had the power to motivate you to create an *identity shift* within yourself that you may or may not have wanted. Perhaps making that shift was preferable to other identities that would follow had you not agreed to leaving the game, such as "**I am** in trouble with my spouse." One person is, symbolically, riding two different bikes: the mountain bike at the game and the stationary bike at church.

How Identity Is Constructed

Building an identity is not as simple as assuming a job title or changing your business cards. Understanding how to build an identity requires looking deeper into how identities form. Additionally, identities can carry different strengths, from weak to strong, that can affect the level of action that flows from that identity. The culture of an organization also defines identities that can take many forms, such as a company mission statement, organizational values, or a job title.

The key ingredient needed to create an identity shift is tension. In this context, a tension is any activity that motivates people to expend the energy required to adopt a new identity. If there is no tension, identities will generally remain as they are, given there is no reason to evolve and innovate a new identity. Unfortunately, there is a natural biological roadblock with tensions in that people often resist them, even unconsciously.

Several years ago we illustrated this point at a seminar when we asked a woman to come to the front of the auditorium. One of us held out an arm and made a fist so that the arm was parallel with the floor. We then asked her to do the same and put her fist right up against the extended fist. A medium amount of tension was applied so that the closed fist pushed against her closed fist. Her immediate response was to push back with the same degree of tension, even though that was not part of the instructions.

We've found that very few people will ever absorb the tension against their fist in this experiment. To absorb tension is, in some ways, admitting defeat, and as a species, humans are wired to survive and conquer. The same is true with identities.

All of us tend to resist identities that feel forced upon us; they are seen as mental foreign bodies. So changing individual and organizational identity requires skill and planning if it is to be not only built but also sustained.

To illustrate the point of how to use tension to alter identity, we'll cite two examples from Mitch's experience in the healthcare industry.

Collective Identity: Being the Company Mission

As a leader it can be daunting to try to determine what collective identity should be created and supported within an organization. Often a good place to start is the company mission statement.

Years ago, I worked for an organization with a fairly typical and uninspiring mission statement. Like most mission statements, a committee formed it years earlier, and its chief aim was to offend no one. It wasn't memorable or inspiring and was nothing more than a form of inexpensive artwork in each office.

During a strategic planning retreat with the company's top twenty senior leaders, I asked if anyone could recite the mission statement. It didn't surprise me that no one could, including the CEO and the president.

I have asked thousands of employees at seminars across the country if they know their company mission statement, and roughly 1–2 percent raise their hands.

Besides being uninspiring, our mission statement was two paragraphs long, difficult to remember, and seemed to only address the segment of the workforce that either provided clinical care or were involved in research and education. If a person swept the floors or was an accountant, how was it possible to connect with that? How could people see themselves in a proclamation that was supposed to be the company identity statement but didn't speak to what they did within the company? Perhaps it was impossible to form a mission statement that called out the contributions of thirteen thousand employees across eleven hundred job descriptions.

This organization prided itself on being mission driven, and so it created a great deal of tension at the thought that employees didn't know the mission statement. The organization contemplated hosting contests for employees to memorize the mission statement as a means of creating awareness. Finally, the organization decided on a different tack. Given the brain's inability to remember more than five to seven things at a time, the statement had to be short and memorable. Additionally, if this was to be a company identity and if identity drives action, an opportunity would be lost if the statement wasn't crafted to encompass everyone. All employees needed to see themselves in a way that was meaningful to each one.

After a few weeks of deliberating, a new mission statement was offered: "We serve, heal, lead, educate, and innovate." This new statement applied to every employee's sense of identity. Each employee could say, "**I am** an innovator" or "**I am** a leader" because, regardless of job title, everyone could produce actions around those identities.

At seven words, the mission statement was short enough that a new employee could remember it after the first day in orientation. In new hire surveys conducted ninety days after orientation, "Do you know the company mission?" was the only question that new employees answered "yes" to 100 percent of the time.

But how was it possible to ensure that this new mission statement didn't become inexpensive artwork like the last one? When the new mission was launched there was a degree of cynicism among some employees who were reluctant to take on a new identity. The organization realized that for old identities to be dislodged and for a new identity to be created, the correct tensions would have to be applied. To make certain this happened, processes and system structures were formed that kept the collective identity front and center. The mission was recited at the beginning of each meeting and was printed on every agenda.

At first, reciting the mission statement was met with smirks and eye rolling, but tension was continually applied until repeating the statement became the normal course of doing business. During employee rounding (a program where senior leaders visited with employees in their work area), each employee was asked to recite the mission statement and might be asked to describe a time when they innovated something at work. The rounding was not conducted as an audit but more as a coaching session. If an employee had a great answer, they were given one of five different mission cards. Each mission card touted either serve, heal, lead, educate, or innovate—the various verbs of the mission statement. When an employee received various combinations of cards, such as two of a kind or a straight flush of all five, they could trade them in for such booty as company hats, mugs, or shirts.

The language of the mission statement even found its way into the day-to-day dialogue of employees. It was clear what the organization was about. It wasn't necessary to dictate every desired behavior, because the mission statement covered everything. It was clear that if there were a piece of trash in the hallway or the parking lot, an employee picked it up because a clean environment was a healing environment. Picking up trash isn't in your job description? Picking up trash could be seen as serving, and therefore it's in everyone's job description.

As the new identity of serve, heal, lead, educate, and innovate was adopted, the tension required to create and maintain that identity lessened. The organization made the transition from mindfully creating an identity to the point where the identity could mindlessly be recruited by the brain for future action.

Pros Versus Amateurs: Individual Identity

Another simple example of creating individual identities at work is one we call *pros versus amateurs*. At a hospital I (Mitch) led in southeast Louisiana, there were concerns that our employees weren't living our service principles of providing each patient (1) with a warm welcome, (2) anticipating their needs, and (3) offering a fond farewell at the end of every encounter. The three principles were adopted from the Ritz-Carlton, and senior leadership really believed in them and had seen these principles work in other industries. The principles didn't rely on heavy scripting, which could sound insincere. Instead, a warm welcome was judged more by the warmth of the greeting than the actual words spoken to patients.

As with most change initiatives, there were immediate resisters who felt that the program was little more than charm school for the nurses. Several nurses, especially those in the higher acuity areas like the ICU, felt their clinical skills were what they should be judged on rather than the fluff of interpersonal skills. In short, the nurses had an identity that said, "**I am** talented and don't need to improve." When they looked at the new proposed identity (i.e., **I am** living the service principles), it didn't produce enough tension to inspire them to change. The idea of responding to the resisters with corrective action or other threatening methods was toyed with, but there was worry that this would unleash maladaptive tensions like low employee morale or increase employee turnover. After realizing this, we started a more disciplined plan around an identity the nurses valued greatly, namely, "**I am** a medical professional."

The healthcare field is full of professionals: physicians, nurses, lab technicians, imaging technicians, pharmacists, and many others. Each of these professionals is required to undergo an enormous amount of training in order to practice in their field. Many are also required to earn state certifications and licenses to ensure they are prepared for their duties. These employees deal with life-and-death situations on a daily basis, yet they manage to keep their cool even under stressful situations. It's hard to imagine an industry with more professionals than the healthcare industry.

It was clear that most employees found the identity of "**I am** a medical professional" meaningful. Because of this, it was decided to use the identities of professional versus amateur in our daily language. In open forums with employees, the following questions were asked as a way for them to understand the new identities that were being referenced.

They were told, "If we all went to the basketball court across the street at the elementary school and took turns shooting free throws and doing lay-ups, some of us could eventually get some in. But what would it look like if a professional basketball player came out and practiced free throws and lay-ups?"

One employee said, "They'd be more consistent."

Another said, "While we could probably get a few shots in, a professional could do the same thing over and over again."

I asked, "Is there anything else you can think of that separates amateurs from pros?"

A surgical tech shot back, "People don't pay to watch amateurs."

Of course they don't. No one who knows his or her job inside-out wants to be referred to as anything other than a pro. Dozens of other meetings like this first open forum followed. No one wanted to be an amateur, as it was currently defined, and for good reason. With time, a desired personal identity of "**I am** a pro" was formed for everyone who worked at the hospital.

During this time, research was shared with employees that showed that patient satisfaction, using all those soft people skills, actually had clinical implications. Satisfied patients were more likely to follow their nurse's treatment recommendations during their course of treatment. No longer was demonstrating good interpersonal skills seen as fluff, because it was demonstrated that the skills supported good clinical care. Patients didn't listen to or follow the treatment recommendations of nurses or other staff they felt didn't care about them as a person. Employees also realized that the actions associated with the pro identity meant they would be required to be consistent with their service principles to patients every time or risk being graded as an amateur during employee rounding.

Another initiative the leadership undertook that determined how to separate pros from amateurs was the implementation of the 10/5 rule. The 10/5 rule was a concept borrowed from retail business models. It stated that if a patient, staff member, or visitor were within ten feet of an employee, that employee would make eye contact and visually acknowledge the other person. If the employee was within five feet of the other person, visual and verbal acknowledgement had to be shown.

A lot of skeptics said that the staff would just make sure they walked around people and stayed eleven feet away so they didn't have to participate. It turns out this never happened. Additionally, all leadership was given strict instruction that if the staff didn't pick up on the behavior, it was because leaders weren't modeling the behavior. This behavior produced tension for the leaders because every employee in the hospital could judge whether or not the leader's identity was that of a pro or an amateur based on adherence to the 10/5 rule.

Within a month something remarkable happened. It was as if the whole facility had changed. I remember being so worried that I would miss 10/5-ing someone (especially a fellow employee who knew the rule) that as I walked anywhere, I was constantly scanning the hallways for eyeballs I was supposed to connect with. The most embarrassing and wonderful thing happened to me during this time. One day I was in a hallway, talking to the chief of the medical staff while patients and employees were walking by. As I moved away from the chief of staff, a housekeeper looked me over and said in a serious tone, "You didn't 10/5 me." Initially I felt embarrassed, but then I got incredibly excited. I realized that staff members were looking for this behavior and comfortable holding others accountable to it regardless of position.

Within a month, patients and visitors were saying that this was the friendliest hospital they had ever been to. Then something quite spectacular happened that wasn't planned. The staff reported that they were 10/5-ing at the mall, the grocery store, and everywhere they went, not because they meant to, but because it was now an authentic part of them—10/5-ing had become mindless. Our patient satisfaction improved over this period from the 15th percentile to the 70th percentile.

Once these identities were formed, they were painstakingly maintained because leadership placed a focus on them through processes, rewards, and recognition. Whether through the mission statement or through organizational values, promoting an identity of "I am an innovator" sends a clear message to employees that the organization has sanctioned the use of mountain bikes when appropriate. This permission to ride mountain bikes may at first yield a high percentage of failure; first-time employees gleefully embrace the exciting and riskier terrain. Even with adequate processes to assist with innovation efforts, first-time mountain bikers will fall off their bikes frequently in early innovation efforts. With time and coaching, the ratio of risk to success will improve, however.

These failures may drive some to advocate that the organization should stick to their road bikes before chaos ensues. It is at these moments that leadership must celebrate the failed attempts and focus individuals' attention on what can be learned by failure. Employees choosing a mountain bike when a stationary bike was needed, or vice versa, may cause some failures. These failures are also useful to learn from as employees learn how to appropriately shift between identities. A useful tool for understanding when we are operating under the wrong identity is called the *Five Whys*.

The Five Whys: The Root Causes of Identity Failure

Every organization is interested in hiring the right employee for the right job. To that end, many companies use psychometric testing such as Myers-Briggs, Birkman, or Hartman profiles to uncover the identities and corresponding future behaviors of employees. While these tools are useful in helping people understand their personality and goal orientation, there is little evidence that sharing this information leads to positive behavior change or improved performance. Given that identity drives behavior, it is often useful to understand what identity lies behind actions so that the root cause of the behavior can be understood. Given that 98 percent of employees have the capacity to innovate at the creative genius level, the question is not one of natural ability but rather can employees' brains recruit the right identity for a given situation.

A very useful tool in diagnosing the root cause of identity failure is the Five Whys, which can pinpoint conflicting identities within an organization. Developed by Sakichi Toyoda, the concept of the Five Whys have been used by Toyota Motor Company to uncover the root causes of defects in manufacturing processes. Remember: the brain doesn't like to juggle more than five thoughts at a time, so questions about why something happened are asked in groups of that number. The following whys are examples of the kinds of questions that can be asked.

An example of the Five Whys was used at the University of Missouri Health Care in 2012 during an employee recognition initiative that Mitch was involved in. Employees were invited to nominate exemplary employees as role models based on a set of criteria established by the human resources department. Employees were expected to exhibit four distinct behaviors around citizenship, teamwork, waste reduction initiatives (Lean Six Sigma), and innovation. Employees who received the role model award would be invited to a recognition dinner and rewarded with a 5 percent pay increase in addition to any other merit increases the employee was due. During the process, over four hundred applications were received. There was no cut-off for award recipients, meaning that if all four hundred were qualified, all would be recognized as role models. Applications were measured against a criteria score sheet to ensure the four behaviors were represented in the employee's application.

The questions were asked of a group of people who were evaluating the role models. Their answers appear below the questions. As the scoring began, an alarming number of applications failed to meet the criteria and were removed from consideration. Even more peculiar, of the over two hundred applications that failed to meet the criteria, more than 80 percent were excluded because of not having enough innovative behaviors. The Five Whys helped to uncover the root cause of the identity failure.

The Five Whys

1. **Why** aren't there more employees being recognized as role models?
   A: Those who were nominated didn't meet the minimum qualifications.

2. **Why** didn't the nominees meet the minimum qualifications?
   A: While most met the criteria for good citizenship, teamwork, and waste reduction initiatives, few met the criteria for innovation and trying new things.

3. **Why** didn't they meet the criteria for innovation and trying new things?
   A: I don't think they see that as part of their job.

4. **Why** don't they see innovation as part of their job?
   A: Our employee evaluations are structured around our company mission and values, and innovation isn't part of our mission and values.

5. **Why** isn't innovation part of our mission and values?
   A: Leadership hasn't set innovation as a priority in our mission and values.

As a general rule, you can get to the corresponding roots of problems or successes by asking five why questions and then matching those to a corresponding Innovation Cycle (stationary, road, hybrid, or mountain). The following examples show a behavior that is driven by a problematic identity.

Five Root Causes of Identity Failure

1. **Why** did our organization miss our sales targets this quarter?
   A: There has been an unexpected surge in our competitors' sales.

2. **Why** has there been a surge in our competitors' sales?
   A. They've got a new line of disposable products that are cutting into our market share.

3. **Why** doesn't our organization have products that can compete with these?
   A: There hasn't been a focus on new product development this year.

4. **Why** hasn't developing new products been a focus?
   A: Because there has been a focus on cutting the costs of our existing products.

5. **Why** has our organization been overly focused on cutting costs?
   A: Because it seemed like the best way to increase our value to customers and shareholders.

Problematic Identity: "We are efficient"—Stationary Bike
Identity Shift: "We are innovative"—Mountain Bike

In the series of why questions, the root problem of an organization's identity structure is exposed. The current identity is

"**We are** efficient" yet the market reality dictates that a stronger identity around innovation is needed, requiring a shift from road bike behavior to mountain bike performance. There is, of course, nothing wrong with being efficient but the Five Whys detected an imbalance in the identity of the organization that will lead to a future failure. A mission statement may say the right things, but the Five Whys have the ability to diagnose the current reality of an organizational identity crisis in real time.

Here is another example of the Five Whys where a company performance evaluation system is establishing the wrong identity.

Five Whys

1. **Why** don't our employees come up with any incremental improvement ideas?
   A: They have a lot of ideas, but it's often difficult to get their ideas off the ground.

2. **Why** is it difficult to get their ideas off the ground?
   A: Because when any of these ideas are tried, they compete for resources from the other departments and no one has extra resources for new ideas.

3. **Why** don't departments have extra resources for new ideas?
   A: New ideas often happen outside the budget cycle, and so they get pushed off for a year, if they get funded at all.

4. **Why** are they pushed if they're good ideas?
   A: No one is willing to go over budget to take on a new idea that is experimental.

5. **Why** aren't people willing to take on new ideas that are experimental?
   A: Because during performance evaluations a higher value is placed on coming in on budget than on trying new ideas.

Problematic Identity: "**We are** risk averse"—Stationary Bike
Identity Shift: "**We are** supportive of new ideas"—Road Bike
(at a minimum)

When Individual and Organizational Identities Collide

Often an organization may strive for an identity that a particular employee has no interest in adopting for one reason or another. In these cases, attempting an identity shift does little more than grind the gears of your Innovation Cycle. In many of these cases, both the individual and the organization find no other remedy than to part ways.

As part of a process improvement initiative at a health system in Louisiana, Mitch was attempting an identity shift where employees could say, "**We are** a process improvement and value-driven health system." The organization was actually fairly good at innovating and had piloted online physician appointments, phone apps to list emergency room wait times, and other firsts for the area. The problem area was in producing stronger processes to scale these innovations to their potential rather than having them be expensive hobbies that didn't work reliably.

A physician was assigned to be involved in one of the process improvement projects around patient satisfaction scores because his own scores needed improvement. After trying to make the physician part of the improvement efforts for months, he sent an email that I'll paraphrase:

Mitch, I am sick and tired of being hounded about my involvement in these process improvement activities. I have the highest clinical production in the department and my low patient satisfaction scores are being compared to people who see a fraction of the patients I do. I'm not interested in going to another demeaning class about how I'm supposed to improve. I've heard we are even using the same book as last year, which is ironic since if it didn't bring up the scores last year, what will make this year different?

This physician's identity could be labeled a few things without even using the Five Whys. Perhaps it's "**I am** too busy to improve." During this time his patient satisfaction scores where at the 7th percentile while the organization had collectively moved from the 45th percentile patient satisfaction to the 99th percentile. Not surprisingly, he left the organization a year later to work in a private practice as the tension between his identity and the new organizational identity became untenable for both parties.

The Five Hows: Root Causes of Identity Success

The opposite of the Five Whys, the Five Hows can uncover what behaviors an identity is generating to make it successful.

As important as it is to diagnose problematic identities so that an identity shift can occur, it is equally as important to understand the root causes of success. By understanding specific positive behaviors that are generated by an identity, others can more quickly learn what behaviors are required to reinforce an identity and make it as strong as possible.

Say, for instance, you visited a company that you heard offered great service. You wanted to get to the bottom of what identity was responsible for driving this behavior so you could use it at your organization. A customer standing nearby comments to you, "This company is great!" The following example shows how the Five Hows can get to the root cause and behaviors of this successful identity.

The questions, made up of three groups of different how questions, can be asked. As they are with the Five Whys, questions about how something happened are asked in groups of the same number. Possible answers appear below the questions. You may get to the answer sooner than the Five Hows, or you may need to go farther than that, but five is a good place to start.

Five Hows

1. **How** is this company great in your opinion?
   A: It's just so friendly and positive! There's lots of energy here.

2. **How** is it friendly?
   A: Well, the people are friendly.

3. **How** are the people friendly?
   A: They're just open and talk to everyone. They make you feel special.

4. **How** do they make you feel special?
   A: I can tell they're interested in me as a person.

5. **How** do they show you they're interested in you as a person?
   A: Every employee looks me in the eye when they greet me.

The behavior that the customer experienced from all employees was the 10/5 rule of customer service mentioned earlier. The reason the customer experienced this behavior consistently is because each employee was acting out the identity structure of "I **am** a pro at customer service."

Here is another example aimed at uncovering the success of an innovative leader. An employee tells his boss, "Sanjay is the most innovative leader in the company!"

Five Hows

1. **How** is Sanjay the most innovative leader in the company?
   A: He's a visionary and really thinks outside the box.

2. **How** is he visionary?
   A: He sees where the industry is going and then plans his moves.

3. **How** does he see where the industry is going?
   A: He's very well informed about the industry.

4. **How** does he become so well informed about the industry?
   A: He finds the time to read more books and listen to more podcasts than anyone I know.

5. **How** does he find the time to read books and listen to podcasts?
   A: During his commute, he listens to books and podcasts rather than the radio.

Here's another example, this time of how Mary is such a great leader.

1. **How** is she a great leader?
   A: Everyone loves to work with her. She inspires confidence.

2. **How** does she inspire confidence?
   A: She makes everyone on the team believe we can achieve great things.

3. **How** does she make everyone believe they can achieve great things?
   A: She paints a picture of where we're going and what everyone's role is in the journey.

4. **How** does she paint a picture of where she wants you to go?
   A: She uses simple language in communicating the vision.

5. **How** does she communicate the vision?
   A: She communicates the vision with passion in a way that you know she's invested and believes in it.

Whether it takes four or six hows to uncover a successful practice, the benefit is that a behavior is uncovered that can be shared so that others can enhance their identity of "**I am** innovative."

Organizations as Recruiters of Identity

Often we see that employees possess an innate desire to innovate, but the organization they work for does a poor job recruiting an identity of innovation within the employee. Often these people will find other venues to express their innovative identity. Several years ago while serving as CEO of a hospital in Louisiana, Mitch was involved in starting a compensation program for physicians to reward greater productivity. A physician in the medical group, however, frequently complained that the plan was flawed and he wasn't making enough money. About once a month, Mitch would get a barrage of complaints from him. One month he complained that he couldn't be productive because he needed more nurses; the next month he complained that the facility wasn't modern enough to attract patients. Other gripes included that his staff wasn't paid enough to work hard.

One evening Mitch received a call from this physician, inviting him to the Louisiana governor's mansion, where he would be recognized for his leadership efforts in an innovative charity care clinic. Mitch was surprised to get the invitation, given the physician's high level of dissatisfaction at work, but he attended regardless.

During the award ceremony, various speakers praised this physician for his pioneering efforts. When the idea for the clinic first came about, a location was needed. This physician found a site where a generous businessman waived the rent, thus keeping the overhead low. The doctor also networked with medical supply companies to donate sufficient supplies to provide care for the patients. Recruiting a labor force of doctors and nurses was no small task. With no money to pay staff, he relied on his passion and powers of persuasion to enlist acquaintances. He had done all of the above for over five years and had been so successful that he drew the governor's attention.

The disturbing fact was that he was more passionate about doing an activity for free in a rundown clinic with staff he often had to coax to help him than he was about seeing patients in our clinic where he was paid, had superior facilities, an able staff, and all the medical supplies he needed to care for his patients. Our clinic had failed him because it was not able to recruit an identity in this physician that would unleash his innovative potential.

But the message he received from our clinic was that production was all that mattered. Production was talked about constantly. Since production was measurable, compensation was based on it. This sent the message "**You are** a means of production" to the doctor.

The identity behind his efforts at the free clinic, however, was the identity he wanted and aspired to. There, his identity was "**I am** a healer, an innovator, a leader."

Matching Identities to the Terrain

Consider the collective identity of your organization to that of your competitors, and then consider where your identity should be in the future if you are to compete effectively. If you are on a road bike today, to make incremental improvements and compete, you need to adopt identities more in line with the actions of a mountain bike. Adapting a strategy to deploy new identities is key.

Whether those identities take the shape of a new mission, values, or job titles, the words will be less important then the routines and processes that establish and reinforce those identities. Identities trickle down over time into the minds of employees, so it should come as no surprise that it can take months and even years for a new identity to become hardwired into an organization. While that may seem daunting, consider that an organization with a weak innovator identity requires supporting structures and practices in order to develop a strong identity. As long as that process takes, it's far superior to not starting it at all.

It's time for organizations to switch to another gear and balance the valuable activities of waste reduction and quality improvement with the messy and exploratory processes of innovation. Basically, that means getting up on a mountain bike. Employees whose work environment recruits an identity of "**I am** a Six Sigma Black Belt" every day will unleash actions consistent with that identity. Exploratory and creative activities that don't fit that identity will not be seen as priorities. When job titles such as chief innovation officer or innovation specialist are as common and as well funded and supported as Lean Six Sigma titles, an organization may well be on its way to building an ambidextrous organization and leadership that recognizes the value of both identities.

Identity: The Brain's Software

In many ways, identity is the software that runs on the hardware of the brain. Understanding how the human brain is wired in order to use both mindfulness and mindlessness at the same time is key to understanding how to balance the two seemingly contradictory processes. By replicating the brain's ambidextrous abilities within your organization, you can increase the volume, velocity, and value of innovation.

The brain is the most complex system in the universe, and as such, a basic understanding of its capacity and limitations is useful if you want to maximize the human potential to innovate. An understanding of identity would be incomplete if we didn't discuss the role of the brain in identity creation as well as the mental processes of innovation.

In the next section we will explore Knowing, which is the second facet of the Becoming, Knowing, Doing (BKD) model. The brain is not only our knowledge repository in terms of memory but also responsible for creating new knowledge through mindful innovation. By understanding the brain's processes, you can learn how to maximize innovative productivity while at the same time integrating the inventive output of coworkers to ensure that well-thought-out innovations are recognized and implemented. That's what chapter 5 is all about.

REMEMBER

✔ Identity is the core of our being and in large part drives our actions. If you are seeking different, more innovative actions, then you must uncover the identity driving your desire.

✔ The key ingredient needed to create an identity shift is tension.

✔ When doing the five whys or five hows, it gets easier when you realize that you are aiming for a certain target, and so the questions should be around the target you are aiming for. With the five whys, the target is getting to questions around identity, values, or mission. With the five hows, the target is getting to a certain behavior that is evidence of a person's identity.

QUESTIONS

> How would you describe your primary identities?

> Which identities drive your daily actions?

> How do you feel about the need or desire to create an identity as a creative genius?

> What tensions are you experiencing in your life that would force you to create a new identity of an innovator?

> What tensions should you add to your life to power the creation of a new identity of an innovator?

> What would the Five Whys reveal as the root cause of your lack of desired creativity?

> What would the Five Hows suggest you should change in order to create such an identity?

knowing

The reasonable man adapts himself to the world; the unreasonable one persists in trying to adapt the world to himself. Therefore all progress depends on the unreasonable man.

—George Bernard Shaw

CHAPTER SIX

Innovating with the Brain in Mind

If identity is the core of being, then the brain is the core of knowing. The relationship between identity and the brain can easily be described by using a map metaphor. All identities are like mental maps in the brain. When the brain encounters a situation, a mental map is recruited; it dictates how you should act in that situation. Many identities are so ingrained that the brain recruits these maps in an almost reflexive, habitual manner. In these cases, the rapid recruitment of an identity can appear *mindless*, given you are not consciously aware of it happening. There is nothing wrong with the brain mindlessly recruiting an identity—so long as it is what the situation requires. If the situation requires a mental map that the brain has not created, the brain must do its own form of innovating by using *mindfulness* to make a new mental map.

Understanding how the human brain is wired to use both mindfulness and mindlessness at the same time is key to understanding how to balance the two seemingly contradictory processes. By replicating the brain's ambidextrous abilities within your organization, you can increase the volume, velocity, and value of innovation.

Companies Don't Innovate

If you are like many of your business peers, you spend a great deal of energy reading about innovative people and companies as well as market innovations. Yet without looking under the cranial hood at what makes innovation happen, it's not possible to really understand how innovation works. That's because the brain does the real work of innovation.

The social sciences use the *iceberg model* to explain the complex dynamics of human and organizational behavior. Picture the visible top of an iceberg, that is, the part we can see above the water, as analogous to the results and behaviors of an organization and its people. The largest part of the iceberg, which is underwater, is analogous to emotions and thinking. Often when people speak of innovation or other kinds of organizational performance, they focus on what they can see, namely, the proverbial tip of the iceberg. But to truly understand a phenomenon like innovation's mental processes, you need to understand the whole iceberg. The tip is merely the end result of a lot of thinking and emotion.

The thinking and emotion that emerges from the heads of innovators drives innovation and makes it possible. Yet the mental aspects of innovation are often put aside while focus is either on what the company does to facilitate an innovative culture or the early childhood influences of pioneering innovators. Elaborate and well-meaning flow charts show how a company harnesses innovation to produce better goods and services, but nowhere on the chart will the role and processes of the brain be represented. It's imperative, however, that brain functions are understood if you want your organization to succeed.

Do you want to harness the creative potential of 98 percent of your people? Then read on.

Soft Sciences Versus Hard Sciences

Why has a discussion about the brain's role in innovation been missing for all these years? For example, very few MBA students take classes about or are given training on the brain in organizational training programs. Traditional management has largely ignored the mental processes of work, labeling them as *soft skills*. The relegation of thinking and emotion to the soft skills bin of management is nothing short of ironic: soft skills are a lot more complex than hard skills.

Consider the following comparison of the hard versus the soft sciences. If you place a piece of magnesium in a beaker of water, it will hiss and fizz until it fully dissolves. If you do that same experiment a hundred times, the result will always be the same. That is hard science. Now consider the soft science of people management. If you hold a meeting today at one o'clock in the boardroom, a certain number of people will come, sit in various places, make small talk beforehand, and react afterward to what was said during the meeting. If you hold this meeting on a different day or at another time, you can get various people attending who may sit next to different people, who will talk about something else and react to the meeting in a different way. These dissimilarities will occur every time a meeting is conducted.

The hard sciences are often seen as the most challenging courses in school, but based on the example above, predictions about the future in hard sciences are fairly easy because they rely on an array of constant laws and rules of behavior. The soft sciences that dictate our mental processes are where a great deal of complexity is found. For example, NASA can determine what the gravitational pull of a star one million light-years away will be ten years from now, but like all of us, NASA can't tell you what will happen at a staff meeting tomorrow.

While the brain is complex and often unpredictable, there are several useful findings that neuroscientists have uncovered that can aid in understanding the brain's role in innovation. While still difficult to predict, these findings regarding the brain can help you discipline your mental process and generate more innovative thought than you otherwise might. Luckily, while the brain is a highly complex organ, a brief explanation regarding its anatomy and physiology can greatly aid in understanding its role in innovation.

Brain 101

A useful description of the brain is often referred to as the *triune brain model*. Formulated by neuroscientist Paul D. MacLean in the 1960s, the triune brain offered a possible explanation as to how brains developed and built upon its existing structures during evolutionary periods. It essentially states that the brain has three parts: the reptilian brain (sometimes called the r-complex), the mammalian brain, and the neocortex.

Each of these three components has a different function. The reptilian brain regulates basic physiological and involuntary activity, such as breathing, heart rate, body temperature regulation, digestion, and anything else the body does that you are not consciously aware of. The mammalian brain is responsible for such things as the limbic system (including the fight-or-flight response) and the many emotions that emanate from it, including reproductive drives. The neocortex includes the prefrontal cortex (PFC), which is responsible for conscious thought, planning, reason, and emotion regulation. The emotions of the limbic system often arise on a nonconscious basis, meaning there is an encoded mental map

Figure 4

INNOVATING WITH THE BRAIN IN MIND

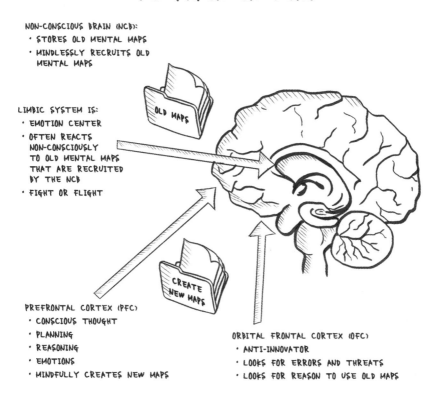

NON-CONSCIOUS BRAIN (NCB):
- STORES OLD MENTAL MAPS
- MINDLESSLY RECRUITS OLD MENTAL MAPS

LIMBIC SYSTEM IS:
- EMOTION CENTER
- OFTEN REACTS NON-CONSCIOUSLY TO OLD MENTAL MAPS THAT ARE RECRUITED BY THE NCB
- FIGHT OR FLIGHT

OLD MAPS

CREATE NEW MAPS

PREFRONTAL CORTEX (PFC)
- CONSCIOUS THOUGHT
- PLANNING
- REASONING
- EMOTIONS
- MINDFULLY CREATES NEW MAPS

ORBITAL FRONTAL CORTEX (OFC)
- ANTI-INNOVATOR
- LOOKS FOR ERRORS AND THREATS
- LOOKS FOR REASON TO USE OLD MAPS

that tells humans to run from a spider, snake, or angry dog before they are consciously aware of doing so. The PFC is often described as the executive function of the brain, as it has the ability to trump the often reflexive and instinctive urges of the limbic system.

When strong emotion is part of a mental map, it greatly increases the speed of map recall and action. In this way the limbic system can help keep you safe from threats by reducing your response time to danger. The limbic system is an important part of the mindless portion of the human brain, along with the nonconscious brain (NCB), where old mental maps are stored. The limbic system reacts to stimuli based on old mental maps that are recruited by the brain. For instance, when a child touches a hot stove for the first time, the brain makes a mental map that a stove equals hot. This map is stored in the NCB so it can be recruited in the future as needed. Mindless mental maps that can be recruited in a split second are important for our survival. Without these maps, we would make the same life-threatening mistakes made over and over again.

Unfortunately, these mindless mental maps can also limit innovative solutions. If in the past you were successful at solving a problem a certain way, your brain may recruit that mental map every time it sees similar situations, even if the map is a poor fit. For example, one evening you leave home to drive to a grocery store. While you're driving, several work-related problems preoccupy your thoughts. Before you know it, you've missed the exit for the store and instead take the exit to your workplace. The NCB thinks it has recruited the correct map based on what the PFC was thinking. However, this map is not correct for the territory you need to navigate.

There is a temptation to accept old mental maps even when they don't fit, because it takes fewer mental resources (in the form of oxygenated blood and glucose) than creating a new map. With respect to innovation, it is important to remember that *the map is not the same thing as the territory*. Every situation is different, and to be innovative you must suspend the initial map the brain recruits and consider if it is a fit or if you should create a new map.

It's easy to cast old maps as bad and new maps as good, but this would be incorrect. Generally a new map is created after several maps were considered during a period of reflection about a given problem. Once the new map is selected, the behavior related to that map is neither efficient nor habitual. Like learning a new dance, a new map takes time to become dependable.

This mental map recruitment and creation process explains why we so often find that our first solutions to new complex problems are almost always wrong. We recruit an existing map that doesn't fit the territory, which perpetuates the failure we are trying to overcome. In essence we choose to ride a stationary bike when a mountain bike is required.

We next will try to address the problem by creating a Rube Goldberg–type of new mental map, some fusion of a stationary, road, hybrid, and mountain bike, but we generally find that our eagerness to solve the problem quickly results in a complicated and overengineered solution that generally fails. The best new mental maps that solve our problems tend to be those that we have thoughtfully created, refined, and streamlined over time so they become elegantly simple. These types of new mental maps fit the demands of the territory.

The PFC is the part of your brain responsible for innovative thought. The PFC not only suspends the reaction to the limbic system's old mental maps but can also draw new innovative maps through a process called mindfulness. Just as mindlessness is the way in which you reflexively react to life without thinking, mindfulness forms a gap in the brain's autonomic responses where you can slow down and reflect. In organizations that are dominated by increasing floods of information, a gap in thinking or a slowing of information flow would appear counterintuitive to the direction an organization needs to go. And yet this gap in thinking is just what the brain requires to function mindfully and produce innovative ideas.

Mindfulness is often characterized by:

- Looking at each situation in the present moment as though it is unique.
- Suspending judgment by keeping old mental maps from being recruited too quickly and used as solutions to a present dilemma.

- Maintaining an openness to novel solutions that would require the creation of a new mental map.

Making new maps is very resource intensive for the brain. That is why, where business is concerned, the brain favors mindless solutions like Lean Six Sigma over mindful innovations. While the PFC takes up 2 percent of your body weight, it consumes 20 percent of your body's oxygenated blood and glucose. And despite being resource intensive, the processing speed of the PFC is very slow relative to the NCB. Think about it like this: the conscious brain can comprehend the coins in your pocket while the NCB can comprehend the U.S. economy. Or the conscious brain can comprehend one cubic foot while the NCB can comprehend the Milky Way galaxy. And from a biking perspective, a stationary bike is analogous to the NCB, where the rider can travel many more miles than someone on a PFC-driven mountain bike. On a mountain bike, the rider must deal with uncertain terrain, changing weather, and the travel patterns of other riders on the trail. The mountain bike requires much more PFC mindful thinking than a NCB mindless-thinking ride on a stationary bike in the gym.

The brain functions utilized in making mindful new maps are similar to organizational innovation efforts. Mentally speaking, mindfully innovating is slower and requires far more physiological resources—oxygenated blood and glucose—than the mindless NCB. Resource and speed issues are the same drawbacks that innovation faces in organizations. Yet once the right innovative solution is formed, this new mindful mental map can have tremendous power because it is added to the toolbox of the NCB for future recall.

Using this understanding of the brain as a foundation, let's take a look at three facts about the brain that can increase our ability to innovate.

All innovation is born of mindfulness, but in order to scale innovation, one must begin to apply the mindless processes of Lean Six Sigma.

The Three Brain Facts Every Creative Genius Should Know

Fact #1: Threat and Reward
The Brain's Simple Organizing Principle

As complex as the brain is, it operates on a fairly simple organizing principle. In general, the brain wants to maximize reward and eliminate threats. However, the ratio of this organizing principle is not 1:1, that is, we don't look for rewards as much as we try to avoid threats. The ratio is more like 1:5 in favor of eliminating threats. This is due, in part, to the fact that the brain possesses five times more wiring dedicated to detecting threats than it does to seeking rewards. This is why innovations are so often focused on eliminating pain points and overcoming failure. As an adult, when was the last time you ran to an activity you saw as a reward? It's probably been awhile for most of us. In this instance, human reaction can be summed up this way: we run from pain, we walk from waste, and we tiptoe toward opportunity.

The brain houses chemical formulas that carry the feelings of threat and reward throughout the body. When there is a sense of reward—whether through food, love, drugs, or enjoyable activities—the chemical the body releases is usually *dopamine*. Threat responses that occur when the brain is under stress are often associated with the chemical *cortisol*. From an organizational perspective, the brain sees certainty as a dopamine event and uncertainty as a cortisol event. When there is too much uncertainty, the limbic system kicks in the fight-or-flight response that actually robs the PFC of resources and renders us unable to think clearly, let alone form innovative maps.

The useful thing about standardization and process improvement is that, when perfected, they give a large amount of certainty that the brain interprets as a dopamine reward. However, organizations are dynamic and change every day. Some degree of disruption is necessary in all systems if they are to adapt and grow. Additionally, too much certainty can lead to boredom and lack of challenge, which can cause employee dissatisfaction and organizational stagnation. It is in this balance between mindful and mindless tensions that the brain feels reward (dopamine) and stress (cortisol) and provides energy (adrenaline) to deal with both.

Conversely, innovative ideas can provide either a reward or a threat, depending on their origin. When our brain generates an innovative mental map, a rush of dopamine is released as a reward. A sense of excitement and energy is often experienced, and we want to share the idea with others. But if we are on the receiving end of another person's innovative thought, quite often this can produce a sense of threat, especially if the idea is coming from someone in authority who can dictate implementation. From a neuroscience standpoint, when another person tries to share a mental map with coworkers, it's seen as a mental foreign body. As with most foreign bodies, the brain will resist it since it has no map in the NCB to match it. In essence, because we don't all possess the same map, we don't see the map as representing our territory. This fine balance between the competing needs of the PFC and the limbic system underscores why it is so difficult for organizations to strike a balance between innovation and Lean Six Sigma.

Quite often innovators are seen as ahead of their time when their particular innovation is not adopted. But what may be more accurate is that some innovators are not skilled in the art of gaining buy-in into the insights that lead to the development of and need for new maps. Instead, the brains of others—perceiving the idea as different, foreign, and therefore uncertain and risky—are awash in cortisol, indicating that the plan will more likely lead to failure than success. The new map is seen as an error that must be reconciled, and the brain does this most often by offering up old maps to explain away the problem. Even though the old map is flawed and not working well, it provides hoped-for or perceived certainty and rewards the brain with dopamine for continuing to use the old plan, even when it clearly isn't working.

Fact #2: The Orbital Frontal Cortex (OFC) The Anti-Innovator

Have you ever wondered why most news is negative, why movies without dramatic tension are boring, and why you jump in a frightening situation before you realize what the threat is? The primary reason for this is that the brain is very good at keeping you alive, and it does so by constantly scanning your internal and external environment for threats five times every second. As a result, real or perceived threats are a major preoccupation of the brain. The region of the brain responsible for this is called the orbital frontal cortex (OFC).

Constantly active, the OFC is the error detection center. The OFC is the reason you notice a missing tooth in someone's smile before you see thirty-one healthy teeth. It is also the reason a parent notices a D- on a child's report card before the A's and B's are recognized. In the workplace, if you have a performance evaluation and 10 percent is around improvements while 90 percent is around things you do well, which part of the evaluation do you most remember? And which part of the evaluation does your boss spend the most time on? Generally you focus on the improvements, since five times more wiring in your brain is dedicated to the threatening part of the evaluation. This is precisely why more is learned from failure than from success: we are wired to focus on failure and to establish maps to overcome it, whereas success garners less attention in the effort to identify threats. Success supports existing identities rather than creating tensions that would force us to learn and create new ones.

When the OFC senses an error or threat, the limbic system kicks in and concocts an emotional cocktail that can prompt us to act quickly and avoid danger. Given our actions are reflexive, they tend to be dominated by mindless thinking that relies on existing mental maps. In the workplace, the OFC is quick to observe problems but fairly useless in solving them in an innovative way. As the OFC detects a threat, it engages the limbic system's fight-or-flight response. When you are in a state of fight or flight, the limbic system robs the PFC of the physiological resources of oxygenated blood and glucose, making it difficult to have innovative thought.

Reactive organizations become this way by allowing individual and an organizational OFC's, out to detect errors and fight the corresponding fires, to set the agenda. An addiction to reactivity is common because it provides a sense of accomplishment. It also prioritizes the day's work in an effortless way by mindlessly reacting to the latest fire. But how can you possibly work on your strategic plan when you must put out today's fire? A mindless reactive organization will struggle to succeed.

Instead, an appreciation of the inner workings of employees' mental resources will greatly aid an organization's ability to switch easily between mindful and mindless processes.

At their heart, organizations are merely a physical manifestation of the internal mental processes of their employees. When organizations don't start with the thought that they may need a new mental map, and they naively work as though they possess all the maps they need, employees waste time treating symptoms rather than wrestling with core issues. This is how you perpetuate maladaptive tensions and continue to generate failure and pain. Those issues include:

- What is our collective identity?
- Is the organization skewed too far toward mindlessness or mindfulness?
- How can a culture of innovators evolve?

Remember: each building, process, program, product, culture, and identity begins as a thought that later took physical form.

Fact #3: Allowing Yourself BAG Time: How Innovation Happens in the Brain

In dozens of seminars we have asked participants to tell us at what point in the day they get their best ideas. The answers are surprisingly similar, no matter what the audience composition is. The top answers look something like this:

1. In the shower
2. Jogging
3. Right before bed
4. Driving to and from work
5. As soon as I wake up
6. Mowing the lawn

It's rare to hear participants say they get their best ideas at work. It's as if people can be innovative in any other place but work. This is problematic, given that the workplace is likely the area most desperately in need of innovation. Luckily, by understanding the brain, it's possible to understand why this occurs and what can be done to improve the brain's capacity for innovation at work.

A great deal has been learned with respect to how one innovates by understanding brain waves. Brain waves are categorized by their frequency and measured by electroencephalograms (EEGs). Waves are measured in hertz (Hz), the cycles per second of a wave's peaks and troughs. While there are five kinds of brain waves—alpha, beta, theta, delta, gamma—only three (alpha, beta, gamma) play a major role in innovation.

- Alpha brain waves, measured at 7–13 Hz, are the brain state of relaxation and meditation. The alpha state is associated with creativity and superlearning, where the brain learns at a faster and deeper level than it does in beta.
- Beta brain waves, measured at 13–40 Hz, are the brain state of normal waking consciousness. Nearly all forms of action, thinking, and problem solving are done with beta brain waves, and it's generally where our brain functions at work and throughout most of the day.
- Theta brain waves, measured at 4–7 Hz, are the brain state of REM sleep (dreams) and the barely conscious state just before sleeping and just after waking.
- Delta brain waves are measured at less than 4 Hz and are the brain state of deep sleep and unconsciousness.
- Gamma brain waves, measured at 40+ Hz, are the brain state of hyperalertness, rapid integration of sensory input, and innovation.

To innovate, it is necessary to turn on the brain waves associated with innovation and creativity on demand. However, there is a sequence that our brain must go through in order to produce these waves. When trying to solve a problem, the PFC is engaged, generating beta waves associated with conscious thinking. For simple problems, the PFC may solve it immediately or in some cases the NCB may pull an old map that the PFC finds acceptable for the current situation.

With more challenging problems, the PFC may generate so many beta waves that the brain is locked up and unable to experience other brain waves. Remember, the PFC can only comprehend simple things like the change in your pocket. To make a real breakthrough, you may need to access the power of the NCB that can process huge amounts of information. So how do you access that part of your brain if it's nonconscious?

The reality is that our NCB has already solved most of the problems we face. The problem is that we aren't consciously aware of it. Back in school, prior to taking a test, the teacher would say, "When in doubt, go with your first answer because that's usually the right one." The NCB is a powerful computer, but it's often very difficult to hear. We tend to hear it best when our brain waves occur in the following sequence: beta (thinking) to alpha (relaxing) to gamma (innovation). We call it *putting innovation in the BAG*.

Figure 5
WE NEED THE RIGHT
BRAIN WAVES TO INNOVATE

MINDLESSNESS   MINDFULNESS

BETA	ALPHA	GAMMA
ALERT WORKING NORMAL JOB ROUTINE	RELAXED REFLECTIVE EXERCISE OR SHOWERING	ACTIVE THOUGHT COMPOSING

OLD MAPS

CREATE NEW MAPS

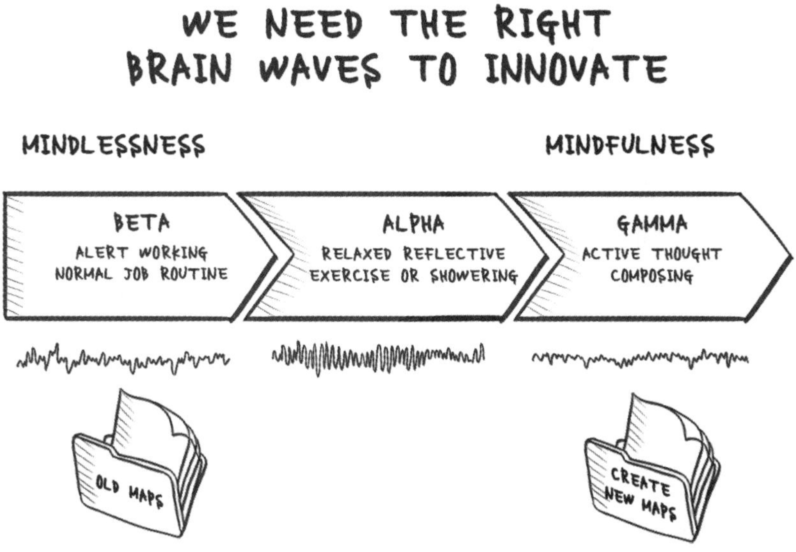

So why not use the PFC's beta waves to go through the above sequence and start generating some blockbuster ideas? Unfortunately, the brain doesn't work that way. While the PFC can generate beta waves (and even, to some extent, alpha waves by disengaging the PFC to relax and start daydreaming), gamma waves arise from the NCB and come on their own timetable.

How many times has someone said, "Don't overthink it?" This generally refers to trying to solve a problem by only using the PFC's beta waves. This is counterintuitive, given most people believe, if they haven't solved a problem, it's because they haven't applied enough thought. Beta waves are, figuratively, noisy waves. Too many beta waves can get in the way of other waves like those used to relax (alpha), sleep (delta), or innovate (gamma). Have you ever had trouble sleeping (delta waves) because you couldn't turn off the stream of beta waves associated with thinking and racing thoughts? The reason alpha waves exist between delta and gamma waves is that they serve as a buffer or doorway to the NCB. We all know how difficult it is to solve a problem with beta wave overthinking. Alpha waves provide some separation from overthinking a problem, allowing the brain to shift into a lower hertz state. In an alpha-wave state, the brain allows new thoughts, similar to a state of daydreaming, which can be coupled in novel combinations with earlier beta thoughts for innovative solutions. At the very moment multiple thoughts are coupled together for an innovative solution, a burst of gamma waves flood the brain, and we become consciously aware of the implications and uses of our new innovation. This is how the brain applies the three complexity processes necessary for innovation: variation, interaction, and selection.

Within the brain, the following process occurs. The PFC, working on a problem, emits beta waves. Then the brain gets tired of working on the problem and shifts its focus to jogging, showering, sleeping, daydreaming, or doing some other activity. In a state of mental relaxation, and with beta waves giving way to alpha waves, the brain is more able to become aware of the insights associated with gamma waves. In essence, alpha waves suppress beta waves to allow the PFC to become aware of gamma wave insights.

In this quiet time, the brain can more easily become aware of innovative ideas that have already been solved by the NCB. As gamma waves increase in the brain, alpha waves plummet, and when the gamma waves become strong enough, the idea is recognized by the conscious mind as a Eureka! moment. At that instant, the body releases a flood of dopamine and adrenaline. The dopamine makes the idea feel good, and the adrenaline gives us a shot of energy to act on the idea. This is why many companies, such as Google and 3M, have adopted the practice of allowing employees 10–15 percent of their time to work on new ideas. As we mentioned above, we call this BAG time. While the remaining 85 percent of the employees' time may be dominated by beta waves, the 15 percent of protected time can allow for states of mindful innovation to generate gamma waves.

However, it is important to note that just because you feel good about an idea it doesn't automatically make that idea one that should be adopted. Like all mental maps the PFC produces, there is a tendency to identify and fall in love with our own creations. The good feelings generated with the new map only make this identification stronger when emotion is linked to a mental map, making its recall more rapid and powerful. In short, we see our map as a solid solution and struggle to understand why others in the room don't immediately get it.

In order to combat this reaction, we offer a three-step process for brainstorming that allows teams to constructively manage employees' innovative thoughts. The process permits the most useful ideas to be considered for implementation. Given that the mental processes of innovation often happen in an undisciplined fashion, having structured BAG time allows employees to harness their innovative potential for a greater volume, velocity, and value of organizational innovation.

The Three-Step Process for Brainstorming

There is a process, using the collective wisdom of an organization, to aid in tempering individual innovative solutions. Committee brainstorming generally gets a bad name (groupthink), as extroverts contribute a disproportionate amount of dialogue and persuade or bully others into agreement. However, if done in the right sequence, group brainstorming can actually yield a significant number of insights. The brain needs the right initial conditions to mindfully innovate. Getting in a group and asking for rapid-fire ideas shifts the mind into beta wave thinking. This results in pulling old mental maps quickly but does not produce as many innovative maps. Three steps that can greatly enhance innovation at work involve:

1. Group questioning
2. Individual brainstorming
3. Group brainstorming

When the brain is presented with a statement such as "Sunshine is important for warmth," the brain only has one mental map in front of it (sunshine equals warmth). The same is true when the brain is presented with a close-ended question such as "Is sunshine important for warmth?" But the opposite happens when the brain is presented with an open-ended question such as "What is sunshine good for?" Then the brain searches for multiple answers that can range from warmth, photosynthesis, suntans, the foundation of all color, or beautiful sunsets. Open-ended questions help build a broad funnel of ideas. A broad funnel is important as it ensures that all meanings and solutions are on the table for consideration.

Figure 6

BRAINSTORMING THROUGH BAG TIME

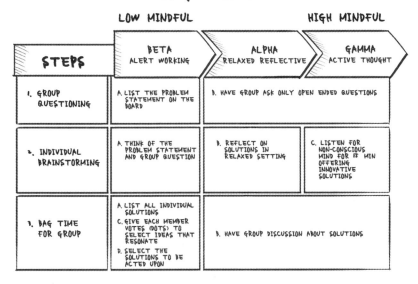

	LOW MINDFUL		HIGH MINDFUL
STEPS	**BETA** ALERT WORKING	**ALPHA** RELAXED REFLECTIVE	**GAMMA** ACTIVE THOUGHT
1. GROUP QUESTIONING	A. LIST THE PROBLEM STATEMENT ON THE BOARD	B. HAVE GROUP ASK ONLY OPEN ENDED QUESTIONS	
2. INDIVIDUAL BRAINSTORMING	A. THINK OF THE PROBLEM STATEMENT AND GROUP QUESTION	B. REFLECT ON SOLUTIONS IN RELAXED SETTING	C. LISTEN FOR NON-CONSCIOUS MIND FOR 15 MIN OFFERING INNOVATIVE SOLUTIONS
3. BAG TIME FOR GROUP	A. LIST ALL INDIVIDUAL SOLUTIONS C. GIVE EACH MEMBER VOTES (DOTS) TO SELECT IDEAS THAT RESONATE D. SELECT THE SOLUTIONS TO BE ACTED UPON	B. HAVE GROUP DISCUSSION ABOUT SOLUTIONS	

If a group sits down to brainstorm, and all that comes out are statements or close-ended questions, the range of possibilities is much narrower. (This is the same logic behind the Five Whys and the Five Hows discussed in the previous chapter and follows the innovation trio of interaction, variation, and selection.)

Step 1: Group Questioning

1. List the problem statement on a marker board (beta waves are used).

2. Have the group ask *only* open-ended questions about the problem statement for thirty minutes (alpha and occasional gamma waves are used).

Step 1 involves asking questions about the problem statement while a member of the team writes down each question on separate cards or sticky notes. It often helps to assign a process checker to disqualify nonquestion statements or close-ended questions from being recorded. What will become apparent immediately is how counterintuitive this exercise is to the brain. The exercise will drag as team members struggle to think of questions to ask.

Many people resist the exercise because they feel they already know the answer and want to declare it. When the brain is faced with a problem, it enjoys pulling maps quickly to reduce uncertainty and variation and gets rewarded with dopamine for doing so efficiently. Just as the brain provides a dose of dopamine when you innovate, it also gives you dopamine when you get an answer right or think you get it right because you answer it capably. Remember that mindlessly pulling old mental maps when confronted with a problem keeps the brain in a more efficient, lower-energy state. In short, the dopamine work-to-reward ratio is better for mindless rather than innovative thinking.

Months after conducting this exercise with a group of executives, Mitch was contacted by a vice president of an information technology department. He reported the following experience.

"My team had a difficult problem to solve and I knew it would take a pretty innovative solution. A lot of people in our company don't see the IT shop as a bastion of innovation, and I wanted to change that perception. As we listed the problem statement and began to ask open-ended questions, the first ten minutes were painful and enthusiasm was low. When an occasional question would surface to be recorded on the board, a team member would roll his eyes and say under his breath, "I know the answer to that." However, things got moving after that, and once the thirty minutes were over, we had a huge list of open-ended questions about the problem statement. Everyone agreed that if we could answer all these questions with our solution, the result would be a stellar product. The open-ended questions helped expand our thinking and see around corners we might not have known were there."

Step 2: Individual Brainstorming

1. Think of the problem statement and group questions (beta waves are used).
2. Reflect on solutions in a relaxed setting, such as walking, jogging, etc. (alpha waves are used).
3. Listen for the nonconscious mind to offer innovative solutions for fifteen minutes, while reflecting, composing, etc. (gamma waves are used).

Although no answers were given during Step 1, the NCB of each individual in the group heard each question and began trying to answer them. Regardless of the number of questions, the remarkable processing power of the NCB can manage the complexity of hundreds of queries. The conscious brain also hears each question, but its ability to remember each one and come up with innovative solutions alone through beta-wave thinking is limited.

In Step 2, each individual is given some quiet time to mindfully reflect about the problem statement. In this state of mindful reflection, alpha waves are emitted. The brain floats from thought to thought, at times linking them or deleting options as it shifts through the mental chaff to find the right solution. During this process, the brain is freed up from noisy beta-wave activity. The brain feels quiet and relaxed, and the process of mindful reflection feels almost enjoyable. In these moments, the brain is calm enough to become consciously aware of solutions housed in the NCB. A burst of gamma waves ensues as ideas flow into the conscious mind as the brain releases dopamine and adrenaline. Step 2 allows for more introverted participants to express a stronger voice in the exercise, given they are not competing with extroverts for speaking time.

Participants then write each idea on a piece of paper, a card, or a sticky note to be shared with the group in Step 3 of the process.

Step 3: Group BAG Time

1. List all individual solutions on a marker board.
2. Combine similar solutions.
3. Have the group discuss solutions.
4. Give each member five dots (stickers or markers) to place on ideas that resonate best.
5. Select the solution(s) to be acted upon.

The group organizes the sticky notes into groupings with common themes. Once groupings are completed, participants discuss each idea, detailing the pros and cons of various solutions. With the ideas listed on the marker board, each person is given five votes (either with a marker or stickers) to place on the solutions that resonate best. This winnowing process will generally show some clear preferences around which innovation is preferred. Interestingly, while each participant may have experienced a reward of dopamine and adrenaline for coming up with an idea, the internal physiological reward often does not translate to the correct external solution.

Even so, the same could be said of a group that brainstorms without reflection by quickly pulling old mental maps through beta-wave activity alone. In these sessions, participants get their physiological reward of dopamine and adrenaline by being the first to give a perceived right answer, even if that answer is the wrong map for the current territory. The difference is that by using the beta-alpha-gamma sequence, ideas generated will generate a higher yield of innovative thought. Think of this brainstorming effort as

Figure 7

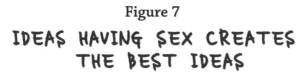

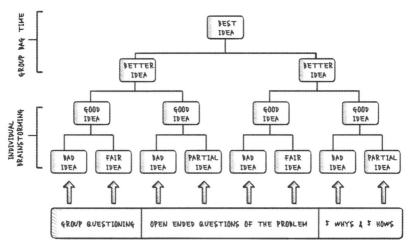

generating ideas that then have sex with other ideas in order to create a baby which is the better idea. As more generations combine, better ideas emerge.

The Next Step

Equipped with the knowledge of the brain's innovative processes, combined with methods for vetting innovative ideas in larger groups, we can now discuss how the organization harvests those ideas for implementation. Given that innovation is a messy process that often leads to failure, companies should have a process for doing the process intelligently. In the next chapter, we will detail how companies can take the innovative ideas of individuals and teams and engage in *fast, frequent, and frugal failure* on their journey to breakthrough innovations.

Figure 8

WHYS AND HOWS TO CREATE GOOD IDEAS

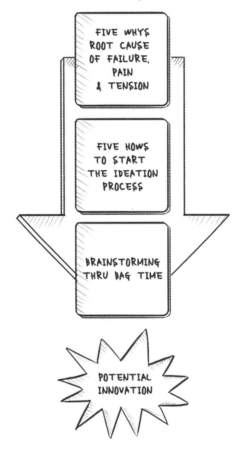

FIVE WHYS
ROOT CAUSE
OF FAILURE,
PAIN
& TENSION

FIVE HOWS
TO START
THE IDEATION
PROCESS

BRAINSTORMING
THRU BAG TIME

POTENTIAL
INNOVATION

REMEMBER

✔ The brain is the core of our knowing.

✔ All identities are like mental maps that exist in the brain. When the brain encounters a situation, a mental map is recruited. It dictates how we should act in that situation.

✔ If the situation requires a mental map that the brain has not created, the brain must do its own form of innovating by using mindfulness to make a new mental map. That is,

  a) Looking at each situation in present moment as though it's unique.

  b) Suspending judgment by keeping old mental maps from being recruited too quickly and used as solutions to the present dilemma.

  c) Maintaining an openness to novel solutions that may require the creation of a new mental map.

✔ If the brain doesn't innovate a new mental map for a new situation, it will often use an old mental map that doesn't fit the new situation—the wrong bike for the terrain. This is often the reason we experience personal and organizational failure since the map doesn't fit the territory, and we end up with maladaptive tensions.

✔ The brain's simple organizing principle is to maximize reward and eliminate threats.

✔ One part of the brain, the orbital front cortex (OFC), acts as an anti-innovator because it scans the environment for real or perceived threats every five seconds. When a threat is detected by the brain, it tries to pull old maps rather than innovate new ones so it can quickly and efficiently eliminate feelings of threat and uncertainty.

✔ In order to innovate, it is necessary to turn on the brain waves associated with innovation and creativity on demand. To do this, the brain must go through a particular sequence labeled BAG: beta (thinking), alpha (relaxing), and gamma (innovating).

✔ Brainstorming can work if done as follows: group questioning, individual brainstorming, and then group brainstorming. This approach magnifies the power of the innovation trio: variation, interaction, and selection.

─────────────── QUESTIONS ───────────────

> ❯ Describe a situation where you needed a new mental map but instead recruited an old one that didn't work?

> ❯ Using a specific example, how have you personally created new mental maps in the past?

> ❯ How has your organization done this in the past?

> ❯ What barriers did you and your organization have to overcome to create new mental maps?

> ❯ How do you incorporate BAG time to ensure your mind is prepared to innovate?

CHAPTER SEVEN

Riding to Succeed Through Failure

Failure is the genesis of innovation, the source of learning, and the basis for creating new mental models. However, the predisposition to mindlessness causes us to shun failure, to attempt to too quickly solve difficult problems, and thereby fail in the wrong way.

This is known as *mindless failure*.

To become an innovator and a creative genius, you need to know how to mindfully fail. It means learning how to be unsuccessful with a purpose and intent in order to accelerate the formation of new mental models necessary for innovation.

As you know by now, existing mental models are mindlessly employed to solve new problems that unfortunately tend to lead to slow, infrequent, and expensive failures. These are the exact opposite types that innovators need to seek. As explained in the previous chapter, this is because, when faced with a new and difficult problem, our first response is to try to solve it quickly and efficiently. Recruiting existing models that have worked well in the past for what appears to be similar problems is the norm. And why not, since this approach to rapid resolution rewards us with a quick dopamine hit?

Then we move on, having reinforced our identity as a smart and efficient problem solver, only to become frustrated later when we see that our quick fix didn't work. Worse yet, we tend to continue with this failed approach for a long time because we are so confident that since the mental model worked so well in the past, it should work again.

After overinvesting in failure through this first approach, the tendency is to move to a second mindless method. Thus a convoluted variation of the first approach is implemented, whereby existing mental models are combined in a complicated, Rube Goldberg manner to solve a complex new problem. This is based on the view that the right models are on hand and we just aren't using enough of them in the proper combination to solve the new problem. While this is a bit less mindless (since we did try to apply creativity to modify existing models), we think of this secondary process as being almost as efficient as the former, but it, too, almost always leads to failure. So mindless failure again results after we overinvest in the wrong solution over a long time and waste more time and money.

For example, sales are low. The last time that happened, discounts helped to bring them up. When that doesn't work now, we offer free shipping, a variation on the first plan. That doesn't work either. But if we employ the Five Whys, we realize that sales are low because our industry has moved on to different and better products. Our product has seen its day and is ready to be retired. Our company needs to innovate to find something new to sell successfully.

Mindful failure, on the other hand, occurs when creative genius is applied to reality so that we can:

- Understand the root cause and primary source of the problem.
- Comprehend it from multiple perspectives.
- Deconstruct it to its primary components.

Applying the Five Whys and Five Hows described in chapter 4 does this. Innovators explore and experiment by using the Innovation Cycle through multiple failure rings in an attempt to learn and innovate rapidly. The more mindful path to failure requires them to perform many failure rings that enable fast, frequent, and frugal failures. They don't try to solve the problem in one fast, simple attempt, but rather pursue the solution through disciplined and purposeful failures. A key outcome of mindful failure is the creation of a minimalist approach to innovation that is both simple and elegant. So why isn't mindful failure an accepted feature of organizations?

The physiological predisposition for individual mindlessness, coupled with organizational mindlessness, results in mindless failure. All this does is waste resources because there is a lack of understanding of *mindful failure with a purpose*. And that is where the Innovation Cycle comes in.

Failure and the Innovation Cycle

The Innovation Cycle consists of three rings: Becoming, Knowing, and Doing. (Being is defined here as what you are today.) In the context of the bicycle metaphor, think of the three rings of the sprocket on the Innovation Cycle. Becoming is the smallest and easiest ring you start on, and as you gain speed, you shift gears to the next larger ring: Knowing. Then you achieve your fastest speeds by shifting gears to the third and largest ring: Doing. In each ring, you will do many revolutions before you are ready to shift gears to the next ring. You only move to the next ring once you have exhausted all you can do in the current one. Read on to discover how this process works at the individual level, but keep in mind that it applies to the organizational level just as mindfulness and mindlessness do.

Note: There is a very good reason why all three rings are explained in the Knowing section. Chapter 6 showed how innovation works within the brain. Chapter 7 shows how to ride through failure in order to succeed. This is the bridge between the innovative mind and innovation within an organization. And this leads to chapter 8, which will show you how to enable innovation to emerge within an organization.

Figure 9

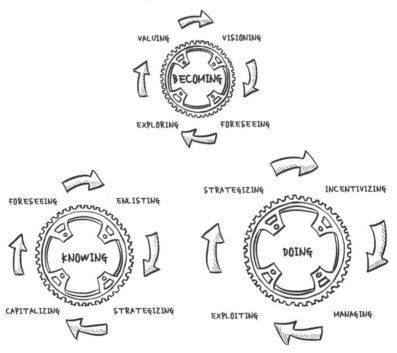

THE FULL INNOVATION CYCLE
FROM BECOMING, TO KNOWING, TO DOING

Becoming

This ring provides the source of your identity discussed in chapter 5. Remember, all of us house hundreds of identities. When a specific identity—for example, the one you use at work—is challenged as a result of some type of failure, you start looping through this ring to form new mental maps to support a new identity. When you fail, a tension emerges because your identity didn't fit the situation. Therefore, you loop through this ring to explore, discover, and develop a new identity that you think will be more successful than your current one. Dissatisfaction with the status quo forms a tension, which is painful to endure. This tension remains until you transform it by either applying an adaptive energy to improve performance or a creative energy to transform performance.

By trying to maintain the status quo, you apply a maladaptive energy that perpetuates and augments failure as you try to maintain the same identity, which isn't working. A new identity emerges as you apply either adaptive or creative energy to the tension. The resulting combination of tension and energy powers the building of new mental models and innovations. Failure and its associated pain act as the cues or triggers for the need to innovate. You remain in this ring until you find and establish an identity you think will be more successful.

For example, when you lose your job, you experience the pain of maladaptive tension. You don't fit in anymore because you have lost your identity as an employee with a certain position in a company. The pain of this tension forces you to explore possible new identities that you think will be more successful.

The maladaptive tension that emerges from Becoming forces you to challenge those things that support your current identity. You review your values and beliefs to determine if they are out of alignment with the current reality. You ask yourself if your vision of yourself is flawed. Then you project your values and vision into the future and foresee who you think you can become in the context of your environment. You try to foresee if the new identity fits better than the old one that failed. Through this process you are applying the *Law of Requisite Variety and Complexity,* and you are trying to harmonize your new identity with external environmental realities.

If you don't like what you foresee, you then begin to explore alternative identities that may require new values and visions that will enable you to predict a more successful new identity in the future. At this point, you explore the environment to test a new mental map for your new identity. You try out the idea of the identity before you actually create it. It is generally necessary to loop through this ring several times until you lock onto an identity that you want to implement for a compelling reason: you visualize that identity becoming more successful than the one that failed. You try to see yourself at another company, in a different position, or with another career. This is not a one-time-only test. Instead, you consider the changes in many ways to determine if you think they will work.

Knowing

This ring starts where the last one left off, by foreseeing the new identity you want to become. It requires understanding the process of transforming the maladaptive tension into either an adaptive one, which requires only modest improvement or incremental innovation, or a creative tension that requires a more transformative breakthrough or radical innovation. An adaptive tension enables small modifications to your identity by tweaking your mental maps, whereas creative tension enables the generation of entirely new mental maps and identities. Transforming a maladaptive tension into an adaptive tension can generally be done within existing similar mental and physical structures.

In contrast, transformation into creative tension requires different and new structures.

For example, if you lost your job as a banker, an adaptive approach would be to find another banking job that might require some improvement or incremental modifications, such as polishing some skills, but it would not require much of a change. However, if, after losing your job, you decided you wanted to become an Internet entrepreneur, you would be forced to transform that maladaptive tension from your job loss into a creative tension. You would need to produce entirely new structures and practices because your new identity would be so different from your previous one.

How do you know when to shift gears from Becoming to Knowing?

You shift from Becoming to Knowing once you *foresee* a new identity, for example, that of an Internet entrepreneur. But to transform the maladaptive tension into a creative one requires you to pedal through the Knowing ring for several cycles. Through this ring you will experiment and test this identity with others in order to know how to proceed. First, you must understand who you need to *enlist* to support you in this transformation, because you can't do it on your own. You then have to develop a strategy for the tension transformation that adds the design of the processes, practices, and structures required. Next, you need to sell the value of your new identity to others who will provide the *capital,* that is, the resources you need to support the people you have enlisted, to implement your strategic plan. Inevitably you will get some of this wrong during your first Knowing loop, which will require you to go through this ring several times until you get your people, plan, and resources secured. But once you do, you can shift to the Doing ring.

Doing

This is the ring where you put your strategic plan into *operation*. This is the plan for the new identity you developed in the Knowing ring. You imagined that identity in the Becoming ring, and you figured out what to do in the Knowing ring. The Doing ring is where you actually become the Internet entrepreneur and you achieve harmony among all three rings of Becoming, Knowing, and Doing because you have finally become the identity you desired. However, if growth is to occur, new tensions must arise as you set your sights on becoming something greater (such as acquiring other Internet businesses to expand your value proposition).

In the Doing ring, you start with your strategy from the Knowing ring to form the structures and practices that ensure the right *incentives* to guide, change, and modify your behaviors as well as the actions of others. You use these structures and practices to *manage* and mitigate the inevitable risks that emerge and threaten this new identity. Then you *exploit* every opportunity to develop, reinforce, and advance this identity.

If the new environment is a better fit for your new identity, you remain in this ring for a long time. You loop through with only minor changes and adjustments from time to time. And as you experience maladaptive tensions, you are able to transform them into adaptive ones with only minor modifications within your existing identity, structures, and practices.

Indeed, this is where mindlessness must now replace mindfulness, because the innovation process has been completed. You need to apply mindlessness in order to scale innovation. For example, as an Internet entrepreneur, you must follow established software development protocols, regulations and laws, marketing programs, and operating practices on an efficient and scalable basis in order to generate a profit and limit errors, costs, and risks.

However, if your new identity and innovations place you in a highly turbulent environment, then you may only loop through this ring for a short time before you experience maladaptive tensions. These will require you to shift back into the Knowing ring to adjust your plan, change your people, or gather more resources before shifting back into the Doing ring.

In more extreme situations, maladaptive tensions may be so strong that you have to downshift all the way to the Becoming ring and begin again to generate an entirely new identity and form new mental maps. The ring you shift to is based upon the magnitude of the maladaptive tension that arises from the Law of Requisite Variety and Complexity. This law states that you must have the same type and level of variety within your organization (or individually) as exists in the outside environment in which you operate. If you lack this requisite variety, then you must change your identity and mental models and innovate in order to survive. (The Law of Requisite Variety and Complexity and will be discussed in more detail in chapter 8.)

Let's see how all these rings work in the real world. The first example is a dotcom start-up within a large organization that Chris was involved in. The second is a medical device start-up Mitch and Chris did together.

Azurix and Mindless Failure

At the height of the dotcom boom in 1999 and 2000, Chris was leading the strategy team at a $1 billion water utility start-up called Azurix. Seeing what was going on with new Internet marketplaces and the stratospheric valuations they were receiving, he convinced the company leadership to launch an Internet business christened Waterdesk.com, and he became the start-up's president.

Unfortunately, none of the Waterdesk.com leadership team had ever been technology entrepreneurs. Chris had done a small retail kosher bakery start-up and helped lead two modest internal start-ups at two large Fortune 100 companies. However, none of these start-ups had ever raised venture capital, and none of the Waterdesk.com partners had ever put their own money at risk on a technology venture.

All of the people leading this new Internet venture, however, were experienced in developing annual business plans and strategies for big companies, so naturally we followed a large company approach to innovation. We studied the competitive landscape, identified new technologies that were driving innovation and forecasted new markets and demand for innovations never before seen. Finally, we approached the Azurix board for funding.

Azurix provided Waterdesk.com with ten million dollars to develop the Internet marketplace business and strategy we had outlined. The expectation was that we would craft and launch a complete solution using expert talent and resources within the next six to nine months. We hired a strategy-consulting firm to further flesh out the business plan. We also engaged a top-five IT systems integrator to manage the technological development process, and we licensed the newest and most expensive applications to integrate into our marketplace solution. No expense was spared in signing up a leading advertising and marketing company to establish a brand and image for the website, the business, and its collateral. All of us at Waterdesk.com and Azurix were proud to say we were one of the earliest customers of the most expensive and cutting-edge technologies. And during these heady early days of the Internet we saw these technology suppliers experience crazy and unrealistic valuation, which we hoped we, too, would receive. After all, one of our technology vendors had already been acquired for four hundred million dollars even though it had only four customers, and Waterdesk.com was one of the four.

Our goal was to build a robust industrial-grade commercial marketplace solution to buy and sell water, water equipment, supplies, and services. We designed and built our solution to be instantly scalable to the entire industry as soon as we launched our website. And we planned to utilize the Lean Six Sigma type of performance our parent company delivered in running its global water management businesses. We were prepared to instantly dominate the global water Internet marketplace.

During this whole process, the entire Waterdesk.com leadership thought we were being very mindful. The aim was clear: develop a new model and identity for the company as a water Internet marketplace. But what none of us appreciated was that the ecosystem we were operating in was so turbulent and dynamic that anything we were focused on doing today could become obsolete within months or even weeks. What we didn't understand at the time was that our traditional mindless approaches to strategy, technology development, operations, and marketing, which relied upon stability and predictability, were obsolete. None of us had ever heard of the Law of Requisite Variety and Complexity, and we had no idea we were violating that law and designing our own demise. We were using mindless processes when mindful ones were needed.

In hindsight, the outcome—mindless failure—was predictable. All that money, time, and effort mindlessly generated something no one wanted.

At the same time, the boyfriend of the Azurix CEO was also experimenting with the idea of starting an Internet marketplace. His was focused on water chemical products and services, which actually overlapped our focus with Waterdesk.com. However, his identity and approach were very different. An entrepreneur, he owned his own business and didn't feel the need to raise ten million dollars to create the perfect scalable solution. Instead, he approached his goal very mindfully by trying to produce the minimal viable product that would enable him to test his ideas quickly, improve them, and figure out what customers really valued.

He immediately set up a web splash page for his Internet marketplace without any of the sophisticated IT back end and capabilities; this cost him virtually nothing. He hired a kid just out of college (who I recommended to him) to monitor hits on the site and then manually fulfill orders. Visitors to his website had no idea what type of back end he had, nor did they care. All they wanted was to buy their chemicals at a good price.

At the time I made fun of what I smugly thought was his charade. He was offering a pretend Internet marketplace whereas I was building a real one that would be a world-beater. We knew it was going to take us longer to come to market, but when we did, we were confident we were going to crush this upstart through our superior technological prowess.

However, unlike us, he conducted many mindless failures on purpose to rapidly learn what customers in the water industry valued about Internet purchases. He followed what Eric Reiss, the author of *The Lean Start-Up,* later called the build-measure-learn approach to innovation. He worked out a very inexpensive minimal viable product (MVP), tested it, learned what did and did not work, and modified it. He then relaunched a better version quickly to offer the next version of his MVP. Through this type of rapid innovation he learned how to build a successful product on a shoestring budget that actually delivered value to customers. By the time we came to market with our solution, he was on version 5.0 and had spent less than one-tenth what we did. Plus, he was making money—something we never managed to do.

Since those dotcom bubble days, Chris has worked with executives from large organizations that are trained in mindless Lean processes, and he's seen this pattern repeated. They approach new challenges with the mindless approach in an effort to ensure quality, reliability, and large-scale success. They fail to realize that such an approach will lead to mindless failure, which is ten times more expensive and takes ten times longer to fail. It also tends to increase risk aversion within the organization to try new innovative ideas because of previous disasters.

Mindful failure is what Mitch and Chris attempted on the next venture.

Tympany: Failures, Innovation, and Identity

We were part of a small company that developed a device that mostly did what audiologists do every day. It worked so well that, on January 17, 2005, more than five hundred audiologists assembled in Chicago for the annual Great Debate in Audiology. And our product was the topic for the debate. These audiologists considered it to be the most disruptive technology to ever enter their field of medicine: automated audiometry.

While Clayton Christiansen's *The Innovator's Dilemma* makes disruptive innovation sound sexy and the inventors behind them look brilliant, we can tell you from personal experience that when you are disrupting an entire industry, market, or profession, you're Public Enemy Number One.

The audience at the Great Debate was hostile. Prior to the debate, audiologists representing the leadership of the American Academy of Audiology (AAA) and the American Speech, Language and Hearing Association (ASHA) sent letters to their congressmen demanding the device called the Otogram—our device—be outlawed. They told the inspector general of the United States that people who used our technology and claimed medical reimbursement for the ensuing procedures were committing fraud because a machine had performed the test, not an audiologist. They also made the same argument to the Center for Medicare and Medicaid Services (CMS). Then they reached out to the American Medical

Association (AMA), which regulates current procedural terminology (CPT) codes for medical reimbursement, to demand that the codes be modified to exclude automated testing. And they made all this public through journals, websites, other media, and conferences.

Our small start-up company named Tympany threatened their identity because the device, called the Otogram, did 80 percent of what they did every day. In addition, the device enabled non-audiologists to simultaneously test three patients and deliver the same quality of test results as those of audiologists. This device was sold to hundreds of physicians and a handful of audiologists with excellent results.

We tried to paint for them a picture of a new identity focused on treating hearing loss that concentrated on the dispensing of hearing aids. We showed them how this was a role that couldn't be automated, offered great value for the patient, and would enable them to earn more money than they could earn through hearing testing. But the audiologists weren't buying the identity of being mere hearing-aid dispensers. They saw that as a second-class profession, and they had no desire to adopt that identity.

As the great disruptors at this event, Mitch and I thought it best if neither of us represented the cause of automated audiometry. We felt that the current animus toward us, as non-audiologists threatening the profession, would distract from the focus of the debate. So we invited two customers who were PhD audiologists to represent the merits and virtues of the device at the meeting.

It was a lively and engaging debate, but the vast majority wanted to maintain the status quo that supported their current identity. But for us it served to highlight how far we had come in forming our identities as innovative leaders on a mission to improve the world's hearing in a field of healthcare that was new to us.

Here's how we changed our identities as innovators. Doing so enabled us to earn a noble moniker as creators of a disruptive technology.

Becoming: We Created a New Identity as Technology Entrepreneurs

After leaving Azurix in 2000, I (Chris) was hired by GEN3 Partners (GEN3), an innovation-consulting boutique, to help originate engagements with Fortune 500 companies that were struggling to innovate as quickly as the Internet was enabling start-ups. In those days, I would often hear the phrase "It's not the big that eat the small but the fast that eat the slow." The mission at GEN3 was to enable large, slow-moving organizations to improve their innovative capabilities to survive in the new Internet-powered world. With the insights gained from this work, GEN3 cofounder Michael Treacy and I were planning to write a book on innovation. During my short tenure at GEN3, we worked through several drafts of our ideas but never really were able to pull all our ideas together before I left.

For the year I was with GEN3, we had some very exciting engagements. But twelve months after the dotcom bubble burst, it was clear that the consulting business model GEN3 had formed, with funding from two leading venture capital firms (Accel Partners and Michael Dell Ventures), was not sustainable. So GEN3 gave me a modest severance package that forced me to rethink my identity. Was I a consultant, an entrepreneur, or should I just go back to corporate America and be a senior-level cog in another hierarchical organization? What should I become?

Several experiences at GEN3 helped me better explore my future identity. As a co-thought leader with Michael, I was often asked to speak at venture capital conferences about innovation and what we saw as driving it. After speaking at an innovation conference in New York City in 2001, I was boarding a plane to Boston when a man behind me asked, "Aren't you the guy that gave the speech at the venture conference today on innovation?"

He explained how he loved what I had to say and mentioned that a client he was working with was experiencing difficulty raising some money for a new venture. He asked if he could get my advice on what I thought they should do.

We had a pleasant conversation and I gave him my card. Frankly, I never expected to hear from him again.

The next day, he sent me a copy of their business plan and asked if I would review it and then share my insights and recommendations.

Later that week I gave them an earful of free advice. Because they weren't paying me, and since I felt they would never have the funds to do so, I felt no need to soften my views. I was brutally honest with my assessment of their business plan and laid out three reasons why I thought their idea was hopeless and would never work.

The essence of their idea was a fragmented industry roll-up. They were trying to do a roll-up of small mom-and-pop audiology clinics around the country, with the idea that once they got big enough, they could eliminate waste through standardization, consolidation, and bulk purchasing. Basically, it was a mindless value proposition. What I found lacking in their plan was the following:

1. **The wrong team.** No one on their team had ever rolled up anything before in any industry, plus they had no experience in mindless Lean Six Sigma operating models. The two principals were a physician and a hospital administrator.

2. **The wrong business model.** I shared with them the assessment of most of the academic research on roll-ups: they

generally fail to generate value for many reasons, but the most important is that some industries, technologies, and services defy the business logic for rolling them up. (I learned this with my kosher bakery. Many people suggested I follow a similar logic in that market, and they thought that since it had never been done before it would be easy. I learned there were many reasons why there were few large national Kosher bakeries.)

3. **The wrong innovation.** There was nothing in their plan that indicated they were offering any new sources of value. In essence, there was nothing novel and therefore nothing innovative. I defined innovation as value-creating novelty, and I outlined how what they produced offered neither novelty nor new value.

I ended our call by expressing the need for them to be more mindful in their approach and to focus on finding the failures that produce key pain points in the marketplace that generate maladaptive tensions. I then encouraged them to figure out how to transform those tensions into creative ones that, in turn, would drive an innovative approach that would provide the foundation for their start-up.

After such a brutal assessment, I never expected to hear from them again.

To my utter shock, they agreed with everything I said. Then they asked if I would visit them in Austin, Texas, and help them identify the failures, pain points, maladaptive tensions, and required innovations. At that time I had a client in Austin that I was visiting regularly, so a time to meet on my next trip was arranged.

I spent half a day at an audiology clinic with the two principals of the start-up: Dr. Michael Glasscock, a world-leading otolaryngologist (an ENT—ear, nose, and throat—specialist), and his hospital administrator partner. They walked me through the entire workflow of an audiologist, demonstrating hearing tests and fitting hearing aids. When we finished, we sat down to lunch and one of them asked, "So what is your great insight? What's the big idea? Where should we innovate?"

I hadn't expected that.

All I knew about audiology was what I had read in their business plan a few weeks before and what I had seen that morning. So I qualified my comments accordingly and told them that what I thought was needed was an ATM-like set-up to test hearing. I described something small, portable, and automated that would enable self-service and eliminate the need for an audiologist to diagnose hearing loss. I went on to describe how they could innovate the hearing health business model by leveraging this new technology. Doing so would enable them to achieve the objectives of their original business plan without the need to do the roll-up. This time, however, they could achieve it through innovations rather than brute force.

They thought that was a brilliant idea and asked me how to do it.

Explaining that I was an innovation consultant, I told them I had no idea how to do it. While I understood how to identify business problems and needs, I was not a technologist. I had no idea how to invent and produce new technology. I certainly didn't see myself as the genius behind a new disruptive technology and start-up I was suggesting they invent. But the problem was that they couldn't see themselves in that role either. Because none of us had the identity of a medical technology inventor and entrepreneur, we couldn't see a way to do what I had outlined.

We chatted further and agreed on some modest next steps to flesh out these ideas, but I doubted any of us thought this was going to lead anywhere.

At this same time, two other things were happening. First, as I mentioned above, GEN3 was restructuring. They were preparing to let me go, which was generating some maladaptive tension in my life. And second, I was teaching a course at the University of Houston on innovation and entrepreneurship where I used the audiology experience as a real-life case study for my class.

My personal failure of losing my job was now causing some pain and forcing me to figure out how to transform the maladaptive tensions in my life into a new identity. At the same time, in the course I was teaching, I was representing myself with an identity as an innovator and entrepreneur. This wasn't completely inaccurate, but it wasn't completely accurate either. Yes, my wife and I started a kosher bakery. I led corporate start-ups at Koch Industries in weather derivatives, at Union Bank of Switzerland in Latin American equity research, and at Azurix in Internet marketplaces for water products. But none of these had required me to start something in my own garage and raise venture capital to make it all happen. To date, I fell short of my own definition of an entrepreneur, that is, starting a new venture with resources beyond my own and growing it exponentially.

I remember the moment when I decided to accept the identity of a true entrepreneur. I was discussing the automated audiometry case study in the university class, and I asked myself, "Do you have the guts to start a technology company from scratch and raise venture capital to fund it and grow it? If not, you really aren't an innovator and entrepreneur."

This was frightening. Accepting such a radical new identity wasn't easy. There were many doubts and fears to overcome.

My first concern was based on a core value I held that any business I started required a noble purpose, that is, it needed to make the world a better place. This wasn't about money but about solving an important problem. I had to believe that automating audiometry would make life better, that diagnosing and treating hearing loss was valuable, and that this was a high enough value I should commit myself to.

My next concern was convincing myself that I could be the creative genius behind a new technology, innovating a business model, and getting others to believe me, fund me, support me, and join my team. And I was supposed to do all this without any experience of ever having done anything like this before. Still, I was forming a virtual identity in my mind, foreseeing what I thought I could become.

This process forced me to accept that there were some huge gaps between my current being—who I was—and my new foreseen identity of who I thought I could be. I was forced to go through the Becoming ring of the Innovation Cycle several times in order to identify two types of gaps: my personal ones and those in the hearing health marketplace that I thought existed and believed I could close if I became a technology entrepreneur.

The maladaptive tensions that cause these gaps must always exist at both the personal and market levels. You need to recognize your own pain points and failures that create tensions, and the marketplace needs to also suffer from its own pain points and failure that drive maladaptive tension you can remove—*if* you successfully change your identity and mental model. Here are the questions I asked myself:

Evaluate Gap

1. Do I value becoming an entrepreneur, inventor, and innovator? Am I willing to pay the price to become one?

2. Do I believe there are maladaptive tensions in diagnosing and treating hearing loss? Do I believe this is a noble pursuit that will make the world a better place by eliminating pain points and failures through innovation?

Envision Gap

1. Can I see myself becoming what I value by aligning my personal values with those of the hearing health marketplace?

2. Do I see how becoming what I value, by eliminating the maladaptive tensions in the hearing health market, will enable me to eliminate my own maladaptive tensions?

Foresee Gap

1. Do I see a new mental model of my identity showing how I can become what I value?

2. Do I see a new mental model of the hearing health marketplace where my personal becoming helps others to overcome the maladaptive tensions they face in hearing health?

Asking your questions in order to create a new mental model for a new identity is crucial. But then you must test that identity to see if you think it will really work.

Explore Test

1. How can I test my new mental maps that enable me to close these gaps and create a new identity to see if they make sense and are possible?

2. How many times do I need to test them before I am satisfied that I can become what I foresee?

I looped through the Becoming ring of the Innovation Cycle several times, testing my new mental maps, refining them until I was convinced that I could become what I envisioned. I found how to align my personal failure and pain with what I saw as a moral value and imperative to help those in the hearing health market-place. I could foresee how I could help remove the maladaptive tensions in that marketplace that arose from the lack of simple, elegant, and sophisticated hearing-loss diagnostic solutions.

I was ready to move to the next ring of the Innovation Cycle.

Knowing: Transforming Maladaptive Tensions into Creative Ones

In order to form my new technology innovator identity that I could foresee in my mind's eye, I needed help from others, a strategic plan, and some financial resources. I had to find out how to transform my personal maladaptive tension from my job loss and lack of entrepreneurial experience as well as the maladaptive tension in the hearing health marketplace into creative tensions that would drive my ability to invent and innovate.

I began to reach out to others to enlist their views, advice, and support. One of the first people I enlisted was Mitch. He led the specialty medical practices, which included the audiology practice, at the Ochsner Clinic in New Orleans. Since I knew nothing about the healthcare industry, let alone audiology, I needed him to educate me on workflow, process, structure, payment, reimbursement, regulation, business models, profit margins etc. You name it, I had to learn it. Fortunately, he had access to all this information. He was familiar with the maladaptive tensions in Ochsner's audiology practice that could be addressed through innovation, such as staffing shortages, foreign language needs, high costs, workflow challenges, etc. His insights and information became the basis of our strategic plan.

More important, Mitch was also dealing with his own maladaptive personal tensions around his professional career and was interested in trying his hand at a more entrepreneurial pursuit. He had already begun experimenting with some new identities and mental maps that could enable him to transform his personal dissatisfaction and tensions.

Still, I needed to enlist more than just business intelligence; I had to engage technology partners. Through a daisy chain of serendipitous introductions, starting with Dr. Glasscock, I enlisted nearly a dozen professionals, including electrical and mechanical engineers, audiologists, physicians, and computer programmers across the country. Each had a unique role to play in inventing our technology. By aligning their own personal maladaptive tensions with those of the hearing health market, similar to what Mitch and I had done, we were able to produce a detailed innovation roadmap and strategic plan.

But a plan and a team were not enough. We needed money to realize our vision. I reached out to dozens of angel investors and venture capital firms all over the country, sharing with them our vision, strategy, and innovation plans in order to raise the capital to develop our technology and business.

And we were raising money at the worst possible time. Less than a year before, in 2000, the dotcom bubble had burst, bankrupting start-ups and venture capitalists alike. Enron, along with half a dozen other Fortune 500 firms, had gone bankrupt. As if these two factors weren't bad enough, within two months of founding Tympany, the 9/11 attacks ushered in the most risk-averse capital-raising environment that any technology entrepreneur had yet encountered.

As a result, the four founders (Mitch, Dr. Glasscock, Dr. Barry Strasnick (a colleague of Dr. Glasscock), and I) invested nearly $200,000 of our own money, which was enough to get us started, but far short of the $2 million we thought we needed to invent the Otogram and launch it commercially. So we went through the Knowing ring several times, making adjustments to each of the mental models and maps. Each ring further advanced and defined our new identities as inventors and entrepreneurs. This is no different than riding a bike. Even when you start going fast, sometimes you need to slow down before you can speed up again.

As in the Becoming ring, each one of the progressions in the Knowing ring opened tension gaps we had to close in order to successfully finish looping through this ring and moving to the next one, Doing. In the Knowing ring, we provided the details of the mental maps and models showing how we could transform maladaptive tensions into creative ones. Here are the questions we asked ourselves:

Enlist Gap

1. Did we have the right people on the team and who else should we add?
2. How would we get everyone aligned to transform our personal and industry maladaptive tensions to creative ones to produce the innovations we needed for success?

Strategize Gap

1. What was our business and innovation plan? How would we get from where we were to what we desired to become?
2. What were the milestones we had to realize? When did we need to reach them in order to deliver our vision?

Capitalize Gap

1. Where would all the resources come from to fund and support our innovative efforts?
2. In what form would they be provided?

Foresee Gap

1. How must our mental model and map of what we are trying to become change based on those we enlisted, strategies we employed, and capital we raised?

2. Do any of these changes produce tensions with our original values and visions that we need to address by going through the Becoming loop again?

We had to loop through the Knowing ring numerous times over many months pre–9/11. And while we had a large investor who committed all the capital we were seeking at the time, within a week of his commitment the Twin Towers came down and he pulled out. This led us all to drop back into the Becoming ring and ask ourselves, given that the world had changed so dramatically with this one event, did we still have the same values and vision? Did we still foresee the same future?

After looping back through the Becoming ring, we decided we could still foresee our new identity as disruptors in hearing health, and so, rather than pivoting to a different approach, we persevered. It took another five months and a capital call among the founders, plus changing our view and definition of our MVP, before we raised the capital we needed to move to the Doing ring. We convinced a small venture capital firm in Houston to believe in our team's ability to become what we all envisioned, to believe in our strategic plan, and to fund us to deliver it.

Doing: Delivering an MVP and Then Iterating New Ones

The Doing ring focuses on making the minimum viable product or products necessary to get market feedback and create value. This is the physical manifestation of a mindful failure: moving fast to implement frequent improvements on a shoestring budget in order to deliver a feasible MVP that generates enough measures and information to learn from and then try again. While this type of failure occurs in both the Becoming and Knowing rings, they are relatively inexpensive there. In Becoming, failures are virtual because they occur largely in your mind and incur little cost. In Knowing, you commit more resources and obtain personal commitments from many others, but most of your failures are on paper. In Doing, failure costs you a lot more because you are building the physical manifestation of your vision. This is why it is so critical to mindfully fail by following the Lean start-up approach to creating MVPs so you can accelerate the volume, velocity, and value of your innovative efforts.

Our first MVP was an Otogram designed for the largest clinical market segment with exposure to the most patients with hearing loss. That market consisted of primary care physicians (PCP). If we were ever going to be big, it would only be by entering this market and getting some portion of the three hundred thousand PCPs in the United States to buy our product. To our great disappointment, when we showed our prototype to PCPs in focus groups and demos, they told us they would never be the first to buy a technology like ours despite the lofty economic value it could deliver to their practice. First, they wanted to see otolaryngologists use it.

We scrambled to create our next MVP that would address what we saw as the failures and pain points of the largest ENT practices. These practices employed the most audiologists, did the most hearing tests, and therefore had the most to gain from the efficiencies that automated, multilingual testing technology could provide. Here we learned the hard lesson about the abilities of those who viewed us as disruptive to their identities to build barriers against the adoption of our revolutionary technology.

The ENTs assigned their audiologists, who were their hearing testing specialists, to evaluate our technology. The audiologists informed us that they didn't need to assess our device to know that it wouldn't work. They claimed to know from years of personal and professional experience that few patients would have the patience to endure an automated test. They also knew it couldn't be as accurate as human technicians despite the fact that our clinical trial data indicated it was. They also knew that no insurance company or CMS would reimburse doctors for an automated test. Therefore ENT practices couldn't make or save any money by using Otograms.

With two strikes against us, we produced what we thought would be our last MVP because it addressed the market needs of a small niche market consisting of one- and two-physician ENT practices. For these practices, audiologists were the single largest expense, and an ENT practice could rarely afford to employ one full time. Even if they wanted to, they couldn't because audiologists were in short supply. Also, small practices often needed multilingual audiologists, but unlike larger practices that were able to hire a couple of audiologists who spoke different languages, they could not afford to do so. In addition, hearing testing was the single largest bottleneck in their practice. But if we could remove that bottleneck, we enabled them to generate an additional forty thousand dollars in revenues for a practice without its hiring an audiologist. Without the test results the Otogram delivered, they couldn't diagnose a patient's problem and couldn't treat them. This small niche market had the most acute pain points of all the market segments we approached.

After three loops through the Doing ring and three MVPs, we launched our first commercial MVP at the largest otolaryngology conference in the United States, which was held that year in San Diego, only fourteen months after Tympany was founded. To our relief, the Otogram was a smashing success. The traffic at our booth was so heavy we were voted best booth in our category. We sold ten devices, some to leading organizations such as Stanford

University's Ear Institute. Our big problem was that we now had $250,000 in sales and accounts receivable, $100,000 in accounts payable, but only $1,000 in the bank.

At this time, Mitch took a leap of faith to join me on a full-time basis, leaving behind the security of the Ochsner Clinic. Then we shifted back to the Knowing ring to modify our team, plan strategically, and raise two million dollars in new funding.

Here are the tensions gaps that occurred as we looped through the Doing ring.

Incentive Gap

1. How do we align the success of our product with that of our physician customers and their staff and in line with that of our sales force?

2. What type of incentives could we offer customers, clinical staff, employees, and third parties to drive our success?

Manage Constraints Gap

1. How do we identify and leverage constraints in our MVPs to guide us to breakthroughs?

2. How does the feedback from our MVPs cause us to determine whether or not we should pivot to a new strategy or preserve with the current one?

Exploit Gap

1. How do we innovate on the fly and create new MVPs to enable continual momentum and constant forward motion?

2. How do we apply build-measure-learn to exploit the next MVP opportunity?

Strategize Gap

1. How do we pivot to change our strategy to adapt to the market realities that emerge from our various MVPs?
2. What changes does our pivot to a new strategy require in all other elements of the three rings?

We cycled through all three rings several times during the four years we ran Tympany before we sold it to a medical device company. As our sales increased from $250,000 the first year to $2 million the second and $5 million in the third, we were forced to shift from mindful failure to mindless success. We had to apply the Food and Drug Administration's (FDA) good manufacturing practices (GMP), which ensured more of a Lean Six Sigma approach to operations. As our discipline moved from Lean start-up to Lean Six Sigma, we found it increasingly difficult to be the ambidextrous leaders we wanted to be. We needed to figure out how to apply more mindful structures and practices to perpetuate the culture of innovation and discovery on which Tympany was founded. However, we never completely figured it out and applied it before we sold the company. The buyer was a new entrant into the diagnostic hearing testing market. This company needed to create a fresh identity by using our company and technology to transform the distribution of its own hearing aids.

Constantly Changing Gears to Maintain Forward Motion

The next chapter will outline how you can enable this kind of mindfulness and creativity on a sustainable and disciplined basis within a mindless organization. We will share some of the best practices we have seen within large and small organizations to engage and free the creative genius in us all to solve complex problems simply and elegantly. It is always important to remember that you have to enable and support change at the edge of chaos so that a new order can emerge. If, however, you set the right conditions, that new order will emerge spontaneously.

- Failure is the genesis of innovation, but mindlessness causes failure to be shunned.
- The Innovation Cycle consists of three rings: Becoming, Knowing, and Doing.
- Becoming is the smallest ring and creates new mental maps. This is where tensions force you to identify a new identity.
- As you gain speed, you shift to the Knowing ring. This is where you foresee the changes needed to assume your new identity.
- You achieve your fastest speed by shifting to the largest ring, Doing. This is where you put your strategic plan into operation.
- You only move to the next ring when you have exhausted all you can do in the current ring. Often you have to downshift to a previous ring when you find the current one isn't working.
- The purpose of the Innovation Cycle is to use creativity to close the gaps between the current maladaptive state and the desired future creative state that emerges from the tensions you encounter.
- These gaps occur at the individual (internal mental maps) level as well as the organizational level. To be innovative, you must have both a personal need to overcome tensions as well as an organizational need to do so.

———————— QUESTIONS ————————

> How do you value becoming an innovator? Are you willing to pay the price to become one? (This is the evaluate gap.)

> How do you see yourself becoming what you value by aligning your personal values with those of your innovation? (This is the envision gap.)

> How do you see a new mental model of your identity that shows how you can become what you value? (This is the foresee gap.)

To explore further, ask yourself:

> How can I test my new mental maps that enable me to close these gaps and create a new identity to see if they make sense and are possible?

> How many times do I need to test them before I am satisfied that I can become what I foresee?

CHAPTER EIGHT

Riding the Entire Innovation Lifecycle

For an innovation to succeed it must be taken from an idea born in mindfulness to a scaled opportunity that is delivered through mindless structures and practices. While the Innovation Cycle explains how to innovate, it doesn't show how to nurture, protect, support, and discipline your creative ideas so you can advance them through all phases of growth.

So how do you ride the Innovation Cycle along its entire lifecycle?

Think of it this way: you ride your mountain bike to explore and experience new vistas on narrow dirt trails, jumping over rocks and logs, riding up and down steep hills, and through hazards. No other type of bike can take the abuse heaped on mountain bikes. If you want to explore risky terrain, there is no better bike to ride.

In time, a popular trail can become so well worn that the park service may decide to maintain, widen, and improve it so that more than just mountain bikers can enjoy it and people can ride it on hybrid bikes. It is not yet safe enough for a road bike, but it is much easier and safer than a mountain trail. To allow these hybrid bikes, the park service will level out the steep grades, remove the ruts, rocks, and logs, and may even add a layer of gravel for extra protection and safety.

A very well-traveled gravel road in high demand will eventually become a paved road, smooth and even, with gentle grades that allow road biking. All these improvements decrease the risks to riders, enable greater speed, and allow bicyclers to spend more time in mindless pedaling rather than mindful stump jumping. You can turn and peddle much faster on a paved road than on gravel, plus rain will have a limited impact as well.

In time, paved roads with high traffic become great locations for commercial buildings. Eventually you'll see gyms with stationary bikes that can allow you to cycle with great efficiency and safety. You can follow the voice of the spin class instructor in a mindless manner. You have a general idea of what you will be doing, but you don't know the exact commands she will shout. However, you know that all you need to do is follow her calls to realize your desired goals.

Applying the Innovation Lifecycle to Meet the Demands of the Law

Just as the nature of the environment you are in dictates the type of bike to use, the *Law of Requisite Variety and Complexity* dictates the structures and practices needed to create the magnitude and volume of innovation required to thrive and survive. When this law isn't followed, it forms gaps and tensions to which maladaptive, adaptive, or creative energy can be applied to transform and drive innovative outcomes.

A company approached me (Chris) a few years ago, frustrated that none of its innovative ideas had yet made it into the market.

The company, a large global financial services organization, was responsible for trillions of dollars of payment processing every day. Mindless operating efficiency is the key capability of the company. With the advent of Paypal, Square, and other disruptive digital money offerings, the leadership realized they needed to become more innovative. A few years before, they had developed a very impressive and robust ideation and discovery capability that had generated hundreds of novel ideas and solutions through various types of open innovation challenges and campaigns.

But despite the promise of the new ideas they had formulated, whenever they approached the leaders of the organization, they heard a hundred reasons why these clever solutions would never work. At its core, the primary concerns of the company's leaders was that these potential new offers would lead to risk and failure.

How is it possible to get the mindless part of an organization to adopt and deploy the novel and new solutions developed through mindfulness? When I first met with the company's leadership, I described how a potential innovation needs to grow through four distinct phases where the right discipline at the right phase of development is applied. Doing so limits the risks of nascent innovation and prepares it for the next phase of growth. I asked them, "Once you have identified the innovative idea and potential, what do you do to de-risk the novel solution?"

When they asked me what I meant, I explained that as innovations emerge and advance through the four phases of growth, certain steps must be taken. They must provide the proper structures and practices at each phase of the Innovation Cycle to **discover, incubate, accelerate,** and **scale** the various risks that arise as they move from the status quo to a new solution. Each phase, in turn, is focused on certain kinds of uncertainty that we transform into risk through the innovation cycle, where the of risk that must be identified, quantified, measured, managed, and mitigated.

Discovery: Feasibility Risk

As you develop the ability to ideate and discover potential innovations, the first risk you need to understand is whether or not
the idea is good or bad. The reality is that most ideas are bad. But
consider: bad ideas can give life to better ideas when two or more
of them are combined. We refer to this as bad ideas having sex with
one another and generating better ideas as offspring. In this continual procreation across successive generations (as brainstorming
is outlined in the chapter 6), you generate good ideas that provide
the foundation for innovation.

My client had developed a very effective discovery capability.
They had also created an effective way to evaluate each idea and
developed a test (a proof of concept [PoC]) to determine if the idea
was feasible. Unfortunately, they encountered resistance when
they tried to pass on the PoC to the operating business. There was
no interest in taking on the burden and risk of developing and
implementing a risky new idea, even if it seemed feasible.

Incubating: Technical Risk

When I asked the client how their innovation team incubated their
ideas to remove technical risk, they were confused. They didn't
view that as the responsibility of the innovation team. They saw
themselves as a very Lean Innovation support team that drove disciplined ideation and discovery. They lacked a technical identity and
related capabilities. I asked them who in their organization had the
responsibility for identifying, quantifying, measuring, managing,
and mitigating the technical risk associated with new solutions that
the operating business had no current interest in. The answer was
no one. So without anyone to pass their POC to in order to advance
them along the Innovation Lifecycle, all their ideas died.

To counter that, I talked to them about how they needed to introduce an incubator that would create MVPs in the form of mock-ups, prototypes, simulations, and pilots to manage and mitigate the technical risks. This is the phase in which the first MVP—of many— is offered within the organization in order to get market feedback as soon as possible. Doing so forces both failure and learning.

Most new ideas must spend quite a bit of time in this phase and go through many versions of MVPs before they are ready for commercial launch. During this phase you will identify your best idea for a commercially successful business model that you can use to launch the business into the next phase of growth.

Accelerating: Business Model Risk

We then discussed how—once risks were removed through more technically oriented MVPs—to identify, quantify, measure, manage, and mitigate the commercial risks found in the business model through the next round of MVPs.

Most emerging innovations are technologies in search of a business model. It is difficult to know how all the dimensions and elements of the business model (described in greater detail in chapter 11, Accelerating Success) need to be configured for greatest effect and success. By launching various MVPs in this phase, it is possible, through trial and error, to go through successive iterations of the business model in order to create the best one for scaling your innovation.

Scaling: Operating Risk

Once the feasibility, technical, and business model risks are removed or mitigated, it is time to scale the innovation by applying mindless disciplines to it. This is the point at which the operating business will be willing to support and deliver the innovation to the broader marketplace on a consistent basis with a focus on standardization and efficiency.

The problem that my client had, as with most companies, is that they wanted to skip over incubating and accelerating. They had their reasons. First, they didn't view removing the technical and business model risks as their job, because they didn't have the identity, experience, and skills to do it. Second, because their organization didn't have an operating model for innovation, there was nowhere else in the organization where the innovation could go to be de-risked.

Figure 10

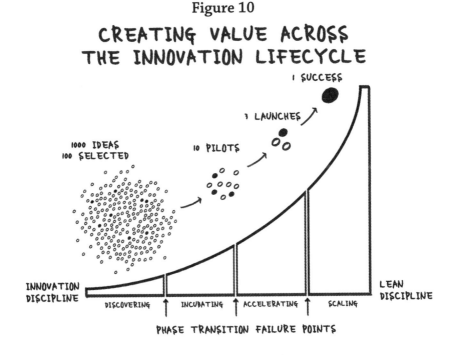

The Four Phases of the Innovation Lifecycle

Figure 10 characterizes the four phases of the Innovation Lifecycle and the funnel-like nature where Lean Innovation discipline takes an initial thousand ideas and advances only the best through three phases to deliver a single scalable innovation.

With each phase of growth, the organization provides different structures and practices that become increasing mindless in nature, thus decreasing risk and increasing profitability. Through each phase, poor innovative ideas get weeded out, combined by having sex, and improved through the application of the Innovation Cycle's three rings. By shifting gears, you apply fast, frequent, frugal failure by creating MVPs that provide market feedback and learning.

Figure 11

RIDING THE INNOVATION LIFECYCLE

MOUNTAIN BIKE   HYBRID BIKE   ROAD BIKE   STATIONARY BIKE
DISCOVERING   INCUBATING   ACCELERATING   SCALING

Discovery Phase

In the discovery phase you ideate and search to discover novel ideas that could become innovations. This is risky and challenging business, requiring a symbolic mountain bike.

My financial services client had an innovation support team to help leaders identify operational challenges that would benefit from some innovative solutions. These challenges would include pain points and failures in any process, product, service, marketing, distribution, business model, or value network that the business unit, division, or group might face. The innovation support team generally facilitates and co-leads with business leaders a process of ideation focused on internal businesses, external groups, or both. Their process was often completely open to enlisting outside customers, suppliers, or third parties to come up with new ideas. Their practice was to use this type of closed and open ideation in innovation campaigns, jams and competitions, and co-creation workshops and programs. The various techniques we have discussed in the previous chapters provide the tools and frameworks for this kind of ideation.

During this phase, the discovery support team, which comprises five to ten full-time employees recruited from multiple disciplines and job function across the organization, help design, structure, and operate the ideation processes employed by leaders that want to apply innovation to their problem solving. At this phase, most ideas are still only loosely defined, and the innovators (those who generated the idea initially) continue to bear full responsibility for their day-to-day jobs. They are not full-time innovators but practitioners that innovated.

A central objective of the discovery support team is to capture and filter ideas generated within the business units and supporting functions. The goal is to help individuals as well as self-organized groups of innovators to produce feasible POCs. Additionally, the team manages the process of selecting which of these ideas should be advanced to the incubation stage of growth. Another key objective for these teams is to hand innovative ideas that may be more incremental or less complex in nature (and therefore do not require a formal incubation) back to the business units and support functions for them to handle internally. This decision is based on the level of technical, business model, and operating risks that the new idea produces.

Those ideas that appear to be merely modifications and improvements or even incremental innovations that improve on current offerings generally don't need to be incubated. Instead, they are passed directly to the Lean Six Sigma operating business to be implemented through its normal process. Only the breakthrough and radical innovations of the innovation support team need to be de-risked through incubating and accelerating.

To ensure excitement and engagement in the innovative process, the client's discovery team developed marketing campaigns that highlighted the challenges in the market and provided visions of a world without these limits. They came up with competitions and scoreboards around how various teams and ideas were doing in the innovation challenge. They conducted one-day hackathons that brought diverse groups together to share ideas in short speed-dating formats to enable self-organized teams to compete. They invited venture capitalists to be the judges of the new ideas and solutions presented by both the internal and external teams.

An important point to understand from their efforts, and that of other clients, is that the discovery phase must capture the imagination and passion of people to launch and liberate their own creative genius. This doesn't just happen without a lot of planning, preparation, and execution. The following is a list of activities the discovery team performed to elevate and engage the passionate energies of diverse groups of people.

Highly engaging and participatory ideation and screening processes: Develop and run flexible and inspired processes to gather and screen innovative ideas from across the company or network (e.g., social media tools, e-suggestion boxes, workshops, conferences, virtual events, cross-functional away days, etc.)

Marketing and communications programs: The discovery team must get people excited about sharing and collaborating. Their focus is on leveraging diverse communication platforms and social media to get people excited about participating. They provide various types of awards (financial, social, recognition, etc.). They also get leadership engaged in the messaging and support for the events and recognize the value of learning through failure and its role in achieving the organization's goals.

Learning and development programs: People love being creative and are eager to learn how to increase their ability to be inventors. The discovery team establishes, provides, and supports innovation training programs.

Knowledge management systems: Silence can kill interest in innovation. If your innovation effort feels like a black box where ideas go in but no feedback comes out, then people's passions will no longer support their participation. The team must make sure that every contribution is acknowledged, valued, and evaluated. This communication includes developing infrastructure for sharing best practices around innovation and transferring knowledge and lessons learned from both successful and unsuccessful projects.

Incubating Phase

To eliminate technical risk through incubation, an organization needs a different set of supporting structures and practices. In this phase, the mountain bike is no longer appropriate, but there are still too many risks to use a road bike. You want to increase your speed, so you need a hybrid bike that can deal with the lack of stability.

For my client, this meant establishing a new governance structure—called enablers—designed and run to select, fund, staff, and review projects. The enablers came from both within and without the company to ensure that diverse and objective perspectives were considered when making decisions. This also required a modest full-time incubation team with start-up and technology experience that understood how to apply the principles of Lean start-up, invent MVPs, and provide project management. These people sat outside the usual lines of business in the larger organization and reported to a head of innovation and the enablers.

During incubation, the level of involvement and engagement expected from the people who invented the idea increased. As a result, they became engaged in providing the details they envisioned their innovation possessing and helped to make their vision a technical reality. This didn't mean that the inventors gave up their day jobs. Instead, they were given the freedom to spend time on their figurative mountain or hybrid bike for a while.

The incubation support team also collaborated with experts from the business to increase their understanding of the business requirements and technical issues that needed to be designed to create the MVP. The key goal of the incubation support team was to support the inventors by providing them with funding, supplementary subject matter expertise, and protection from the broader organization. Combining forces, the incubation team and the innovators conducted additional product and market research to come up with a business plan that outlined the expected business model to be used in the next phase: accelerating.

Accelerating Phase

The object of the accelerating phase is to move quickly toward commercial success. You are *now* ready for a road bike. The technical risks have been removed, prototypes are in place, and pilots are completed. Now it's time to remove and/or mitigate the risks associated with bringing a new business model to the market. (Some risks can't be removed, but it's possible to decrease their negative impact through a mitigation strategy.) This requires the introduction of a new governance structure that differs from those used in discovery and incubation. The acceleration teams are full-time management groups that live and breath the business on a full-time basis. Because the financial risks are bigger, the consequences of failure are larger.

To succeed in this phase requires wrapping a complete business model around the most successful MVP developed in incubation. This requires the design and configuration of the four primary dimensions of the business model and their underlying elements to launch the next MVP. The following outlines these dimensions and elements and the questions that need to be answered.

1. ***Capabilities: What you do.*** What capabilities are required to generate value? Capabilities represent the primary inputs to a business model and are defined as a set of actions that create value and support the delivery of the value proposition from the customer's perspective. Capabilities are comprised of technology features, key activities to deliver the features, resources necessary to produce and support those features, and a relationship with the customer to deliver the capabilities and associated value.

2. ***Stakeholders: Where you play.*** Which stakeholders are involved with and impacted by the business model? Stakeholders include customers (who can be buyers, users, or beneficiaries of the value proposition), partners who support the value proposition, and channels to communicate, educate, and deliver the value proposition.

3. ***Benefits: How you win.*** What are the differentiated value proposition benefits that the business model provides to each of its stakeholders? The benefits are based upon the use case for eliminating pain points, waste, failure, or providing new opportunities. All these offerings are delivered through particular types of customer experiences that yield specific value that generally falls into five types of benefits: cost, convenience, confidence, compensation, and connection.

4. ***Economic impact: What you win.*** What is the expected economic impact of the business model? The costs required to operate the business model and deliver the value proposition, the margin earned above these costs based upon the level and type of differentiation, and the revenue streams based upon the revenue models used are all driven by economics.

An important insight gained from our Tympany experience was that new innovations generally lack the characteristics to be successful in a large mass market. They tend to be too expensive, too large, too slow, or too burdensome for the masses. Therefore, they are only adopted in niche markets where the performance characteristics of the new innovation significantly overcome the pain points within the market.

The most critical goal and activity in this phase, therefore, is to find those initial small niche markets that will be the early adopters of the innovation and will pay for it through a successful business model. Finding those acute pain points that the innovation addresses will result in a market quickly adopting your product. But it is likely that before you are ready for scaling, you will need to further modify your business model. With Tympany, it required us to get commercial success first with the niche market of small ENT physicians and then move to the next market of large ENT practices. Finally, we moved to the mass market of PCPs with our offering once we had succeeded with the previous two smaller markets.

Scaling Phase

The goal of every innovation is to become successful enough that it can be scaled. So let's look at a few case studies that both show how large innovations struggle to apply the Innovation Lifecycle and what you can do to learn from their failures and apply it within your organization.

Catastrophic Failure by Missing the Innovation Lifecycle

Most failures of existing successful business occur because the leaders didn't understand the Innovation Lifecycle and apply it to their businesses. Here are three iconic examples that illustrate the insights necessary to know how to overcome the barriers that all large companies have.

Amazon versus Barnes & Noble

Discovering. In 1994, Barnes & Noble (B&N) and Borders led the book retailing business by controlling 25 percent of the market share of what had traditionally been a highly fragmented industry. Their value proposition focused on delivering an attractive and comfortable retail location with a much wider selection of books than most other chains or mom-and-pop shops. At this time, the Internet was growing at over 2000 percent per year, and Jeff Bezos, the founder of Amazon, was exploring various markets he thought were ripe for digital disruption. He discovered that book retailing seemed to carry all the pain points and waste he could remove through an innovative new business model. That year he wrote his business plan for Amazon based upon his point of view that consumers wanted an infinitely large selection of books they could find in virtual space rather than physical place. He believed that customers would forgo the comforts and immediacy of an attractive local store if the selection, benefits, and price were right. At the same time, the incumbent book retailers did not undertake a discovery process.

Incubating. B&N and Borders increased their commitment to their torrid store growth, driving all of their top-line growth with new superstore openings across the country. While these superstores could offer an impressive 170,000 different titles, the selection paled in comparison to what Amazon would be able to deliver within a two years of its launch, namely, 1.1 million titles. Borders began to experiment with the Internet in ways that it felt would be less threatening and disruptive to its existing physical retail business model. It provided a website to allow customers to find Borders stores and to search for titles online. However, it didn't allow customers to buy books anywhere except within a store. After incubating his technology for less than a year, Bezos launched Amazon in July 1995. The site quickly jumped to 2,200 daily visits.

Accelerating. By 1997, Amazon's stunning and rapid success captured the attention of other retailers, causing 14 percent of them to state they planned to launch web stores. B&N decided not to enter ecommerce directly and instead announced a partnership with America Online to start an online bookstore. Other online bookstores like Book Stacks, Internet Bookshop entered ecommerce, as did Crown Books. Amazon's daily visits hit 80,000, an amount equivalent to the daily visits of dozens of physical B&N or Borders stores. Both B&N and Borders continued to mindlessly invest heavily in bricks and mortar rather than clicks. Bezos said he would reinvest all of Amazon's profits into the growth of the business and launched its IPO in 1999 to raise $54 million.

Scaling. As B&N and Borders struggled to replicate Amazon's success, the latter entered other retail markets to become a dominant ecommerce company. Within ten years of its IPO, Amazon had a market capitalization of $40 billion versus $1 billion for B&N and $163 million for Borders.

Google versus Microsoft

Discovering. In 1995, Scott Banister invented the business model of paid search, an approach to advertising where retailers pay a search engine for sending customers to their website based upon his search criteria. He launched Keywords Inc. as the first paid search engine company. Banister joined Ali Partovi at LinkExchange as a programmer and within a year it was sold to Microsoft for $265 million. As employees of Microsoft, Banister and Partovi tried to convince Steve Ballmer and other leaders at the company of the future potential of the paid search business model. Unconvinced by Banister and Partovi's pitch to launch a paid search business, Microsoft decided not to enter paid search itself, but instead signed up with Goto.com to experiment with its own products on paid search and earned an impressive $50,000 the first day. But Banister was unwilling to wait for Microsoft leadership to come around, and he left the company in 1998 to found IronPort, which he sold to Cisco for $830 million in 2007. Meanwhile, Larry Page and Sergey Brin were completing their doctorates at Stanford and exploring ways to link academic citations to content searching on the Internet. In 1998, they started Google as a search engine business without a revenue model.

Incubating. In 1999, Goto.com generated millions in revenues for Microsoft products that used its paid search services, and some at Microsoft began to believe that the paid search business model could be valuable. Microsoft launched Keywords paid search, and it quickly delivered $1 million in revenues despite the fact that Microsoft placed severe restrictions on it so it wouldn't compete against its larger and more established banner ad business. Microsoft midmanagers reviewed Keywords' performance and decided to shut it down, concluding that it could never become a big enough business to interest Microsoft. In 2000, Partovi threatened to quit if Ballmer didn't intervene and reverse the decision to pull the plug on Keywords, but Ballmer stood by his managers and shut down the business. Partovi left Microsoft to shop the paid search business model to Yahoo and Google. Google listened to Partovi's pitch and decided to pass since they had already developed and incubated their paid search business and revenue model as the means to monetize their search engine. In October 2000, Google launched AdWords and offered it on AOL.

Accelerating. In 2001, Microsoft met with Goto.com (now rechristened Overture) and decided to buy it, but Ballmer balked at the $1–$2 billion price tag and decided that Microsoft could build it for a lot less. This provided an opening for Yahoo to buy Overture for $1.8 billion, which placed them as a strong number two in the paid search market. Google's business was accelerating rapidly, becoming the market leader. In 2004, Google came to market with one of the largest IPOs in history, valuing the company at $23 billion. That same year, four years after it had run off Partovi and three years after it sent Overture into Yahoo's arms, Microsoft launched its own search engine (code named Moonshot), and two years later it offered its paid search solution.

Scaling. In 2005, Microsoft's Moonshot search engine performed poorly while Google continued to dominate, reaching a 70 percent market share and fueling the paid search revenue model. While in second place with a 20 percent share, Yahoo was still such a contender that Microsoft explored a strategic relationship with Yahoo since Microsoft's paid search market share continued to hover in the low single digits. By 2009, paid search was an annual $13 billion business, and Google had a market capitalization of $120 billion. Microsoft offered to buy Yahoo for $50 billion to compete in the market in which Microsoft had been the first mover before they discarded their efforts, believing search engines would never amount to much. Ballmer said, "The biggest mistakes I claim I've been involved with is where I was impatient—because we didn't have a business yet in something, we should have stayed patient. If we'd kept consistent with some of the ideas . . . we might have been in paid search."*

The end result was that Microsoft was first in the paid search market but failed to follow the Innovation Lifecycle. Google and Yahoo both entered the market and beat them.

Netflix versus Blockbuster

Discovering. In 1996, the home VHS video rental market was highly fragmented with thousands of mom-and-pop retail stores offering a very limited selection and availability. One large market leader, Blockbuster, offered twenty-five hundred titles per store and good customer service. At that time, 70 percent of the business arose from new releases, and DVDs were just becoming an affordable option for most people. After experiencing a large late

---

* Robert Guth, "Microsoft's bid to beat Google builds on a history of misses," wsj.com, April 14, 2009, accessed May 23, 2014, http://online.wsj.com/article/SB123207131111388507. html#printMode.

fee from not returning a video rental, Reed Hastings decided to experiment to see how well the U.S. Post Office could deliver DVDs in the mail. It turned out that the post office could handle the delivery very well, and he realized that a video business based on DVDs and the post office could enable a new kind of service that could eliminate late fees.

Incubating. In 1997, Netflix transformed its business model from what had been an entertainment destination business to video rentals. It then started a succession of innovations that built the technical foundation for the future business. It invented the queue, where renters could email a list of movies they want sent to them along with their priority, making the entire selection process more efficient and easier. It changed its pricing service from pay-per-rental to unlimited rental subscription. It also offered a recommendation engine to help people find movies they might know little about or had never heard of that seemed to be a good fit with the customer's interests. And they began revenue-sharing agreements with movie studios to align the incentives of both parties. From 1998 to 2001, DVD penetration increased to 13 percent and became a regular feature in rental stores. But despite Netflix's moves and the changes the DVD market enabled, Blockbuster declared that customers would never value online service over immediate gratification available at a nearby retail store.

Accelerating. Over the next four years, DVD penetration nearly tripled to 37 percent of all U.S. households. Blockbuster continued to claim that online rentals were only serving a niche market and that it was not a sustainable business model. But within two years, they reversed themselves and launched an online service integrated into their physical store retail model. The results of this approach, combined with removing their late-fee policy to compete against Netflix, caused Blockbuster to suffer its first operating loss.

In 2006, Netflix reported that it had 6.3 million subscribers. With only 30 percent of its revenues coming from new releases, it had transformed both the video rental model and consumer appetites. Netflix's IPO raised $83 million and positioned itself to scale the business.

Scaling. By 2009, Netflix's nearly 10 million customers had access to over one hundred thousand DVD titles, and it started a video-on-demand service through Internet streaming. Blockbuster continued to try to compete with Netflix on a feature-by-feature offering basis but found that it lacked the technology platform and business model to execute the upgrade effectively.

By the end of 2009, Netflix's market value was $3 billion, while Blockbuster's hovered around $200 million.

Riding the Entire Lifecycle to Avoid Catastrophes

These three case studies are used because they are well documented and relatable. From these three brief narratives it's possible to start to diagnose how an organization's failure to ride the Innovation Cycle along the entire lifecycle will inevitably lead to similar catastrophic results. This is true whether or not you need to become more innovative on a personal, group, or organizational level. Let's follow how these organizations took their falls.

Ignored and Suppressed Tensions When They Emerged

All three market leaders used successful mindless business models and supporting mental models that enabled them to become market leaders. That identity defined them. They were anything but lean, scrappy, and disruptive start-ups. Their mission was to deliver reliable and predictable value to their customers, employees, shareholders, and other stakeholders in a proven business model. Unfortunately, their success resulted in huge blind spots regarding weaknesses within their existing business models. These weaknesses began to emerge as tensions when the new start-ups figured out how to overcome those flaws through new types of innovations fuelled by new technologies packaged in innovative business models. Ballmer's managers at Microsoft attempted to eliminate these tensions by driving off the employees who were trying to innovate in new ways and closing down their experimental business activities. Blockbuster and B&N both tried to reassure stakeholders the new technologies could only provide innovative solutions for a small niche but wouldn't affect their core businesses. These market leaders all found it unfathomable that new technologies, new innovations, and new entrants could upset their business models. Additionally, they failed to see how these new entrants were changing the marketplace to force the larger players to suffer the consequences of violating the Law of Requisite Variety and Complexity.

Applied Maladaptive Energy to Perpetuate Failure

Once the Law of Requisite Variety and Complexity caused these tensions to emerge, it became clear how new entrants like Amazon, Google, and Netflix were harnessing them by applying creative energies to drive new innovations. As a competitive response, the three market leaders decided to double down on their existing mindless business models rather than mindfully innovate. Rather than mimic the emerging early success of the new entrants, B&N and Blockbuster continued with rapid expansion through the old bricks-and-mortar business model. Microsoft focused on banner

Figure 12

MALADAPTIVE TENSIONS OCCUR WHEN YOU DONT MATCH THE BIKE WITH THE TERRAIN

ads, refused to continue to build its own paid search model, and then later failed to acquire one that would eventually end up in Yahoo's hands. All three companies seemed to lack the mindful curiosity to explore how new technologies could enable new mental and business models. And they all believed that more of the same mindlessness would solve problems better than the application of mindfulness.

Restricted the Creative Energy to Transform the Tensions

The singled-minded focus on running the business of today, rather than designing the new business of tomorrow, led the mindless incumbents to initially prohibit and/or restrict the creative energies of their own employees who wanted to ride the Innovation Cycle to help the companies adapt. Then, after they decided they needed to become more innovative, the companies placed severe restrictions on that innovation so as to not compete and disrupt their current business model. Microsoft limited the features and functionality of paid search in order not to compete with banner ads. B&N and Blockbuster limited their online features to finding books and stores and thereby restricted commerce. As market leaders, they were not focused on keeping happy and satisfied customers. Instead, they focused on sustaining a status quo. This meant they were unwilling to disrupt themselves by providing the same features, functionality, and business models of the new entrants. By putting limits on creative energy, they were continuing to apply maladaptive energy, and that perpetuated their failure.

Did Not Apply Discipline to Continually Harness Tensions and De-Risk Creativity

As the new entrants and market forces from their customers, employees, and stakeholders required them to become more innovative and abandon their old business models, the three companies did not adopt a disciplined process outlined by the Innovation Lifecycle. More specifically,

1. **Discovering**: They had no place to send and develop new ideas. There was nowhere outside the day-to-day mindless business operating model for discovery in order to pitch novel solutions and new innovations. There was no place for good ideas to be evaluated, refined, and further developed into a viable PoC.

2. **Incubating:** They lacked a disciplined process to eliminate technical risks by developing MVPs in the forms of prototypes, pilots, and plans that could inexpensively identify, quantify, measure, manage, and mitigate the technical risks prior to introducing them commercially.

3. **Accelerating:** They provided no business model development process to identify, quantify, measure, manage, and mitigate the commercial risks associated with bringing a new business model and related innovations to market. The next needed step—modifying them through an iterative MVP process to find the right models that could eventually be scaled—was impossible to do.

This final chapter in the Knowing section outlined what you need to know about innovation in order to do it most effectively. It is essential to

- Understand the role of mental models and create the identity of an innovative thinker.
- Recognize the Innovation Cycle and how you must be able to change your bikes and shift gears to enable you and your organization to become something new and different by harnessing the tensions that emerge in adaptive and creative, rather than maladaptive, ways.
- Comprehend how to move those ideas forward along the entire Innovation Lifecycle and to do those things that make them successful. This includes knowing that the outputs from the Innovation Cycle progress along a lifecycle that starts with their discovery. Then it requires you to incubate, nurture, and de-risk them and then move them into the marketplace to discovery the best business model for their success.

Now the focus will move to Doing. The next section will provide a more detailed discussion about how you can apply best practices to enable everyone to ride the Innovation Cycle and advance their innovations across the lifecycle toward a successfully scaled innovation.

REMEMBER

✔ A failure to innovate is a failure of leadership to follow the Law of Requisite Variety and Complexity along the entire Innovation Lifecycle.

✔ The Law of Requisite Variety and Complexity states that if you (a person or organization) fail to possess the same magnitude and volume of variety as the ecosystem in which you operate, you will not survive.

✔ To satisfy the demands of this law, you must create the innovative structures and practices needed to create the magnitude and volume of innovation required to thrive and survive.

✔ While Lean Six Sigma operating model structures and practices can act as barriers to innovation, the Innovation operating model provides those necessary to provide the structural foundations so innovative ideas can emerge, take form, and advance.

✔ Without the appropriate structures and practices in all four phases of the Innovation lifecycle, you won't succeed in harnessing the tensions that power your creative genius and deliver innovation.

✔ The four phases of the innovation lifecycle are the *discovery phase* (mountain bike), the *incubating phase* (hybrid bike), the *accelerating phase* (road bike), and the *scaling phase* (stationary bike).

—————————— QUESTIONS ——————————

> How would you describe your organization's Innovation discipline?

> How well does your organization follow all four phases of the Innovation Lifecycle?

> How does the Law of Requisite Variety and Complexity operate within your organization?

Doing

Life is like a ten-speed bicycle.
Most of us have gears we never use.

—CHARLES M. SCHULTZ

CHAPTER NINE

Disciplining Serendipity in Discovery

In this first chapter in the Doing section, you'll learn how to liberate your creative genius and engage large groups of people in the process. The result will be the ability to hop off the stationary and road bike and, when needed, climb onto a mountain bike to discover, develop, and deploy innovation.

Riding at the Edge of Chaos

The Law of Requisite Variety and Complexity is the primary law that drives change in the complex systems you operate in every day. It explains how all people, organizations, and systems function between the two conditions we constantly find ourselves: the edge of chaos and the edge of equilibrium.

The edge of chaos is like a mountain terrain. The environment is uncertain, unstable, turbulent, and dynamic. It requires constant mindfulness, improvisation, and creativity in order to secure survival. At the edge of chaos, you are on a mountain bike. In this environment, you cannot predict or forecast with accuracy what may happen, which means that stable operating models based on mindlessness cannot function here. Instead, participants must be flexible and agile in order to constantly reinvent themselves and develop new mental models and identities to ensure adaptation. At the edge of chaos, tensions continually emerge. They form requisite variety gaps that present themselves in the form of pain points, failures, waste, and lost opportunities amid the constantly changing environment. This requires the mountain bike rider to be mindful to continually change gears across all three rings of Becoming, Knowing, and Doing.

The other edge state, where you spend most of your time, is called the edge of equilibrium. In this more stable environment necessary for road and stationary biking, where you can predict events with precision, it is possible to plan with high degrees of certainty. On this edge, you can plan a route with an existing map. Here Lean Six Sigma thrives.

All of us operate between these two edge states, never in total equilibrium or total chaos. The environment is neither completely at rest nor completely chaotic. Large organizations operating in stable markets can use existing roads, but start-ups chart new paths through the mountains. To meet the demands of the Law of Requisite Variety and Complexity, you must be ambidextrous enough to ride the right bike for the terrain. Doing so will enable you to harness the tensions around you in order to adapt and generate new innovative outcomes.

Most of us lack the ability to switch back and forth between edges. There is comfort in operating at the edge of equilibrium because this is how evaluations are made and rewards are given.

This is where your organization's critical mass, people, capital, customers, and profits reside. But if you want to survive and succeed, you must ride, at least some of the time, at the edge of chaos.

Crashing into Lucky Accidents More Often

The most powerful tension gap between the two edge states arises between running the businesses of today and innovating the businesses of tomorrow.

To survive in the short term, you must focus on running today's business. This means that you must spend most of your waking hours operating at the edge of equilibrium, far from chaos, where the environment is stable and predictable. Here you can plan for the future by introducing Lean Six Sigma processes and scaling activities, processes, and structures for long-term success. Mindlessness is the order of the day and rightfully so.

Futurist Ray Kurzweil calculates that we have experienced roughly two hundred years of change within just the first decade of the twenty-first century. So consider this perspective: businesses are experiencing two hundred years of tensions in ten years. This phenomenon is apparent in the double exponential growth in technologies like information technology processing power, bandwidth, storage, and genomic sequencing. The disruptive impact of these technologies on industries and companies is easily observed around us.

So ponder this: while technology has grown exponentially, the human brain is roughly the same as it was twenty *thousand* years ago. This mind gap highlights even more the need for mindfulness, which simplifies things and keeps the brain from being overrun with complexity.

As humans, we struggle with the exponential rates of change because they are difficult to comprehend. The mindless approach to life allows the understanding of and planning for linear change, but not exponential change. It is only through mindfulness that such exponential change can be comprehended and responded to. Remember, the mindful brain can comprehend the universe, whereas the mindless brain can only plan for the next logical step.

So how can you enable yourself to spend more productive time on a mountain bike, exploring and discovering creative ways to harness the many tensions that impact you on a daily basis? The answer is found in applying the three processes that provide the foundation for transformation in complex adaptive systems: **interaction, variation,** and **selection.** By applying them, you will increase the volume, velocity, and value of your innovative efforts.

Interaction

Interaction requires constant engagement with other participants, groups, and organizations in the ecosystems in which you operate so that requisite variety gaps in the Innovation Cycle can be identified. Once the identification is made, it is up to you to find ways to close the gaps by transforming your identity and adopting new mental models to create the innovations that ensure survival. This requires you to break down and penetrate organizational silos and go beyond borders and boundaries. It means sharing ideas about new identities you think you need to use and also testing them. It also means establishing and testing new mental models based on this feedback.

In contrast, in a stable system at the edge of equilibrium, interaction is less important and tends to be a source of waste. It causes unnecessary distractions since the mindless processes yield the most efficient and effective outcome in stability. At the edge of chaos, mindfulness demands greater interaction.

In our own experience in leading large organizations as well as the work we have done as consultants with our clients, we have experienced the challenges associated with enabling greater interaction. Large organizations are so internally focused that they lack a clear understanding of the emerging requisite variety gaps between their environment and themselves, and they spend too much time on internal speculation rather then external exploration and discovery.

For example, while working with a client, we spent a year trying to convince the most senior leadership to move forward with a modest experiment to test some new digital health ideas and technologies in the marketplace. Months were spent developing and polishing PowerPoint presentations to present to the CEO based on the internal organization's knowledge and understanding of the emerging tension gaps. The team working on the project was barred from access to customers by those who owned the customer relationships, thereby limiting the team's insight regarding the actual pain points and tensions in the market.

During this same time frame, over a dozen start-up companies, without any big-company organizational barriers, engaged directly with prospective customers and applied creative energies to harness these tensions and launched new solutions to address this problem. These start-ups quickly attracted customers and worked to evolve their solution to MVP versions 1.0, 2.0, and 3.0. These start-ups were riding mountain bikes while our larger client was stuck on a stationary cycle that never left the confines of the office.

Variation

Interaction helps accelerate the process of variation. By exposing participants to one another, you can observe the differences between them and what features seem to lead to better success and survival. Through variation, you can also mindfully fail by mimicking variation seen in the business ecosystem and trying them out to see how well they work. It's simple: variations in the marketplace that fail are avoided, and others that seem to work are copied. If these latter ones fail, they are discarded. Now you copy and replicate variations that lead to success and survival.

Variations arise through interactions outside the primary ecosystem that are copied and introduced. For example, consumers have often been frustrated by the difficulty and length of time it takes to make a doctor's appointment and have asked, "Why can't I set up an appointment online with a doctor as easily and as quickly as I make an airline reservation online?" By copying the online booking innovation in airline ticketing and applying it to healthcare, Zocdoc created an innovative new business, and Mitch's healthcare organization did the same. Much of the variety necessary for innovation emerges by exploring how similar problems have been solved in different markets, situations, and times and then figuring out how to modify them so they can be reapplied in a new context.

Variation is the process of creating new mental models and identities. Through variation, you combine the differences of old maps in novel ways that provide the building blocks and outline for creating a new identity and new mental maps. In a Lean Six Sigma world, variation is the source of errors and failure and is to be avoided at all costs. In Lean start-up, it is the source of the next great invention.

In large organizations, variation brings about powerful tensions because it introduces something that is different that is initially seen and treated as a potential threat. The organizational antibodies attack it as a threat and try to drive it out of the system. I (Chris) was told the following by an executive at a company where I was hired to drive more innovation: "We don't have to respond to these tensions you are creating. You have been here for a year. I have been here for twenty. You will soon be gone, but I will be here another ten. We have been successful in the past, and we can continue to do what we have done in the past to be successful in the future."

Often leaders seek to eliminate the tension that this new variety induces through brute force (demoting, transferring, or even firing an employee). Since leaders are most comfortable with mindless processes that seek to drive out variation, they treat change and its associated tensions and discord as threats to their survival. The longer the tenure of the organization leadership, the more established their mental models for stability, standardization, and normal operating procedures are. This is especially true if there is no identity of innovation in the organization. Such people quickly access existing mental maps that have been successful in the past to solve problems rather than look for new ones that require innovation. They stay on their stationary cycles—represented by the organization's established structures and practices that support solving yesterday's problems. Unfortunately, doing so will not solve tomorrow's problems.

Selection

This process follows interaction and variation because, without selection, the other two have no real value. Selection enables freedom of choice. If you can't choose interaction outside the boundaries of your current system, as well as select the variations you believe are more valuable in closing the requisite variety gaps, then you can never create new mental models or identities to adapt and survive in a turbulent world. Selection represents a critical process to conduct mindful failure. Not surprisingly, it is also a process where you don't want to allow mindfulness because it means that you will not get the same result on a reliable basis from the same process, regardless of who is operating the process.

The paradox is that, as the system moves from the edge of equilibrium to the edge of chaos, mindless processes will not yield the predictable results of the past because the larger system in which you operate is no longer predictable. Yet organizations continue to apply mindless process, expecting to be able to determine outcomes. When they fail, they often assume it's because the mindless process was not implemented correctly. They then increase their focus on improving implementation and executing mindless processes. This only increases failure, which then leads to more of the same. This is how maladaptive tension leads to mindless failures. Apply a mindless process in a dynamic environment, and you will experience failure that will continue until you apply mindful failure to innovate the approach. You have likely heard insanity described as doing the same thing over and over while expecting a different result. Only mindfulness breaks this cycle.

Selection requires the participants in the organization and larger systems be given freedom to interact with the variation without a lot of restrictions. This is the key point behind the idea of creating MVPs in Lean start-ups: come up with something quickly that seems good enough, put it out in the market, and let the participants in the market vote with their dollars and feet as to whether or not the MVP offers value. Then measure their response, learn from it, build the next MVP, and try again.

At the edge of chaos, the selection process must enable rapid learning with limited structure and practice barriers. This means that those on mountain bikes are not operating in a rigid, tightly coupled system with lots of formal standard operating procedures, but rather in a loosely coupled system that allows for greater freedom in exploration, discovery, experimentation, interaction, and selection. Within most large organizations, this rarely happens. Too few people get the rights and freedom to select variations to experiment by interacting with others in the environment. With the typical large company, the selection process is very limited, and consequently learning is very slow, if it happens at all. This policy stifles interaction and variation. No such organization can compete with more agile smaller players in the market that lack these selection barriers and rapidly learn how to close their requisite variety gaps.

A word of warning: these three processes ensure that you are going to crash more often. After all, you're on mountain bikes in rugged terrain. However, since these three processes increase failure, they also *accelerate* learning and *increase* your chances of lucky accidents. Luck is often defined as the intersection of opportunity and preparation. By enabling these three processes to operate within your organization, you are preparing to identify and innovate more opportunities. In essence, you are making your own luck. These three processes are the core of disciplining serendipity and increasing your innovative capacity.

The Trouble with Switching Bikes

As you know by now, having most people ride the same type of bike all the time is the most efficient operating model, and this is the foundation for Lean Six Sigma. But should efficiency be the primary driver of all organizational objectives? A 2013 CEO survey conducted by PwC indicated that, for the first time in history, CEOs now believe that operating efficiency should be of equal importance as innovation.

How can you do both of these things with the same level of effectiveness?

A perfectly efficient system lacks the slack and resources for creativity. To overcome this constraint, there is generally a small cadre of specialists who are allowed to focus exclusively and efficiently on creativity and innovation. These are the mountain bikers in R&D and business development. The rest of the staff is usually informed that they don't have to be innovators. They can remain on their stationary bikes where there is no risk of taking a wrong turn or crashing into another cyclist.

There is no doubt that enabling everyone to switch bikes from time to time decreases efficiency. It takes time to get off one and onto another, plus it takes time to learn how to ride a different kind of cycle. Cyclists have accidents. They crash. Sometimes they crash for stupid reasons that could have been foreseen and prevented. However, with the double exponential rate of change all of us now experience in our lives, employees must be encouraged to tap into their creative genius. Basically, everyone should be able to switch bikes from time to time in order to spend more time taking the risk of exploring dangerous territories and terrains on mountain bikes.

The goal and purpose in expanding innovation capabilities should be to enable spontaneous order to emerge from riding at the edge of chaos.

In this context, *enable* means that leadership should be the catalyst for change, the place where good ideas can go to and come from, both inside and outside the organization. It should protect innovative ideas, nurture them, kill bad ones, and help better ones to emerge and then grow. Leadership must enable employees to use their brains to do these things. Remember, it isn't people, teams, or organizations that innovate. The brain innovates, but it must be in the right environment with the right supporting structures and practices to do so. This is because the brain doesn't innovate alone or in a vacuum but by having the freedom to chose how to interact with other diverse brains. Therefore, the role of leadership is to produce tensions, provide innovative structures and practices, and empower people to harness tensions through these structures and practices as follows.

Leadership

1. **Foresees and generates the requisite variety gaps that induce tensions.** Leadership anticipates future gaps, failure, and pain and brings them to the attention of and imposes them on the organization. This forces people to address future failures, pain, tensions, and gaps in the present. Doing so enables a creative and adaptive response to future problems now instead of waiting for future problems to emerge and then being reactive to them.

   This is how leadership applies the Innovation Cycle discussed in the previous chapter. Leadership that fails to do this can't recognize brilliant innovations even when their teams deliver it. When leaders lack foresight, they are unqualified to identity, understand, select, fund, nurture, and support innovation. A lack of a clear vision and point of view of the future and the ability to foresee your role in it is a critical barrier to innovation.

2. **Provides the structures and practices to harness these tensions.** With these in place, you can move toward creative and adaptive ends and outcomes as opposed to maladaptive ones that lead to continued failure and pain. This requires building and supporting a robust ideation platform, innovation practices, and structures to engage those within and without the organization. This also requires a disciplined approach to evaluating ideas against the vision to see which ideas the organization and people within it can select and nurture. You must then provide an incubation structure and practice to move the best ideas forward to an MVP or several iterations of MVPs. Rapidly learning and adapting are crucial. This means spending much less time polishing PowerPoints and more time on doing experiments, launching MVPs, and

getting real market feedback. Rapid experiments, prototypes, and pilots accelerate learning and commercial success.

3. **Enables others within and without the organization to leverage these structures and practices to innovate rapidly.** When you see the structure of the many incubators and accelerators in the market, it is interesting to see how quickly they learn and adapt. In the time that a large organization polishes its PowerPoints, a dozen or more companies in these incubators have launched solutions, obtained customers, generated revenues, hired employees, raised capital, and gone on to the next version of their product. This is the pace of learning all organizations need to enable. Leadership's role is to create and deploy an innovation operating model that allows this pace of adaptation and creativity.

By doing these three things, leadership will allow a new order to spontaneously emerge from what looks like a chaotic process. People will be hopping on and off their various bikes to take a turn at innovation. This fresh order will be in the form of new businesses, business models, products, services, and solutions. Leadership should be the key enabler of this emergent process. While they do not directly create the businesses, products, or services, they increase the velocity, volume, and value of interaction, variation, and selection.

Enable Anyone to Ride the Innovation Cycle

Generally, when we talk to leaders of organizations about tapping into everyone's creative genius, they get very worried. Their experience is that most people aren't very innovative, and giving them license to spend time trying to be that way will be a waste of time. The ingrained belief is that the new ideas will not bring any value to the organization. But fortunately we know that 98 percent of employees have the hardwiring to be creative geniuses, so it's merely a matter of recruiting that identity from the mind.

Still, many organizations have attempted to open the floodgates of imagination by starting very open-ended, all-comers innovation programs where they invite everyone to provide ideas about anything. As we previously pointed out, these organizations invariably suffer from innovation fatigue. They are unprepared for the flood of random and varied ideas that people have been holding. They also invariably find that after the initial cathartic deluge of ideas, released by everyone at the same time, the idea flow collapses to a mere trickle. The paucity of follow-on creativity after the initial release requires very little supporting innovation infrastructure to accommodate the few ideas that are shared after the initial flood. This justifies the initial skepticism of the naysayers who said that most people are not creative and have few good ideas.

The problem is that you need to have important problems to solve and constraints and tensions to overcome in order to have good ideas. The all-comers approach above allows people to release ideas that have built up over many years to address the pain points and tensions they have experienced. But once they have communicated them, there isn't much more to share unless you help them focus their creative energies on new problems and pain points.

So what do you do if you know your business badly needs more innovation and you recognize the need to tap into everyone's creative genius?

Just as mindlessness has supporting structures and practices to support Lean Six Sigma operating efficiency, mindfulness requires its own discipline—albeit a very different type—to do the same.

This discipline can operate in an open system extending beyond the boundaries of your organization, in a closed system within its own walls, or on an individual basis. By promoting innovation challenges and campaigns, it is possible to engineer focused activities and events that can engage large or small groups for years, months, weeks, days, or hours, depending on the design of the campaign. Here are a few examples of how this is being done.

Qualcomm Tricorder Challenge: Dozens of non-Qualcomm organizations and teams are competing to construct the first device to diagnose a dozen different medical conditions using a single, simple, small mobile technology device. It would be like the tricorder that Bones used in *Star Trek*.

Netflix Recommendation Engine Challenge: Dozens of teams around the world competed to develop a more effective recommendation engine for the Netflix website that must be 10 percent more accurate than the current one. The winning team emerged by combining two competing teams who operated virtually during the competition and met for the first time in person when they received their one-million-dollar prize.

PwC New $100 M Practice Challenge: This was an internal challenge that did not allow any of PwC's partners to participate in providing ideas to create a new consulting practice that could generate $100 million of revenues within five years. Associates, managers, and directors competed over twelve months and through three rounds to design new consulting practices.

Kaggle Challenge Business Model: The company's business is to help organizations design external challenges and campaigns to attract the brightest scientific minds in the world to solve specific problems through competitions to win awards and prize money.

Datapalooza Hackathons: Under the leadership of Todd Park, the U.S. government has become a leader in enabling greater ingenuity to emerge from within the government. At these events, innovators partner with the government to generate new creative solutions by leveraging government data and information.

These are just a small handful of the thousands of examples of how different organizations identify challenges that need innovation and then structure campaigns to achieve the challenge objective and thereby provide the necessary discipline to liberate the creative genius. As we reviewed many different kinds of challenges and related campaigns—and supported others in implementing a number of them ourselves—we found they follow certain best practices in their structures, implementations, and operations in order to be successful. These are outlined below. Our focus here is not to provide a detailed how-to guide for every type of challenge but to summarize the key principles and elements that underlie these best practices. These follow a Lean Innovation operating model approach consistent with the Lean Start-Up approach in which the least amount of resources are invested in order to yield the most creativity, failure, learning, and invention by applying the three innovation processes of interaction, variation, and selection.

Lean Innovation Supporting Structure

The Lean Innovation approach to enabling everyone to contribute their creative genius to solve important problems has its own set of specific structures and practices. But this mindful approach requires much less structure and support than that found in mindlessness because most of the inspired work is done on a part-time basis by people hopping off their stationary and road bikes and riding mountain bikes for short periods of time. However, Lean Innovation requires a Lean full-time team (similar to Lean Six Sigma Black Belts) to train and support others who are doing the bulk of the innovative work. In many organizations, the supporting structures and practices generally look something like the following.

Chief Innovation Officer (CINO): This is generally a full-time role focused on supporting leadership in getting innovation into the DNA of everyone in the organization and liberating their creative genius. This person leads the enterprise innovation efforts and the innovation support team.

Innovation Support Team (IST): This is a small full-time team, generally five to ten people, depending on the size of the organization and the breadth of services provided. This team enables others in the business to apply innovation best practices within their areas of activity to ensure and make possible greater mindfulness, inventiveness, and innovation.

Campaign Executive Sponsor: This leader works with the IST on a part-time basis to identify and propose challenges that require innovation and provides support on a part-time basis throughout a campaign. This person must have a passion for innovation and will select the Campaign Sponsor.

Campaign Sponsor: This leader works with the IST on a part-time basis to identify and select the core campaign team and helps to further refine the challenge as well as define, design, run, and wrap up the campaign.

Core Campaign Team: This group of three or four senior managers work with the IST on a part-time basis and generally have accountability around the selected business challenge. Ideally, these people are drawn from cross-functional areas of expertise in order to increase the diversity of insight and perspective they bring. This team does most of the heavy lifting in the campaign. They work with the IST to design the campaign, develop the evaluation criteria, and perform many of the operational tasks in running the campaign as well as support the communication strategy, evaluation, selection, and development plans for the better ideas.

Extended Campaign Team: This is a part-time role for people who act as advisors to the IST and Core Campaign Team and can be any number of people, but generally between five and ten. Ideally, these people also represent a diverse background of experience and expertise from both commercial and functional areas.

Idea Stewards: These part-time roles are filled by senior managers who have meaningful experience in the area of the challenge. They are responsible for championing the development of the light business cases used to further evaluate ideas that seem to have merit and represent strong candidates for future innovations. The job can include working with the person or team that submitted the idea to further explore and develop it by conducting interviews, gathering expert opinions, and coming up with market tests, prototypes, pilots, etc. The idea is to support the person or team in developing an MVP that can be quickly tested and evaluated. The number of idea stewards is based on the number of good ideas selected to be refined and developed.

Ambidextrous Supporting Leadership and Participants

The outline above makes it clear that this approach to innovation requires ambidextrous leadership at all levels of the organizations. With the exception of the CINO and the IST, everyone else has a mindless day job they continue to fulfill. To participate in this process, they must also add an identity as an innovator. This identity is critical in enabling others to become more creative and mindful. By engaging many layers of leadership and management, you are able to make it clear throughout the organization that creativity and innovation are valued and that your organization expects everyone to be ambidextrous and to operate under both mindful and mindless disciplines. You are committed to getting innovation into the DNA of all your people.

It is also important to point out that just as Lean Six Sigma provides training and support to and from Black Belts and Green Belts, the IST provides similar support to leaders who lack experience in mindful activities like innovation challenges and campaigns. This support ensures that the discipline is consistently applied and refined.

Lean Innovation Processes to Support Best Practices

The following eight stages represent what we have developed with clients in our consulting work and have regarded as best practices for running an innovation challenge and campaign. The timing for each of these stages is flexible and depends upon the type of challenge faced and the kind of campaign being run. Some go on for years, others months, and some, like hackathons, can last just a few hours. Regardless of the time frame, the eight stages tend to follow this general approach.

Stage One: Define the Campaign

Here you work with the Campaign Executive Sponsor to identify a challenge they or their customers are facing that could be addressed by coming up with a more innovative solution to the problem or

Figure 13

EIGHT STAGES OF DISCIPLINED SERENDIPITY AND CREATIVITY

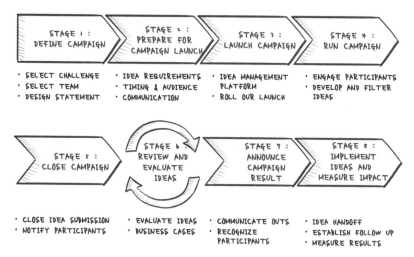

opportunity. You look for tensions that heretofore were maladaptive, because no novel solutions eliminated the pain or waste in the system. The challenge needs to have a strategic alignment with the organization and needs to appeal to those participating in the campaign. The challenge must be defined in scope, and its impact must be measurable.

You generally start by looking at macro trends that are generating requisite variety gaps for customers, competitors, the organization, teams, or yourselves. You then identify the key challenge that the participants need to overcome through the application of innovation. This enables you to identify the specific area of focus for the campaign.

Generally, the most difficult activity in this stage is forming the campaign problem statement, objectives, and associated constraints. Constraints are a key component of defining the campaign because innovation loves constraints. To force innovation, you must impose constraints that can only be overcome through novel solutions. For example, when Netflix launched its recommendation engine campaign, the company applied the constraint that the proposed innovations had to be at least 10 percent better than the current solution. The campaign statement and constraints must be broad enough to enable creativity yet focused enough to elicit actionable insights.

An example of how this process works could be the following.

Macro trend: Social, mobile, and analytic cloud (SMAC) technologies are changing the way customers interact with companies

Business challenge: How do you improve your relationships with customers?

Specific innovation application: How do you link an innovative customer experience with these technologies?

Innovation campaign: What are the eight most effective SMAC solutions you can work out to deliver a better experience and increase customer retention by 10 percent?

Stage Two: Design the Campaign

Each campaign should be designed to achieve specific goals and objectives, which requires answering the following questions.

How do you determine the target community and time frame? The type and size of the challenge will determine the target community and time frame. The Qualcomm challenge required a working product with specific capabilities to overcome predefined constraints. Achieving this required an open process to engage a very broad community over the course of three years. Others may have specific business challenges limited to an organizational department that can be realized in just a couple of months.

How do you establish idea submission and evaluation criteria for the ideas submitted? You generally provide successive filters to screen ideas. The first filter will be high level and will put ideas into three or four buckets based on their level of attractiveness. The most attractive will go through additional evaluation, assessment, and business case development.

How do you determine incentives for participation? You will find the most creative people don't participate for money, and providing more money doesn't necessarily increase participation, although it can increase media exposure and interest. Even when you look at the big public challenges and campaigns, where millions of dollars are on the line, you find that the winning team often spends more to win the prize than they earn in winnings. Money awards, however, do capture the imagination and help get people focused, but they are not enough on their own to drive participation. This is especially true if the participants look at the challenge rationally and realize that any one of them has a very low probability of winning the big reward. So why do they do it? Recognition and praise from peers, superiors, and strangers is one answer. Others do it from a passion to contribute through creative freedom. Some enjoy the challenge of the game and the sociality and camaraderie that comes with it. For these reasons it is important to support multiple incentives to capture participants' imagination, engagement, and passion.

How do you develop communications plans? These plans need to address all aspects of the challenge along the entire time line. This includes how you promote it to get visibility and engagement.

How will you share progress updates? What type of feedback will you provide participants along the way? What will be the final announcement and rewards? Since you are trying to enable large communities to engage their creative genius, you need to employ comprehensive communication strategies that generate the highest level of participation. All systems, whether they are biological or social, require information feedback for growth. When employees don't get feedback, the social system around innovation dies. Some organizations run a communication campaign called "You said it, we did it," where employee innovations are listed and leadership actions and dates of completion are listed next to them. In this way, employees feel more engaged, the social system thrives, and more innovations are presented.

Stage Three: Launch the Campaign

Most campaigns will employ some type of social media technology to facilitate dissemination and the collection of information to support the campaign. This will include guidelines for submission, the evaluation criteria, and ongoing communication. It will also include some type of leaderboard to indicate who is participating and how various ideas are moving through the system, being evaluated, gaining traction, and performing.

Stage Four: Run the Campaign

During the running of the campaign, communication continues to be important. The evaluation, scoring, ranking, and selection process must be coordinated. A social network can be used for the scoring, experts can monitor scoring, or both approaches can be used. In the PwC campaign, PwC employees individually selected a certain number of ideas, and an expert panel of partners also selected others. Engaging in direct dialogue with participants to answer questions and support them in their efforts is another option.

Stage Five: Close the Campaign

You must determine how to close the campaign and notify each participant of their current status and the next steps, such as a time line for review and feedback.

Stage Six: Review and Evaluate Ideas

This is one of the most labor-intensive processes of the campaign and requires engaging the core and supporting teams as well as other leaders. Some of the longer campaigns, like the one run by Netflix, require the participants to deliver a final product. Some are more focused on quickly developed MVPs that gather market feedback but are short of a truly commercially viable solution. Other campaigns merely deliver ideas that could become MVPs and eventually innovations. The following are criteria to use for making a selection:

- Does the idea meet the campaign requirements?
- What strategic opportunity does it align with?
- What is the time required to develop and implement the idea or solution?
- What is the economic impact of the idea or solution measured in revenues, costs savings, or value creation?
- What type and size of investment is required to implement the idea or solution?
- How feasible is the idea or solution?
- How innovative is the idea or solution?

- What is the coolness factor of the idea or solution?
- What is the risk of the idea or solution?
- What level of further analysis is required?

Based upon the ratings and rankings above, you will select the most attractive ideas, MVPs, or solutions to be evaluated. Then you will use a simple business model innovation canvas to understand at a high level how the idea or solution could be brought to market. This is where the Idea Stewards step in. They help to complete the canvas with the idea or solution team to co-create a high-level view of the key elements of the business model in order to commercialize it. This includes an assessment of the stakeholders and market opportunity (where the business participates), the capabilities required to deliver the value propositions (how the business plays), the benefits derived from the value proposition (why the business wins), and the economic impact from commercial success (what the business wins).

Stage Seven: Announce Campaign Results

This provides a great opportunity to reward everyone in some way for participating by acknowledging their contribution, thanking them, and announcing the winners and the process used to select them. This enables you to provide various types of incentives as well as to indicate the next steps in moving the innovation forward along the Innovation Lifecycle.

Stage Eight: Implement Ideas and Measure Impact

In this final stage, you hand off the ideas that are ready for further development and incubation to the next team in the Innovation

Lifecycle. You evaluate your performance with this campaign in order to identify things that did or did not work so you can further enhance your practices. Then you measure your performance using the innovation scorecard. This will tell you how you performed in engaging everyone's creative genius and generating new sources of novel value.

Many Ways to Ride the Innovation Cycle

This is not the only way to ideate and discover inspired solutions when riding the Innovation Cycle. Nonetheless, it has become an increasingly popular way to engage large communities of people in disciplined innovative activities to dismount from their road and stationary cycles and spend some time on mountain bikes.

These structures and practices employ the complexity processes necessary to develop solutions to close the gaps that emerge from the lack of requisite variety. But this approach merely starts applying innovation discipline at the start of the Innovation Lifecycle. In order to actually deliver innovation, you must advance creative ideas and then nurture and incubate them.

The focus of the next chapter describes the next phase of growth: incubation.

REMEMBER ─────────────────────────────────

- ✔ Innovation requires serendipity (i.e., luck), and you can increase your luck by applying the structures and practices of the Innovation Lifecycle.

- ✔ The Law of Requisite Variety and Complexity is the primary law that drives change in the complex systems in which you operate every day. It explains how all people, organizations, and systems function between the two conditions we constantly find ourselves: the edge of chaos and the edge of equilibrium.

- ✔ To survive in the short term, you must focus on running today's business. This means that you must spend most of your waking hours operating at the edge of equilibrium, far from chaos, where the environment is stable and predictable. Here you can plan for the future by introducing Lean Six Sigma processes in order to scale innovative ideas using processes and structures that will aid in short-term success.

- ✔ The mindless approach to life allows the understanding of and planning for linear, but not exponential, change. It is only through mindfulness that such exponential change can be comprehended and responded to.

- ✔ Exponential change can be achieved by applying three processes: interaction, variation, and selection. Applying them will increase the volume, velocity, and value of your innovative efforts.

✔ Interaction requires constant engagement with other participants, groups, and organizations in the ecosystems in which you operate so that requisite variety gaps in the Innovation Cycle can be identified.

✔ Variations that have failed in the marketplace are avoided. Others that seem to be working are copied. If the latter fail, they are discarded. Then you copy and replicate variations that lead to success and survival.

✔ Selection enables freedom of choice in both interactions and selection.

—————— QUESTIONS ——————

> How well do you understand the central role of serendipity in the innovation process?

> How would you describe your discovery process to create more serendipity in a disciplined way?

> How well does your discovery process incorporate interaction, variation, and selection?

> How well do you explore the effects and impacts of exponential change that creates tensions and drives innovation?

CHAPTER TEN

Incubating Creativity

Disciplining creativity that takes place during the Discovery phase of the Innovation Lifecycle, as outlined in chapter 9, will release a flood of new ideas but not innovations. During Discovery, many bad and mediocre ideas are combined to develop new and improved ways of creating value. But the reality is that the vast majority of these novelties will be merely improvements on existing products, services, processes, and business models. They won't spur innovations; that is, they will not create new sources of value in new ways. Many may go beyond improvements and become incremental innovations that add new features, functionality, applications, and benefits to existing innovations. While both improvements and incremental innovations are valuable, both can generally be developed and commercialized by current businesses through existing R&D, product development, and other mindless structures and practices. This can happen because they generally improve efficiency, eliminate waste, decrease defects, and thereby enable one to realize mindless objectives.

But what do you do about the 10–15 percent of the creative ideas with the potential to be more than mere improvements or incremental innovations?

In our experiences, we have seen that these 10–15 percent of new value creation ideas that are identified and refined into POCs possess the capacity to become breakthrough or radical innovations that could disrupt both the inventor's business as well as others in the marketplace. In most organizations, there is a struggle to advance these disruptive ideas along the Innovation Lifecycle because of the lack of nurturing organizational structures, including a significant shortage of leadership support and vision as well as an inadequate understanding of the how-to practices that can turn a good idea into the next great success.

Promising potential innovations require incubators. They require a structure with the appropriate governance, process, and people to ensure the discipline to continue fast, frequent, frugal failure, but on a larger scale than was done during Discovery. This Incubation phase of growth is actually the most difficult to manage of all the phases in the Innovation Lifecycle. The reason is that it's necessary to continually move back and forth through all three rings of the Innovation Cycle to eliminate conceptual, technical, and operating risk through prototypes, virtual pilots, and physical pilots. Effective incubation will enable you to select and test your first business model and then generate your first customers and revenues.

Riding a Hybrid Bike in Unpredictable Terrain

Hybrid bikes are the only bikes with all three rings. Because the hybrid's three rings enable you to travel across all kinds of terrains, inclines, and grades, a hybrid bike is the most adaptable of all bikes. So, in incubation, which requires the most flexibility and adaptability of the Innovation Lifecycle, riding a hybrid makes the most sense.

Hybrids are equipped with the two rings used in mountain biking to allow you to ascend and descend steep trails and hills. They also feature the two larger rings of a road bike in case you find yourself on gravel or paved roads. (While this may sound like they have four rings, the middle ring in a hybrid bike is the large ring of a mountain bike and the small ring of a road bike.) The frame of the hybrid bike is similar to that of a mountain bike, but the other components and wheels look more like those of a road bike. This ensures that you will achieve the maximum flexibility of all the bikes you ride.

Incubation requires this same flexibility to let you quickly change speed and direction as you adapt to an unpredictable and evolving market opportunity with your innovative ideas.

While the primary objective of incubation is to eliminate technical risk and to come up with the first viable business model, you can only do this through lots of trial and error, a.k.a failure. This will require you to sometimes realize that what you foresaw initially, which was the basis for incubation in the first place, was so flawed that you need to shift down to the Becoming ring again and take a few loops. When you do this, you will get the chance to reassess the core values, further refine or redefine the vision, foresee a different future, and explore these new ideas to test them before you are ready to shift to the Knowing ring. It is very common to see an idea that successfully emerges from Incubation focus on an entirely different problem and solution than it started with.

For example, Jiff, a Silicon Valley start-up now focused on corporate wellness programs, began the incubation process focused on digitally completing patient intake forms on tablets in doctors' offices. During Incubation, they realized the technology and capabilities they were developing would be more valuable in addressing a different market opportunity that had greater potential, so they pivoted to this new opportunity.

The primary objective in Knowing is figuring out how to identity, quantify, measure, manage, and mitigate the technical risks associated with the innovation so you can reliably package them into an initial business model you can test with customers to see how they will vote with their dollars and feet. This means that, in Incubation, most of the time will be spent in the Knowing ring: creating pre-commercial MVPs, enlisting the support of others, forming a strategic plan, and gathering capital and other resources. The goal is to generate and manage MVPs to see what works and what doesn't, refine what you foresee as the future potential, and loop through this ring again and again until you are ready to put your innovation into its first business model to test its commercial attractiveness.

Once you think an MVP will work well enough, you will then be ready to turn your novel offering into an innovation by beginning the search for the best business model to generate commercial value from early adopter customers. This requires you to shift to the Doing ring and take an initial loop through that ring in preparation for the next phase of growth: Accelerating.

Despite What You May Hear, Every Novel Idea Isn't Radical or Breakthrough

Many of the lessons learned were gained in our own start-up and incubation efforts. After selling Tympany, Mitch went back to his previous employer, Ochsner Clinic, to become the CEO of one of their businesses as well as executive sponsor and faculty of the Ochsner Leadership Institute responsible for training hundreds of leaders on the neuroscience of innovation. Chris decided to create a medical technology incubator called SimplexityMD.

To create the incubator, we assembled some of our Tympany investors and shared our business plan to develop a novel type of medical technology incubator that would evaluate hundreds of technologies to find those we thought had the greatest promise. We would then apply the Innovation Cycle and Lifecycle to move them toward commercial success. The name—SimplexityMD—was based on our view that we were simplifying the complexity of medical technology innovation.

Once we launched our business, we were surprised at how quickly we were inundated with inventors pitching their ideas. What surprised us even more was how frequently they invoked the words "breakthrough," "radical," and "disruptive" to describe their inventions.

This was a problem. We realized you couldn't justify a new business—with all that it entails regarding raising money, hiring people, etc.—based on an incremental idea. Incumbents are generally the only ones who can really justify investments to bring incremental ideas to market for a fundamental reason: for them it's only an incremental investment to extend their current offerings.

Our incubator could only justify starting a new company if the ideas were big. Additionally, the big ideas had to be disruptive and radical in order to introduce a large enough opportunity to be worth our while. In fact, few breakthrough innovations could justify the heavy lift of new venture creation.

As we listened to the inventors' pitches, we asked them, "Why do you claim this is a radical innovation? It doesn't seem that novel. It seems to be just an improvement over an existing technology or solution." They would respond vaguely, which was never very satisfying, but there was no objective way to challenge them. We needed a framework to evaluate each innovation in order to identify its core elements, quantify the amount of new value it could generate, measure that value across a comprehensive value proposition, and then classify it as a potential incremental, breakthrough, or radical innovation.

We developed the following framework to support the selection process for our incubator. Since then we have provided this approach to others. We think of this as a funneling process whereby we start broad, get more specific with each step, and eventually end up screening out those opportunities that clearly are not candidates for incubation.

Identifying the Source of Novel Value by Minding the Ps and Qs

When we first met with someone to explore their ideas and inventions, we often found they would be so excited about telling us about the features of their technology that they failed to get to the key points. For example, what problem was the person trying to solve? We discovered that we needed to provide a framework to help them focus and mind their Ps and Qs. To do so, we developed the ten primary elements and related questions we needed in order to get a good quick-and-dirty summary of the opportunity. We call these the Ten Ps and Qs of New Value Creation. These questions take a long time for inventors to figure out, but once that is done, they don't take long to share them with investors, partners, customers—anyone they are trying to get interested in their idea. These questions force an inventor and innovator to establish a crisp, straightforward description of the need for and new sources of the value they believe they can deliver.

Answers to these ten P categories are, in essence, the "light business case" referred to in the previous chapter. They should be part of the disciplined discovery process that determines whether or not an idea and POC needs to be incubated.

Problem	What problem are you trying to solve? What are the pain points you are addressing? Who has the problem and pain points? Why do they want it solved? How acute are they? What is your vision of the future if they are removed?
Point of view	Why is this solution needed now? Why should you develop and deliver the solution? What is your key insight that is different than others? Why will it be better than alternative solutions? What is your secret sauce? Do you have patents and/or patentable technology?
Proposition	What is your key value proposition? How will it decrease costs? How will it increase convenience? How will it improve performance and create greater confidence in quality, access, etc.? Who will be compensated and make more money from the solution and how will they do it? What type of technical, social, and emotional connection does it create?
Possibilities	How big is the initial early adopter market? How large is the larger opportunity market? How much of it could you get? How big could the business or offering become in terms of units, customers, and revenues?
People & Partners	What type of people would you need for this business? What type of partners would you need in order to build out, offer, and support the solution? Who would they be?
Plan & Process	What type of plan in terms of timing and process do you have to move the business forward? What type of resources (money) do you need to get to prototype, pilot, and early commercial launch? What would be the timing of these milestones? What does your MVP 1.0, 2.0, 3.0 look like?
Position	What is the competitive landscape? What companies are already working in this space and what are they doing? What type of position could you achieve in the market? How is the industry structure changing? Who will you threaten and disrupt and how much power do they have to stop you?
Promotion	What is your go-to-market strategy? What channels would you access and leverage? What type of direct and indirect marketing will it require? How will you leverage digital and social media?
Products	What are the products, services, programs, solutions, and/or platform offerings you envision? How would they compare to alternatives?
Profits	What is the business model? How do you make money? What type of margins could you earn? What would be your cost structure? How much could you sell your company for in the future? Who would be the likely buyers?

Figure 14

TEN PS & QS OF POTENTIAL INNOVATION

PS	QS
1. PROBLEM	WHAT FAILURE, PAIN, TENSION AND PROBLEM ARE YOU ADDRESSING?
2. POINT OF VIEW	WHAT SECRET SAUCE DO YOU HAVE THAT IS BETTER THAN ALTERNATIVES?
3. PROPOSITION	HOW DO YOU ADDRESS THE 5 CS OF THE VALUE PROPOSITION?
4. POSSIBILITIES	HOW BIG COULD THIS BE IN 1, 3, 5, 10 YEARS WITH WHICH SEGMENTS?
5. PEOPLE & PARTNERS	WHO DO YOU NEED TO MAKE THIS SUCCESSFUL?
6. PLAN & PROCESS	HOW WILL YOU EXECUTE YOUR SUCCESSIVE MVPS?
7. POSITION	WHY AND HOW WILL YOU IMPACT THE INDUSTRY STRUCTURE?
8. PROMOTION	WHAT IS YOUR GO-TO-MARKET STRATEGY, CHANNELS AND DISTRIBUTION?
9. PRODUCT	WHAT IS YOUR PRODUCT, SERVICE, OFFERING AND/OR SOLUTION?
10. PROFIT	WHERE AND HOW DO YOU MAKE MONEY FOR COMPANY AND INVESTORS?

Most of these questions can be answered by anyone who has gone through the Innovation Cycle as we have described it in the previous chapters. While thorough answers to these questions could clearly fill the pages of a detailed business plan, this is not what we're after. We want an executive summary, a clear and succinct understanding of the key elements of the idea to identify the key sources of new value creation.

Quantifying the Amount of Value Created

Identifying new sources of value through the Ps and Qs helps us to begin to quantify that value. Now we can measure and classify it to know whether or not to incubate the new invention. We also want to quantify it across several different dimensions and understand what we are doing to create the value. To do this, we borrowed a

Figure 15

NEW VALUE CREATION MATRIX

	REMOVE	REDUCE	RETAIN	REFORM	REPLACE
COST	$100k IN AUDIOLOGIST	NA	$35k EXISTING DEVICE	NA	NA
CONVENIENCE	10 MIN TIME AUDIOLOGIST	NA	PATIENT TIME SAME		DOUBLE TIME HEARING AIDS
CONFIDENCE	HUMAN GEN REPORT	50% HUMAN ERROR		ARTIFICIAL INTELLIGENT	AUTOMATED REPORT
COMPENSATION	NA		EXISTING CODE	NA	$10k INCREASE REVENUES
CONNECTION	AUTO INTERACTION	NA	NA	CLOUD DATA AGGREGATION	SIMPLE, INTUITIVE, MODERN

NEW INVENTION VERSUS CURRENT ALTERNATIVES

framework I (Chris) had used in the energy industry to quantify the value generated from commodities and financial securities. We call this a New Value Creation Matrix. Here is how it works.

We look at five different dimensions in which we can produce new value: cost, convenience, confidence, compensation, and connection. We then look at what we are doing in each dimension to create the value, based on our Ps and Qs light business case. Are we removing something, reducing it, retaining it (which does not add new value), reforming something, or replacing it? The two dimensions at the extremes (remove and replace) enable radical and breakthrough innovations, but the ones in the middle are more aligned with incremental innovation. However, there are cases where, if we have enough incremental value creation mechanisms across many dimensions, they can, in total and in combination, be the basis for a radical or breakthrough innovation.

As illustrations of how this is done, see the following examples, one for the Otogram that we sold through Tympany and the other for Amazon's book business. One key point about using a new value creation matrix is to understand that few things have inherent and independent measurable worth. Value is almost always measured by comparing one thing to another.

In the case of the Tympany Otogram, this comparison pitted our automated hearing-testing product against the manual approach of an audiologist conducting a manual testing.

Tympany's Otogram New Value Creation Matrix

	Remove	Reduce	Retain
Confidence	Human-generated reports	Human error reduced by 50 percent by removing the audiologist and only retaining patient errors	Basic and accepted testing methodology
Compensation			Existing CPT payment codes
Convenience	30 minutes of audiologist's testing time Requirement, size, and cost of sound booth Audiologist constraints of time and language		Patient time to test remained the same
Connection	Audiologists' direct judgmental interaction with patient during testing		
Cost	$100K per year in audiologist costs and 1000 sq. ft. of space for sound booth		Tympany equipment costs the same as traditional equipment

Reform	Replace
Added artificial intelligence to improve accuracy	Created new standardized color-coded reports integrated in the electronic health records
	$30K in additional revenues for clinician; $100K in additional hearing aid sales
	Doubled the audiologist's time to treat patients and dispense hearing aids Testing in any quiet location Enabled testing 24/7/365 in 11 languages
Data aggregation and monitoring through cloud connectivity	Simple, intuitive non-judgmental interaction and relationship with the Otogram Sense of hi-tech, cutting-edge technology

With Amazon, we compared the online book business to the most successful bricks-and-mortar retail outlet: Barnes & Noble.

Amazon's Book Business New Value Creation Matrix

	Remove	Reduce	Retain
Confidence	Limited selection, uninformed sales clerks, comfortable seating, ability to touch books Shelf space limitations of 170K books	Number of books returned to retailer from 30 percent to less than 1 percent	Quality of books purchased and ability to return book for full refund
Compensation			
Connection			Created a virtual space to replicate the physical experience
Convenience	Restraints of store hours 9 a.m. to 9 p.m., immediate book ownership Physical store limitations (B&N had just 1,008 locations), rental space, and furniture	Time spent on searching for books or bookstores (2 hours) Inventory of books kept on hand	
Cost	10–30 percent lower than suggested retail		

Reform	Replace
Reputation for online service with 44 percent repeat customers, variety of different editions and specialty books	Intelligent online sales assistance, rich online reading experience, synopsis, 3rd party reviews 1.1 million book catalog
New one for small book stores to access a broader market to sell books	
Gathering place for communities, use computers at home instead of info desks	Ubiquitous location on the web
Expedited services at different price points, ease and speed to download on the web	24/7/356, one-day turnaround
Premium options for additional services like gift wrapping Inventory turnover increased from 2.7X to 70X	Shipping price per order $3.95

When using a new value creation matrix to quantify the type and source of the new value, try to quantify as many as possible. By quantifying them, you can use this information in the next step, which is creating value propositions.

Measuring the Value Across the Entire Value Proposition

The detailed output from the New Value Creation Matrix is used to craft the value proposition along the Five Cs of the value proposition. When crafting a value proposition, we found that people hold more confidence in value propositions that are based upon quantified and documented sources of value collected in a New Value Creation Matrix than mere platitudes.

Costs: How much can you decrease costs versus my current alternatives?

Convenience: How much easier is your solution than my alternatives?

Confidence: How much more accurate or better is your proposal than my alternatives?

Compensation: How much more money can people make over the alternatives?

Connection: How much more fashionable, cool, social, emotional, and avant-garde is it than the alternatives?

As we said before, people ascribe greater validity to quantified value propositions. For example, with the Otogram we found little enthusiasm for a value proposition that stated "We can decrease your testing costs and improve your testing accuracy." Instead,

Figure 16

FIVE C$ OF A VALUE PROPOSITION

	VALUE PROPOSITION
CO$T	HOW MUCH CAN YOU DECREASE COT AND PRICE VERSUS THE CURRENT ALTERNATIVES?
CONVENIENCE	HOW MUCH EASIER AND SIMPLER IS YOUR OFFERING OR SOLUTION VERSUS THE CURRENT ALTERNATIVES?
CONFIDENCE	HOW MUCH MORE ACCURATE, EFFECTIVE OR BETTER IS YOUR OFFERING OR SOLUTION VERSUS THE CURRENT ALTERNATIVES?
COMPENSATION	HOW MUCH MORE MONEY CAN PEOPLE MAKE SELLING OR SUPPORTING YOUR OFFERING OR SOLUTION VERSUS THE CURRENT ALTERNATIVES?
CONNECTION	HOW MUCH MORE FASHIONABLE, COOL, SOCIAL, EMOTIONAL, TECHNOLOGICALLY INTEROPERABLE, AND AVANT-GARDE IS YOUR OFFERING OR SOLUTION VERSUS THE CURRENT ALTERNATIVES?

more quantified and specific statements, such as the following, had more powerful effects:

The Otogram can

1. Decrease your hearing testing costs by 75 percent, or about $100,000 per year.

2. Increase the convenience for patients by testing in eleven languages and at any time of the day without an audiologist.

3. Deliver the 99 percent accuracy of an expert audiologist, based upon side-by-side clinical trials.

4. Increase your practice revenue by $30,000 per year in hearing testing and double your hearing aid sales to $100,000 per year.

5. Demonstrate that you are at the cutting edge of the hearing health technology field with an intuitive and elegant design

that connects the patient to the clinician and delivers a better user experience.

By simplifying the value proposition into these five elements and quantifying the value and its source, We found it makes it much easier to classify an innovation by simplifying the value proposition into these five elements and quantifying the value and its sources.

Classify the Innovation to See If It Requires an Incubator

Is it possible to objectively classify an innovation as incremental, breakthrough, or radical? Are these merely intuitive classifications? Or is it possible to quantify them? We consider an incremental innovation as one that gives limited value while a radical one produces a lot of value. But how much is a lot or a little?

This was an important question for us to answer when running our incubator. After identifying, quantifying, and measuring the new source of new value creation, we wanted to use this information to classify each innovation we reviewed and place it in a bucket. This way we could determine whether or not it was worth any additional focus for further development.

To gauge this new value creation potential and classification, we looked at innovations in the marketplace that existing companies launched and the new value they claimed to deliver. We paid attention to statements like "new and improved with 20 percent more. . . ." We also looked at new products that appeared to be very disruptive. On average, we saw they were delivering value that was at least 50 percent better than incumbents, and in many cases their increased value was a multiple of the existing solutions. For example, in the mobile telephone handset market, we saw exponential improvements from one generation to the next in storage,

Figure 17

THREE CLASSES OF INNOVATION ARE BASED UPON NEW VALUE CREATED OVER ALTERNATIVES

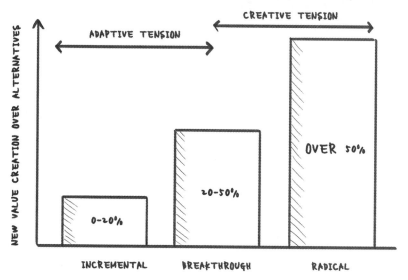

processing power, bandwidth, and peripherals as we moved from feature phones to smartphones. In contrast, incumbents who innovated incrementally never seemed able to successfully transition from the status quo to the next paradigm by merely improving things by 10–20 percent in each new version.

Based on this analysis, we decided to originate our own "bright lines" to demarcate and classify innovations as follows:

Incremental innovation creates 0–20 percent new sources of value over alternatives.

Breakthrough innovation creates 21–50 percent new sources of value over alternatives.

Radical innovation creates in excess of 51 percent new sources
of value over alternatives.

With this classification scale, we were ready to know what technology and new business models we believed required an incubator to make them successful (radical), which were on the bubble and might be worth our efforts (breakthrough), and which were clearly not going to be the focus of our attention (incremental).

The other insight we gained is that the more radical the innovation, the more likely it required a new and differentiated business model to bring it to market. In contrast, it makes sense to commercialize an incremental innovation through an existing business model. Breakthrough innovations can often go either way, but generally they come to market through more traditional means. Because radical innovations tend to be the most disruptive, they require new models that enable the innovators to harness all the capabilities and potential of the innovation.

Structuring an Incubator and Defining Its Practices

Making the right selection decisions about which technologies to incubate is only half the challenge. The other half is introducing the right supporting structures and practices to advance the invention and POC toward a launched MVP in the marketplace. To do so requires applying best practices for governance, processes, and people.

Scope and Scale Is Driven by Size and Need

Not all incubators are the same, so when creating an incubator, it is necessary to take into consideration the size and needs of the organization and stakeholders you represent. For example, an internal incubator of a global multinational corporation may need to span many industries, market segments, and product platforms across multiple countries. A small independent incubator will likely maintain a narrow focus on a single technology platform with a limited focus on selected programs. The scope and scale of the incubator will naturally be driven by these important organizational requirements. However, we have seen that the following best practices can apply regardless of scope and scale. The reason is that these represent the design elements and principles that can be thought of as modular in nature. They can be added in a Lego–building block manner to construct multiple modules to address the organization's needs.

Also, since incubation is one of the four phases of the Innovation Lifecycle, it applies to all successful innovations whether they are stand-alone innovations or performed within an incubator. A successful start-up will go through this growth phase and apply the same practices and structures outlined here. What we describe below is the application of the best practices that both start-ups and venture capital firms can use.

This is why we borrow and apply the approach of the Lean Start-Up.

Governance

An incubator will generally have three governance levels that address the strategic, portfolio, and operating management needs in moving creative ideas forward.

Strategic Innovation Board: This board identifies which technologies, geographies, market segments, and platforms to focus on. The overall strategy of the larger organization will usually govern and drive these decisions. This board will generally be comprised of senior leaders from within the larger organization and often include the CEO. This board seeks funding from the corporate board to fund the incubator and reviews budgets and key hiring decisions. In smaller and independent incubators, or in a lone start-up, the board of directors of the enterprise plays this role.

Advisory Board for Portfolio Management: The Advisory Board operates under the direction of the Strategic Innovation Board and focuses primarily on portfolio decisions, such as deciding which technologies and business models to fund, the level of funding for MVPs, staffing, MVP milestones, and conducting MVP milestone reviews. This board also determines whether or not to persevere down the current path or pivot to a new path and chart a new course because the current one is leading to a dead end. Members of this board will include a couple of executives from the senior incubator leadership. Often times the bulk of the members of this board come from outside the organization. They are there to increase objectivity, expand the scope of experience and talent, and access insights from other markets, industries, technologies, and companies (a.k.a. variation and interaction). These non–executive board members generally serve without compensation or for modest compensation and provide their services in exchange for learning about and getting exposure to cutting-edge innovations and thinking. This board allocates the funds for MVPs within the programs, whereas pivot or persevere decisions are made on a milestone basis.

Program Advisory Committee (PAC). This is an operating committee focused on the project management of MVPs within specific programs being incubated. This committee applies the Lean Start-Up discipline, a key element being Loop Reviews, where they review the progress of an MVP through the Innovation Cycle Loop. The members of this committee are the senior leadership of the incubator as well as the general managers of each innovation platform. They make the selection recommendations and present them to the Advisory Board. They manage the platform, the underlying programs within each platform, and the individual MVPs that test the program goals, objectives, hypotheses, technologies, markets, and opportunities. Program managers present their MVP ideas and plans to this committee for approval and funding. The program managers also provide MVP milestone updates and seek advice from the committee to decide whether to pivot or preserve.

Processes: Lean Start-Up, Innovation Cycle, and MVP Loops

The primary practices performed during incubation occur by applying the Lean Start-Up methodology in the Innovation Cycle to execute MVP. Each loop requires you to test your innovative ideas by going back and forth through all three rings in the Innovation Cycle (Becoming, Knowing, and Doing) in search of the best business model to launch the innovation. This process permits you to identify, quantify, measure, manage, and mitigate the technical, operational, and commercial risks of the innovation.

The Program Advisory Committee (PAC) imposes the Lean Start-Up methodology and discipline to ensure rapid learning through fast, frequent, and frugal failure in each MVP loop. Through periodic Innovation Cycle Loop reviews performed by the PAC for each of the four primary types of MVPs developed and executed during incubation, the team **moves the innovation forward through the lifecycle toward Accelerating.**

Conceptual MVP: This is where you take the creative idea and proof of concept and begin to test the value proposition and identify the technical requirements necessary to deliver it to the customer. This is often a paper or digital storyboard or electronic prototype that may have the look and feel of the future innovation but lacks the technical functionality. For example, in chapter 8 we discussed the water chemical company that formed an e-commerce site that looked like it had all the functionality of a robust site like Amazon. However, behind the scenes, people were performing manually all the operational functions expected from a fully automated e-commerce site. This was okay because this was all that was needed to test whether or not there was sufficient demand by customers for this type of offering. In this example, the value proposition was tested and then the outcome and learning was used to justify the investment to create a full functioning e-commerce offering.

Technical MVP: This is where you develop prototypes to determine if your innovation is technically feasible. You focus on those minimal technical requirements necessary to test the value proposition. This third-party test will or won't validate that your hypothesized value proposition can be technically delivered. A prototype can take many forms and need not be a complete operating prototype with all the technology stitched together. What this means is that the prototype is often ugly but works. For example, the first technical MVP of the Otogram looked awful, with wires hanging out all over it and various computer parts held together by wire and duct tape. But it worked and we were able to get several doctors to use and test the Otogram to validate that it performed as accurately as a human audiologist in measuring hearing loss.

Virtual Pilot MVP: It is possible to find that you can identify commercial risks of market adoption by conducting virtual pilots. In many situations, we developed agent-based computer simulations to test the configuration of our business model and the level of likely market adoption. For instance, we designed and configured original business models for a new pharmaceutical drug to see how patients, physicians, and payers would respond to two different business model offerings: (1) the traditional model of just a pill and (2) a broader program that added value beyond the pill to address a comprehensive set of needs associated with a health condition. Through a virtual pilot simulation, we were able to test the impact that various elements of the business model would have on patient adoption, physician prescriptions, and payer reimbursement. This allowed us to modify and refine our business model in a low-risk computer model environment prior to a commercial launch in a riskier real-world setting. Virtual pilots could also include any other type of low-cost and low-risk tests of a value proposition. As an example, providing your innovation through Kickstarter or Indiegogo is another low-risk way to test the value proposition by demonstrating the potential future offering but not actually delivering a physical working version to evaluate.

Pilot MVP: The purpose of incubation is to develop an inspired idea into an innovation that can be commercially tested through a new business model. This is generally done through a pilot MVP where a small sample of the target customer population experiments with the offering. Ideally, you want all elements of the business model to be tested. This means that the economic dimensions are operating and tied to the value propositions and supported by the capabilities to deliver it. For example, with Tympany we created MVPs that were demonstrated with all their features at trade shows. They were then sold at the show to a limited number of early adopters to test all aspects of the offering on a limited and controlled basis. Other examples include selecting a small sample of your employees as surrogates for future customers to test all the elements of your innovation and business model in a controlled environment. For instance, one of our clients wanted to bring a new disease management solution to the market, but they decided first to see if it actually worked with their own employees. So they included their health insurance company in the pilot to test the economics of the solution. The company provided economic and other incentives to their employees to use it and provided all the supporting capabilities to deliver it. By so doing, they were able to identify the many failures and risks that needed to be addressed before they brought it to market.

People

In the Discovery phase of the Innovation Lifecycle, we explained that most of the people involved in social innovation are doing this on a part-time basis and retain their day jobs. The exception is the small innovation support team that helps various parts of the organization apply innovation tools, methods, and processes to tap into everyone's creative genius. This is a highly leveraged model where you are trying to generate hundreds and thousands of imaginative ideas that, in a large organization, could possibly yield ten or twenty candidates to be incubated.

Incubating is different. In incubating, you deal with just a few ideas with people who are fully committed to moving these through the four types of MVPs to continually test the offerings within the program and drive the learning process. The following are the key roles, responsibilities, and expectations during incubation.

Program General Manager: This person owns the overall program that may have within it several underlying programs. As a sample, look at many of the new healthcare incubators. They generally focus on a specific area, such as mobile healthcare. This defines the focus of their program. The Program General Manager is then the CEO of these small and focused incubators and is part of the selection process. This person is also part of the PAC and ensures that Lean Start-Up discipline is applied. Within larger corporate incubators, there could be several Program General Managers focused on separate platform areas of focus. Under each will often be several programs, each run by a separate Program Manager, focused on different and individualized value propositions and requiring unique capabilities, stakeholder segments, and revenue models.

Program Manager: Think of this person as the CEO of a start-up. He or she owns the responsibility for moving the team through the three rings of the Innovation Cycle. This includes moving the potential innovative offering through the four types of MVPs. Then the person leads the decision process on whether to persevere or pivot, based on market feedback on the MVPs. This person must have very strong project management and leadership skills and remain undaunted in what is often considered irrational outlook, enthusiasm, passion, and vision in order to drive the program forward, despite very long odds of success.

Program Teams: The small cross-disciplinary teams should consist of three to five members. Often the group is a bit of a virtual team for several reasons. Some of these team members may have some specific skills, experience, and talents that may not be needed on a full-time basis on any one program and can be of value across programs. Therefore they will split their time across multiple programs. In other situations, team members may be more of a subject matter expert or advisor with a full-time day job in or outside the organization, who supports the program as needed. You also often find that the people with the best skills and experience are not located at the same site, so you need them to operate as a virtual team across geographies and time zones.

Ready to Accelerate

A successful incubator will generally kill two-thirds of all ideas and POCs it initially accepts. This means that for every ten ideas that move along the Innovation Lifecycle from Discovery to Incubation, only three will survive the four MVPs loop reviews and be ready to be accelerated. In this next phase of the lifecycle, a full-time team will operate the new venture as a commercial enterprise. The team will aggressively search for the best business model configurations necessary to achieve rapid revenue and profit growth. Once it locks into that business model that enables stable and predictable operating performance, it is ready to be scaled.

The next chapter will describe how to move from your hybrid to your road bike and then accelerate growth in the next phase of the Innovation Lifecycle. You will be pushing yourselves to accelerate and increase your biking speed to a faster, more stable, and predictable rate. Doing so will validate the business model you will need to scale your innovation and achieve significant success.

Figure 18

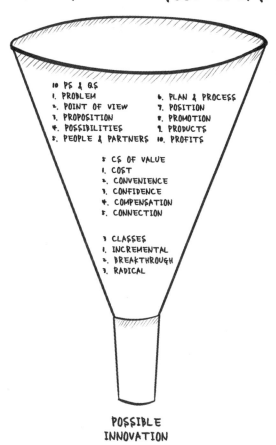

10:5:3:1 TO IDENTIFY AND SELECT GOOD IDEAS

10 PS & QS
1. PROBLEM
2. POINT OF VIEW
3. PROPOSITION
4. POSSIBILITIES
5. PEOPLE & PARTNERS
6. PLAN & PROCESS
7. POSITION
8. PROMOTION
9. PRODUCTS
10. PROFITS

5 CS OF VALUE
1. COST
2. CONVENIENCE
3. CONFIDENCE
4. COMPENSATION
5. CONNECTION

3 CLASSES
1. INCREMENTAL
2. BREAKTHROUGH
3. RADICAL

POSSIBLE
INNOVATION

REMEMBER

✔ Most of our creative efforts yield improvements or incremental innovations that can often quickly and simply be added to our existing structures and practices.

✔ Only 10–15 percent of creative and novel ideas have the potential to be breakthrough or radical innovations, that is, ones that provide a meaningful new source of value. That's why every novel idea isn't radical or breakthrough.

✔ These more promising potential innovations require incubators to de-risk them and move them forward along the Innovation Lifecycle. Incubators are structures with the appropriate governance, process, and people to ensure the discipline to continue fast, frequent, frugal failure on a larger scale than was done during Discovery.

✔ Because incubating requires flexibility to move back and forth through the Innovation Lifecycle, a hybrid bike is used.

✔ There are ten primary elements that can summarize the value of an opportunity. They are called the Ten Ps and Qs of New Value Creation.

✔ The New Value Creation Matrix, in turn, uses cost, convenience, confidence, compensation, and connection to assess how value can be produced.

✔ The best practices that organization can use involve governance, processes to build, measure, and learn if a MVP will work, and people in specific jobs—including Program General Manager, Program Manager, and Program Teams.

—————————— QUESTIONS ——————————

> How well do you use a structured incubation process to eliminate the technical risks associated with new ideas?

> How disciplined is your incubation process to describe new opportunities, understand their source of new value creation, and measure the impact for your customers and business?

> How well do you apply a fast, frequent, frugal failure discipline in your incubation and other innovative efforts?

CHAPTER ELEVEN

Accelerating Success

Y ou've come a long way. The incubation of your innovation is a success. Technical risks were eliminated. An initial business model was selected, and a trial launch completed. Your innovation is now ready for the growth phase known as Accelerating. It is time to continually experiment to find, create, and invent the business model you think can scale.

And here is the reality: *your first business model will fail.* But that's okay. The key is to fail fast, adjust, adapt, iterate, and re-launch quickly.

Innovations at this stage of development are always in search of the right business model that can scale. But it is never obvious up front during incubating what that business model should be. You do your homework and think you have it figured out, but as Sun Tzu wrote in *The Art of War,* no plan survives contact with the enemy. The same is true of early business models. Initial business models are generally too complicated and complex. They lack the simple elegance of more refined innovations and business models that have the potential to scale.

In this chapter we will share our approach to business model innovation and reveal how we and others apply this Business Model Innovation and Transformation (BMIT) framework to accelerate and realize commercial success.

Biking Up and Down in New England

Acceleration reminds me (Chris) of bike rides in New England. Being on a road bike in very hilly terrain requires the rider to constantly shift gears to adapt to the undulating network of small and narrow roads. The heavily forested lanes make it almost impossible to find one's bearings and know directional coordinates and distance.

On these rides, all kinds of challenges will be experienced. There will be long steady climbs of a mile or so where one can't get above 10 mph. Short, steep climbs might take the rider down to 5 mph. But on the flat straightaways, it's possible to accelerate to nearly 30 mph. On steep downhills, speeds of over 40 mph are not unusual.

Biking on any new route on these country roads is impossible to predict. You need to be prepared for anything. You must be flexible, agile, and adaptable. This requires you to constantly shift gears, using both the big and little rings.

Going downhill allows you to go the fastest and is the most invigorating, but it is also the most dangerous. It is easy to lose your perspective, and with your eyes watering from the wind so you can't see well, you lose control and crash. I have seen the same thing with start-ups that seem to achieve early easy success that can lead to catastrophic failure.

All these experiences in New England biking are repeated in the Accelerating phase of innovative growth. Because you are always in search of the best business model, you are constantly changing rings and gears to adapt. It's necessary to constantly shift back and forth between the Knowing and Doing rings in order to fine-tune and experiment with your business models. And many times, when you think you have found the best business models because they enable you to go fast, you find them to be dangerously unsustainable.

What Is a Business Model?

Just as there are many different and conflicting definitions of innovation, the same phenomenon exists when discussing business models. When most people talk about a business model, they are really referring to the revenue model and how a company and innovation ring the register. But a business model is much more than just the revenue it generates.

We developed the BMIT framework to simplify a business model into its four primary dimensions—capabilities, stakeholders, benefits, and economic impact—that answer the four main questions you need to ask:

- How we play?
- Who we play with?
- Why we win?
- What we win?

Capabilities: How We Play?

What capabilities are required to generate value? Capabilities represent the primary inputs to a business model and are defined as a set of actions that create value and support the delivery of the value proposition from the customer's perspective. Capabilities are comprised of technology features, key activities to deliver these features, resources and the associated governance necessary to support and create those features, and relationships with customers to deliver the capabilities and their associated value.

Stakeholders: Who We Play With?

Which stakeholders are involved with and impacted by the business model? Stakeholders include customers (who can be, both separately or combined, buyers, users, or beneficiaries of the value proposition), partners who support the value proposition, and channels to communicate, educate, and deliver the value proposition.

Benefits: Why We Win?

What are the differentiated value proposition benefits that the business model provides to each of its stakeholders? The core premise of the benefits is to eliminate pain points, waste, and failure or to provide new opportunities. All these are delivered through customer experiences that yield value that can generally be described by the five value creating elements: cost, convenience, confidence, compensation, and connection.

Economic Impact: What We Win?

What is the expected economic impact of the business model? This is driven by three underlying elements: the costs required to operate the business model and deliver the value proposition, the structure and nature of the margin earned above these costs based upon the level and type of differentiation, and the revenue streams based upon the revenue models used.

All of these dimensions and elements are used in designing and configuring the initial business model in Incubating. As you see, they are also all in play during Accelerating as you seek to discover the best business model for scaling. This iterative approach to BMIT, see the figure below, is similar to the MVP approach when developing your product. But here the product may remain the same and the MVP becomes the business model.

Figure 19
BUSINESS MODEL INNOVATION AND TRANSFORMATION (BMIT) FRAMEWORK

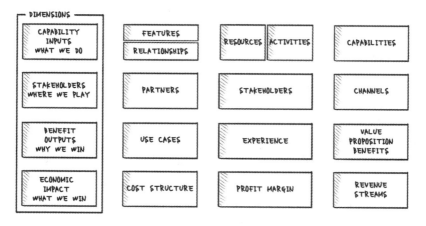

Here are two examples, one with our company Tympany and another from Fitbit, one of the earliest and most successful digital health ventures.

Tympany's Struggle to Discover the Best Business Model

The razor–razor blade business model has generated the most value in the medical device industry over the years, attracted the most venture capital, and set the expectations for many start-ups. This is because companies were able to make money on the sale of their initial device (the razor) and then earn recurring revenues every time it was used (the razor blade). A classic example is the simple glucometer used to measure blood sugar levels. It has two components, a device, the glucometer, and the disposable strips used to collect the blood necessary to measure the glucose with the device. So this was the type of business model we attempted to launch after we completed our incubation and started selling our first Otograms.

MVP 1: Razor/Razor Blade: This is how it looked for us. We charged $25,000 for the Otogram device, and then planned to charge $1,000 per year for calibration services and $5 per patient for disposable foam testing ear inserts, with the expectation that a customer would test about a thousand patients per year. This would allow us to generate a total annuity of $6,000. To put our prices in the context of the client's revenue-generating potential with our device: 1,000 tests per year would generate $160,000 in reimbursement. They paid us $25,000 for the device and $6,000 annually for the annuity items. It was not quite like giving away the razor for free in order to make money on the blades, but given this very strong value proposition for physicians, we were clearly trying to push things in that direction.

We had two problems. First, we didn't manufacture the ear inserts, although we tried to be the supplier to our clients. Unfortunately these disposables were broadly available in the market at deeply discounted prices. We tried doing some individual packaging with per-patient-use bags to differentiate our offerings versus buying a big bag of hundreds or thousands, but we struggled to get traction with this type of approach. We found some clients washing the earwax out of the inserts to save the $5 we charged per test on inserts on the $160 reimbursed test they administered.

Our second problem was that they didn't really value our calibration services and felt that this service should cost no more than the $500 calibration fees others charged to service other manual testing devices. They couldn't figure out why we would charge twice as much for our device.

As a young company of inexperienced entrepreneurs, we found ourselves sucked into discussions and rationalizations about pricing based on costs not value. Clearly we were delivering abundant value to our customers, but the amount of value we extracted was very small. When the customers would start a time-and-materials debate with us to see how they could beat us down on price, we often caved. So we decided to pivot from this model to one focused on delivering and paying for the value of a solution.

MVP 2: Bundled Solution: Rather than get caught in these debates about cost and time, we came up with a new business model where customers would not buy the Otogram but lease it on a per-use basis. Here they would only pay for as much of the Otogram as they used, and only if they created value from it. For example, the customer would enter into a pay-per-use contract where the Otogram would keep track of the number and type of tests performed and automatically send this data to the Cloud on a daily basis. Then we would send clients a monthly bill. So for a $160 reimbursed test, we charged $30. The client had no up-front costs and earned an 80 percent margin on each test.

While this appealed to some customers, those that expected to do a lot of testing didn't like this model, because they realized they could save money by purchasing it outright. The offering appealed more to those that were less familiar with this type of testing and were more likely to be timid and therefore not really focused on maximizing the potential of the technology. This meant less revenues for both of us, since the machines weren't generating as much income as possible, and so we didn't earn our expected volume of per-procedure fees. There were several devices we were forced to take out of doctors' offices because their testing volumes were too low for us to make money on this model. The irony is that the doctors were leaving a lot of money on the table. But because this was a new offering, they weren't accustomed to doing it and thus it wasn't at the top of their priorities. Our previous business model of selling doctors the Otogram ensured they had enough skin in the game to make use of it, while our bundled solution offering looked more like a free option, which they didn't value.

MVP 3: Total Solution: In our third iteration, we tried to focus on a broader value proposition of hearing health and not just diagnostic testing. We looked at how hearing loss was both diagnosed and treated and found ways to integrate the technology into this broader value proposition. We also looked at the value this technology could deliver to hearing aid dispensers, audiologist clinics, and ENT physicians in identifying and generating new customers.

In this business model, we used these hearing health professionals as both customers and channel partners. They would buy our Otograms, put them into primary-care physician offices, train them how to use it, and in some instances provide a testing technician to do the testing and patient management. In return for this, the patients tested in the primary-care office that needed further treatment would be referred to the hearing health professional's practice.

This was a win-win for everyone. We could sell our technology on a per-use basis and decrease the capital outlay for the hearing health professional. They became an extension of our sales force. They were able to provide value-added service for the physicians. And they were able to capture the downstream solution and treatment revenues.

It was this last business model that excited the hearing aid medical device company that bought Tympany. They saw the technology and related total solution business model as a new channel for selling their hearing aids.

We ended up selling our company before we were ready to scale. Nonetheless, our different MVPs brought us increasingly closer to a model we felt could scale by delivering greater value to all the stakeholders. During this growth phase, we were constantly experimenting with and refining our business models, developing new benefits and capabilities, and trying to target specific business models for different customer segments.

Fitbit and the Emergence of Digital Health Business Models

In 2007 a team of engineers and health and wellness entrepreneurs approached more than sixty-one venture capitalists (VCs) with an novel idea: what if they provided consumers with a small digital pedometer that would tell them how active they were? It could also be connected to the Cloud to allow them to share their activity information with friends, family, and healthcare providers. They could provide analytics to create and improve the feedback loop and encourage people to be more active and to eat better. In short, it could be part of a cure for the exploding global obesity crisis related to diabetes and heart disease that represent most of the deaths and costs of today's healthcare system.

Sixty VCs turned them down. These VCs couldn't see consumers paying a hundred dollars out of their own pocket for this device, nor did they think it feasible that theses entrepreneurs could pull together a social community to share the information and motivate consumers to be healthier. The VCs who understood healthcare and incentives knew that it was almost impossible to get overweight and obese patients to change their habits and behaviors. They fully expected this new device, called the Fitbit, to be a failure.

MVP 1: Good Enough: One VC heard the story and thought it had some merit and gave the team $2 million for a 50 percent stake in the company. With this, the team created a device that retailed for $100 and cost about $10 to make. While these margins seem impressive, the initial device was buggy and unreliable. It frequently fell apart. It couldn't survive the abuse of average consumers. The mobile app wasn't native on either of the two dominant mobile device platforms, which meant it was just a mobile instance of the company's web page and delivered a mediocre-to-poor user experience. Still, the MVP device was good enough to test the market and clearly better than any of the alternatives also testing the market. Soon the Fitbit began to get some consumer traction.

MVP 2: Better User Experience and Execution: The team focused on execution of the initial launched device to increase quality and customer services. They developed a very flexible and lenient replacement policy so that customers would have a good experience even when their device broke. They focused on decreasing production costs to $5 per unit while improving quality. With 95 percent margins on their product, they had lots of room to invest to make happy customers. They created a native app version of their software to further improve the customer experience. They also began to provide interoperable application programming interfaces (APIs) to third parties and the ability to use other APIs to provide an interoperable data exchange capability to share information back and forth. These features further improved customer experience and developed a mutually beneficial and reinforcing network and ecosystem in the digital health market among their partners. This all led to significant customer and revenue growth that, in turn, enabled them to obtain greater traction so they could raise $9 million of VC funding.

MVP 3: New Channels and Expanded Features: Then they began to focus on many new channels for distribution through retailers like BestBuy and through employers and health plans that wanted to use this device to augment their wellness programs. The team began to add more features and services. For example, they added an altimeter to the accelerometer to measure stairs climbed as well as steps taken. (We burn four times more calories going up stairs than walking on flat ground.) They added sleep tracking because sleep has a large impact on diet and weight loss. They began to partner with other health and wellness app companies to add Fitbit data and calories burned to nutrition apps so users could better budget their eating behaviors. They first integrated with digital wireless scales and then eventually added their own scale so they could provide more parts to the solution. They provided an analytics services for an annual fee of $15, and they continued to drive down their cost of manufacturing to $4 per unit.

MVP 4: Expanded Offering: Their success began to inspire competitors that were competing on many dimensions and elements of the business model. To address this, they developed the next version of their flagship premium product, dubbed the Fitbit One, along with the Fitbit Zip, a lower-priced version that included new products with different form factors. They also added an online premium coaching service for $15 per year to support people in achieving their weight-loss goals. They also began to partner with employers in using the Fitbit to promote greater engagement among employees by tying an employee's insurance premium to the number of Fitbit steps they took. They worked with organizations like Aetna in its efforts to build its digital health platform called CarePass so that a larger community could benefit from the seamless collection and integration of their fitness and wellness information. This additional market traction helped them to raise $12 million of additional VC funding.

MVP 5: Approaching Scaling: They had now become the most visible and highly integrated digital health device on the market. Many employers and health plans were integrating the Fitbit technology into their broader solutions. Healthcare providers like the Mayo Clinic were integrating the technology into clinical medical trials to demonstrate the value of activity in recovering from surgery. Cardiovascular prevention programs began to incorporate the Fitbit as a prescribed medical device that the practice monitored daily to provide coaching to patients focused on weight loss and better cardiovascular health. All this traction enabled the company to raise an additional $30 million of VC financing and valued the company at $300 million just five years after its initial launch.

Fitbit provides a clear example of how all elements of the business model are constantly in play during Acceleration. Pricing models and services change, customer segments and channels grow and overlap. Features keep changing to develop the set required to deliver on expanding value propositions. All this requires the company to constantly expand and upgrade its capabilities.

Business Model Versus Technology Innovation

Too often, too much time is focused on technology innovation and too little on how to innovate and transform the business model. The reality is that the most successful companies are the ones that use technology innovation to invent new and transform old business models. Disruptive companies seek to find ways to leverage new technologies in ways that alter many or most of the business model dimensions and elements. They do so to find new markets and alter competitive dynamics that change the playing field, giving them a comparative and competitive advantage over incumbents and new entrants.

A classic example of how new technologies can facilitate the transformation of a business model is the role that social, mobile, analytic, and Cloud technologies (the aforementioned SMAC) are being used to create new business models focused on delivering a total solution that generates greater value.

For instance, General Electric (GE) used these technologies to change its business model in the aircraft engine market from selling expensive pieces of equipment to selling uptime, that is, the number of hours the jets are used. They realized their customers really didn't want to buy jet engines. What they really wanted was reliable and safe propulsion. In response, GE changed their business model to deliver this total solution. By so doing, they now provide all elements of the propulsion products and services necessary to keep planes flying. Their customers pay them for uptime. This has required a total rethinking of risk and risk management on the company's part. They needed to add many mobile sensors to their engines that continuously monitor and share information via the Cloud. Analytics on this data are run to gain insights that allow them to predict and prevent adverse, costly, and dangerous events. They aggregate these data, information, and insights in order to see patterns across a broad network of customers, geographies, use cases, and experiences to gain further insights that lead to new technology innovation and design.

The same phenomenon is playing out in industry after industry. By applying social network, mobile sensor, and communication, along with analytic tools, Cloud data archiving, and sharing, business models are being radically transformed. The most profound impact of these technologies have been documented in travel, media, publishing, entertainment, banking, finance, retailing, and telecommunications. But now the lessons learned in these industries are impacting the new emerging business models in industries that carry a reputation for being the last to adopt new information technology. One of those industries is healthcare.

Owning the Disease: Healthcare Business Model Innovation

Innovative healthcare leaders that studied business model innovation enabled by SMAC have started to construct similar models that focus on delivering customized, integrated, and comprehensive solutions to address the various challenges found in healthcare. We call this new business model *owning the disease*, because it allows a healthcare company to deliver a total solution that solves a health-related problem. It gives them the ability to be paid for delivering outcomes and value rather than being paid for merely the volume of pills or devices sold or procedures performed.

An interesting example of an owning-the-disease business model comes from Merck Serono in the growth hormone therapy market.

Merck Serono was struggling to make a profit in the generic drug growth hormone market. They were close to last place in their field, with 10 percent of the market share and losing money. Their leadership expected they would be forced to exit the business to stop the hemorrhaging of cash. The managing director of the business realized he had few options and little time to turn things around. He also knew that since they were competing in a generic product market with five other companies, he couldn't improve his fortunes by focusing on the drug. Instead, he had to create value beyond the pill and deliver a highly differentiated program that could leverage SMAC to offer a solution through a new business model.

MVP 1: Mobile Connectivity and Insight: Merck Serono began asking the Five Whys to understand why patients who used their generic growth hormone drug did not have better outcomes and consistent performance. They asked questions about how the drug must be injected, ways in which patients or physicians can do it poorly, and why people forget or neglect to do the procedure. They continued this line of inquiry until they came upon their first MVP for a new business model solution.

They realized if they could provide a mobile device that could do the injection in the patient's home—remotely controlled and monitored by a nurse in a call center who could intervene by either communicating directly with the patient or by manipulating the mobile drug injection device—they could get better outcomes.

Therefore they invented a new mobile medical device called the EasyPod that would inject the drug into the patient and could be controlled remotely. A nurse would take the EasyPod to a patient's home, install it, and show the patient how to use it. Next, they had nurses in a call center provide the monitoring and management services to help achieve better adherence to and manipulation of the EasyPod device to get better results from the drug.

The outcome from this MVP was that all these patients experienced significantly higher levels of adherence and much better health outcomes. With this data in hand, they approached the healthcare payer to ask if they could be paid a premium over the traditional drug price for health outcomes using their program rather than for the volume of drugs they sold.

The payer said they would be willing to provide this upside benefit if the company would be willing to accept the downside risk associated with patients who didn't perform as well.

MVP 2: Predicting and Preventing Risk: To manage both the upside and downside risk, the company realized it needed to eliminate from the program any patients who did not have the genomic and physiological profile to benefit from their drug. Consequently, they invented a molecular diagnostic screening device that they gave to physicians for free. The goal was to test all growth hormone therapy patients to know whether or not the Merck Serono drug would work for them.

This addition to their business model worked very well and enabled the company and doctors to predict with near certainty who would benefit from getting the drug. The company then provided their devices and call center services to the physician and patient for free to improve adherence. The company also provided free in-office nurse consulting services to help the physician practices to better manage these patients. They collected the data generated from the diagnostic, device, and services to perform analytics to continually fine-tune their business model and provide the electronic health record information to support their payments.

MVP 3: Selling the Program, Not the Pill: Through an iterative business model innovation approach that took some incubated technologies and then incorporated them into progressive versions of a new business model, Merck Serono was able to move toward solutions where they were selling a program, not just a pill. This was in a generic drug market where the traditional view was that the only dimension of competition and differentiation was price. However, by creating and selling a total-solution program, Merck Serono was able to increase its market share from 10 percent to 50 percent. It turned its losses into a 20-percent profit margin, and they found their program so attractive to physicians that it literally sold itself, thereby requiring a minimal direct sales effort.

There are a few other noteworthy insights from this company's business model innovation. They never replaced the doctor in the delivery of care. Instead, they delivered many free services and technologies in a new business model to the physician and patient. They didn't charge either for the molecular diagnostic, the EasyPod, the call center service, the nurse visits, or the data analytics and integration. All of these were free. What they did was provide a single invoice to the payer that showed how their performance exceeded the benchmark of their competitors, and they were paid for the additional value they delivered based upon patient outcomes.

Many other healthcare organizations are now transforming their business models toward a solution like this to leverage the innovative power of SMAC. They are starting solutions units, divisions, and teams. These include pharmaceutical, medical device, provider, and payer organizations. Additionally, new entrants into healthcare see this type of business model innovation based on SMAC technologies as key to their becoming a disruptor in the market.

The key to success for all these organizations, however, is to realize that they are in the Accelerating phase of the Innovation Lifecycle. Their first business model will fail and must be continually iterated and improved before they discover the one they can scale.

Business Model Innovation and Transformation Process

The challenge most companies face is that they possess only a framework and process for innovating technologies and not business models. So not only do leaders need to be ambidextrous in being both mindfully innovative and mindlessly efficient in promoting a Lean Start-Up and Lean Six Sigma approach to growth and operation, but they must also be ambidextrous within innovation to pursue both technology and business model innovations.

We have identified ten challenges leadership faces when promoting this kind of ambidextrous approach to technology and business model innovation.

1. Expanding the value proposition for customers is the crucial part of business model innovation. This requires both a more focused effort on innovation and a greater tolerance for risk

and failure, because your first new business model will fail. You will only be able to achieve success during Acceleration by constantly exploring better business model choices that expand the value proposition.

2. Concern about destroying cultures that have been successful in the past is merited, but business model innovation ultimately entails the creation of a new, convergent culture to generate new sources of value for customers. Because new business models require new stakeholders, capabilities, and benefits, along with different economics, the culture of the organization must change. The challenge is doing this in a productive manner to avoid maladaptive tensions while at the same time harnessing creative ones.

3. Business model innovation entails breaking down silos to better understand customers' total needs while decreasing the complexity in providing solutions. Many companies look at their broad-based capabilities and conclude they possess all the necessary pieces to build and deliver a better business model. Yet when they try to execute, they fail because the existing business model has generated severe organizational barriers to transformation.

4. Scale matters in business model innovation, but not in the way many expect. Some large organizations may find it difficult to transform their business model because they are too large and complex, too divided into silos, and unable to leverage resources. This is why we see new entrants and start-ups as more disruptive business model innovators than incumbents. The latter have too much scale and can't harness it effectively.

5. Business model transformation changes a business model from selling products and services to selling solutions. As a result, the mix of revenues will gradually shift to a roughly

equal split between products and services, where information will become the key differentiator and driver. In discussions with many leaders, we find they will agree in the need for them to move to solutions and services. However, then they confess that the transition is too painful because it results in maladaptive tensions, and they lack the ability to transform these into creative tensions that lead to innovation.

6. Business model innovation and transformation is generally a platform strategy. It requires you to control the platform core and at the same time interoperate with a broad set of partners that provide various types of peripherals that enable the total solution. This also means that a new business model can enable you to control channels so the company becomes the essential conduit and platform through which others sell their products.

7. Information and analytics strategy drives business model transformation. As value migrates from physical things (atoms) to digital information (bits), organizations that harness data most effectively will have a competitive advantage. This requires rethinking what data and information are and where they come from by building a sophisticated SMAC technology networks. Then it is necessary to harness SMAC capabilities to collect, archive, and curate data in the Cloud, where you draw insights and action through analytics.

8. Business model innovation and transformation is not a diversification play. Instead, it is focused on integration and cooperation to bring an integrated solution to the customer. The key is not possessing or owning all the capabilities but integrating them (both your own and those of your partners) into a synthesized solution that delivers a new value proposition.

9. The application of SMAC often requires you to think very differently about where, when, and how to target economic impact. For example, many new business models are not B2B or B2C or B2B2C but instead B2C2B, where the value proposition is delivered to a consumer for free through some kind of free digital data hook. Then, once these free hooks enable you to achieve critical mass, you find creative ways to monetize that data, information, insight, relationship, and opportunity.

10. Analytics are the secret sauce to business model transformation because the key to success is better risk management by predicting risk and then knowing how to either mitigate or take advantage of it. The challenge in creating analytics is mashing up a comprehensive set of underlying data and information (much of which must come from third party and public sources) needed for studying and developing the tools through computer modeling, simulation, system dynamics, agent-based design, etc. to draw insights, change feedback loops, and improve performance.

Organizations and leaders who can overcome these ten challenges associated with transforming and innovating their business models will be paying the PRICE necessary for success:

- **P**redict the risks customers face in their business or face personally and provide solutions to mitigate and manage them. This means leveraging SMAC to predict, prevent, and manage risk is the primary purpose of big data-based strategies. Business model simulations can help to de-risk business models during incubating and accelerating before you launch and iterate them in real life.

- **R**un a doubly ambidextrous organization that has both a Lean Start-Up innovation operating model and a Lean Six Sigma operational efficiency model as well as the ability to do both technology and business model innovation. Most organizations limit innovation to R&D. Today, companies need an operating model that requires innovation to emerge and develop across and throughout the enterprise so that the business model innovates too.

- **I**ncentivize people to do the right thing. This means rewarding failure, which ironically also means rewarding people for always telling the truth, even if it does not result in sales and profits. Incentives need to focus on experimentation, learning, trial and error, rapid iterations, and selling solutions (that often include products and services from others). For example, some employers require their employees to engage in innovation challenges (outlined in chapter 8) with certain threshold constraints of performance. One is that the idea must improve performance by at least 10 percent above the current threshold. To not penalize employees for failure, which is the most common outcome of most innovative endeavors, they rate an employee as successful if the person completed the challenge and failed. Employees who achieve the 10 percent performance threshold are rated "exceeds expectations," and those who do even better are rated "outstanding."

- **C**onverge mindlessness and mindfulness. See them as being symbiotic to enable you to support successful identities to drive efficiency to provide the resources for growth *and* create new identities that will become the future engines of growth at both the individual and organizational levels.

- **E**xpand programs, products, and services into solutions on a common platform. This requires co-creating and delivering solutions with partners and channels on a common technology and operating platform and applying a comprehensive business model innovation framework to design and simulate converged offerings.

People, Process, and Governance in Accelerating

Unlike the virtual and supporting teams and organizations outlined in the Discovery and Incubation phases of the Innovation Lifecycle, Acceleration requires a full-time team. During this phase you are in the market, constantly searching for the best business model to accelerate the growth of your innovation. This requires a venture capital board governance structure that provides some flexibility not found with more traditional Lean Six Sigma governance. It must also provide mentoring, coaching, and insights from those who have accelerated businesses themselves. Generally, large organizations won't have these kinds of people and will need to recruit volunteers or partners to help provide this type of governance and impose the Lean Start-Up approach to innovating the business model.

Moving to Measuring Innovative Outcomes

In the final chapter in the Doing section we will outline how you can know if your innovation operating model is working and how, when, and where you can provide the discipline necessary to improve it. Innovation requires measurement to manage it, just like any other discipline. The challenge is that they are different measures than are normally used for running the businesses of today.

REMEMBER

✔ All good ideas and potential innovations struggle to find the right business model to drive their commercial success.

✔ While your first business model will likely fail, the key is to fail fast, adjust, adapt, iterate, and re-launch quickly.

✔ The most successful companies use technology innovation to transform their business model.

✔ All business models are comprised of four dimensions: stakeholders, capabilities, benefits, and economics.

✔ The Business Model Innovation and Transformation (BMIT) framework describes the underlying elements of all four dimensions and how they all interoperate to drive commercialization of new innovations.

✔ Therefore companies must pursue both technology and business model innovation.

✔ The BMIT enables you to pay the PRICE necessary for success:

> **P**redict the risks that arise from failure, pain, and tension that customers face in their businesses or consumers face personally and then provide innovative solutions to mitigate and manage them.

> **R**un a doubly ambidextrous organization that has both a Lean Start-Up innovation operating model and a Lean Six Sigma operational efficiency model as well as the ability to do both technology and business model innovation.

› **I**ncentivize people to do the right thing. This means rewarding failure, which ironically also means rewarding people for always telling the truth even if it does not result in sales and profits.

› **C**onverge mindlessness and mindfulness. Seeing these as symbiotic enables you to both *support* successful identities to drive efficiency to provide resources for growth and *create* new identities that will become the future engines of growth at both the individual and organizational levels.

› **E**xpand your disciplines beyond Lean Six Sigma and provide programs, products, and services that can deliver solutions on a common platform.

Figure 20

BUSINESS MODEL INNOVATION AND TRANSFORMATION CANVAS FOR DESIGNING NEW BUSINESS MODELS

STAKEHOLDERS		
CUSTOMERS	**PARTNERS**	**CHANNELS**
CUSTOMERS REPRESENT THOSE THAT CAN BUY, USE, OR BENEFIT FROM THE VALUE PROPOSITION, WHICH CAN BE FOCUSED ON MASS MARKETS, NICHE MARKETS, SEGMENTED MARKETS, DIVERSIFIED OFFERINGS OR MULTI-SIDED PLATFORMS	PARTNERS ARE STAKEHOLDERS THAT SUPPORT THE VALUE PROPOSITION BY ENABLING: OPTIMIZATION AND ECONOMY OF SCALE, REDUCTION OF RISK AND UNCERTAINTY, ACQUISITION OF PARTICULAR RESOURCES AND ACTIVITIES	CHANNELS PROVIDE THE PATH TO COMMUNICATE, EDUCATE, DELIVER AND SUPPORT THE VALUE PROPOSITION TO VARIOUS STAKEHOLDERS

ECONOMIC		
COST STRUCTURE	**REVENUE STREAM**	**PROFIT MARGIN**
THE COSTS NECESSARY TO CREATE THE INPUTS AND OUTPUTS FOR THE STAKEHOLDERS	THE CASH GENERATED FROM EACH PERSON/CUSTOMER FOR VALUE DELIVERED THROUGH THE BUSINESS MODEL	THE MARGIN ADDED TO COSTS TO GENERATE REVENUES AND BASED UPON VALUE ADDED IN EXCESS OF CURRENT ALTERNATIVES IN THE MARKET

CAPABILITIES		
SOLUTION DESIGN	**RESOURCE/ACTIVITIES**	**CAPABILITIES**
FEATURES HELP IDENTIFY OR NAME MULTIPLE TECHNOLOGIES THAT ENABLE A USAGE TO BE REALIZED. RELATIONSHIPS DESCRIBE THE TYPE OF INTERACTION YOU HAVE WITH A PERSON THAT DRIVES ENGAGEMENT AND SUSTAINABILITY.	KEY RESOURCES TO MAKE THE BUSINESS MODEL WORK, PROVIDE CAPABILITIES AND DELIVER THE VALUE PROPOSITION KEY ACTIVITIES TO MAKE THE BUSINESS MODEL WORK, PROVIDE CAPABILITIES AND DELIVERY THE VALUE PROPOSITION	THE ABILITY OF A SYSTEM TO PERFORM SOME MEANINGFUL ACTION IN PURSUIT OF A USER'S GOALS DESCRIBED FROM THE USER'S PERSPECTIVE

BENEFITS		
USE CASES	**EXPERIENCE**	**VALUE PROP.**
IS HOW AN OFFERING, SOLUTION OR SYSTEM IS UTILIZED BY A PERSON, GROUP OR ORGANIZATION FOR A PARTICULAR PURPOSE OR NEED	IS WHAT A PERSON THINKS, FEELS, OR PERCEIVES BEFORE, DURING, OR AFTER USING A PRODUCT OR SERVICES	IS A PROMISE OF VALUE TO BE DELIVERED AND A BELIEF FROM A PERSON THAT THE VALUE WILL BE EXPERIENCED. IT IS SUMMARIZED IN THE 5 CS OF THE VALUE PROPOSITION

—————————————— QUESTIONS ——————————————

> How would you compare your technology innovation efforts to those you must apply to business model innovation? How well do you do both?

> How well do you understand that the greatest challenge of all innovation is discovering and creating a new business model that will enable it to eventually scale?

> How well does your organization understand and apply the BMIT framework?

> How willing is your leadership to truly pay the PRICE to accelerate innovation?

CHAPTER TWELVE

Mindfully Measuring Innovation Discipline

If you don't measure innovation, can you really discipline it? Will doing so trigger the observer effect and alter the innovation's outcome as a result of the measurement?

Why wouldn't you measure innovation? Nearly all of the tried-and-trusted business measures support mindless operational efficiency. Annual budgets, earning forecasts, variance analysis, financial, managerial, and activity-based accounting, and all of their derivative measures allow businesses to provide a rich and descriptive understanding of the past and present. And in periods of predictable stability and certainty, they provide very accurate measures to help those businesses navigate the future. Unfortunately, these traditional performance measures become less useful in helping you chart your course in uncertainty and applying innovation's discipline.

The problem is that innovation is tough to measure, and the more uncertain the environment, the tougher it is to measure. But the need to measure mindful innovative disciplines still remains.

With measurement, you can ensure that you are enabling and supporting the emergence of the innovations necessary for survival by creating the business of tomorrow while running the business of today..

In this chapter we provide two useful tools for measuring and managing innovation. The first is an innovation assessment survey we have developed that follows the BKD framework and Innovation Cycle outlined in chapter 7. It provides a baseline of your current mindfulness and mindlessness when it comes to innovation so you know where you should focus in implementing and transforming your innovation operating model. The second is a framework for measuring effectiveness in applying the disciplines associated with an innovation operating model. Theses measures require looking at the entire Innovation Lifecycle as well as the inputs, activities, outputs, and impact that support your efforts.

Beware of Over-Measuring That Kills Innovation

There is a word of caution about measuring discreet innovations as opposed to the portfolio across the phases of the lifecycle. Too often we have seen organizations try to impose a rigid and harsh measurement discipline early on in the lifecycle of the innovation. The unfortunate result killed off many would-be great innovations. The collateral effect sapped the creative passion and energy from their people.

In previous chapters we discussed ways to measure the quality of good ideas that deserve to be incubated and accelerated. The fundamental principles behind these types of measures are basically to gauge the outcomes and risks you are trying to address in each phase of the lifecycle. For example, in Discovery, we are primarily measuring the number and quality of the ideas to determine whether or not the proof of concept or principle seems reasonable, feasible, and possible as a new source of value creation. Incubation is focused on measuring technical risks, while Acceleration determines commercial risks. The underlying logic of measuring is that as the innovation advances across the lifecycle, the measurement dimensions and rigor increases.

Measures When Spinning Versus Outdoor Riding

Before you start your first spin class in a gym, you often take time to conduct a baseline assessment to measure your maximal oxygen consumption, heart rate, weight, endurance, and general fitness. This baseline helps you know how to design your spin-training program to achieve specific fitness goals and objectives. As your spin-training progresses, you can compare your results to measure how far you have progressed and how close you have come to meeting your goals.

During each spin session in the gym you find there are many measures you can take to understand your level of performance. You can measure heart rate, cadence, tension on the flywheel, time, and length of activity. You can compare these measures to other people's or your past performance. In a gym, the environmental factors such as wind resistance, temperature, lighting, noise, road conditions, etc. are all constants and controlled.

In the real world of biking, however, all the environmental variables are in play and produce significant uncertainty in determining outcomes. Add head wind, rain, and cold, and you will not only slow down the biker but also increase the danger and risk of accident. Without proper nutrition, protection, and training, hills, intense sun, and heat can lead to dehydration and heat stroke.

Some of the most interesting measures when biking involve the variability of pace, cadence, and heartbeats created by changes in elevation, temperature, and wind resistance.

When road biking, the variation in these measures will generally fall within a limited range since the road surfaces and routes are known, fixed, and predictable. But once you head onto a mountain path, all bets are off. Rain can wash away a path, and water can make an existing path impassable. The ease of taking new or any number of alternative side paths, any of which could end up taking you to the final destination, makes measuring and comparing measures more difficult. New sensor technologies and GPS have provided ways to gauge many of these dimensions of activity to help you detect patterns and maps never seen before.

Similarly, the measure we developed for the equivalent of the stationary biking in a gym, where the Lean Six Sigma approach permits the elimination of and control for many variables are inadequate for the more rough-and-tumble outdoor biking activities. That's where so many additional variables are in play, producing greater uncertainty and risk. All types of biking would benefit from conducting an initial fitness assessment in order to structure your bike training strategy and program, select specific goals and objectives, and measure those in a disciplined and objective manner. So let's start with creating your innovation baseline with an initial assessment and then discuss innovation measures and the application of an innovation scorecard.

Finding Your Innovation Baseline

We have found that many organizations and leaders need to first understand their starting point regarding their innovation capabilities and capacities to know how they can better ride the Innovation Cycle. They need to answer questions such as "How do we enable our employees to *become* innovators?" "How well do we enable them to *know* how to innovate?" "How well do we support them in *doing* innovation?"

We have created a fifty-three-question survey instrument to assess an organization's overall BKD score along the spectrum between mindful and mindless. The instrument also provides scores in each of the BKD dimensions to see the relative strengths and weaknesses in each dimension. Some organizations we have worked with have used this type of instrument with thousands of employees across all geographic, functional, and hierarchical levels within the organization to see where their greatest innovation challenges lie. While we have provided the questions to this survey below, you can also access it at www.innovationcycle.com. That's where you can use this electronic version to administer it across your organization and see your calculated scores to help you know where to start in creating or transforming your innovation operating model. Such an assessment provides an accurate measure of the cultural climate, capability, and capacity toward innovation across the organization.

This assessment provides several statements regarding each of the ten dimensions of the Innovation Cycle and asks the respondent to complete a 1–5 Likert scale to indicate if they: (1) strongly disagree, (2) disagree, (3) neither agree nor disagree, (4) agree, or (5) strongly agree with the statement.

Becoming: Enable the Creative Identity to Emerge

Valuing Innovation: Our organization and leadership values promote and enable innovation.

1. Leaders demonstrate a willingness to challenge the status quo and take calculated risks on innovative ideas and activities.

2. Leaders are tolerant of failure and see failure as a necessary part of the learning and innovation process and seek to enable fast, frequent, and frugal failure.

3. There is a culture of openness to new ideas and a willingness to take calculated risks to achieve innovative objectives.

4. Processes are designed in such a way to support and nurture creative thinking and innovation activities.

5. Employees are encouraged to take free and unstructured time to think and collaborate creatively to develop innovative new opportunities.

Visioning Innovation: Our organization and leadership create and promote visions requiring innovation.

1. There is a shared vision of what innovation means for the organization and what could be achieved.

2. Leadership demonstrates a commitment to innovation vision through its behaviors and day-to-day activities with staff and stakeholders.

3. The organization continuously generates, gathers, and screens creative ideas from staff, customers, suppliers, and competitors to drive innovative activities.

4. The organization continuously scans for trends, emerging ideas, and technology developments *within* and *outside* the industry sector.

5. The organization has a clear understanding of the innovation landscape that its innovation activities are focused on addressing.

Foreseeing Innovation: Our organization and leadership create tension gaps between the current and foreseen future.

1. The organization regularly identifies opportunities for new and improved products and services.

2. The organization has processes in place for ensuring that the opportunities and risks of creative ideas and innovation activities are created, selected, evaluated, and developed.

3. The innovation process requires the application of scenarios to explore various perspectives and alternatives regarding the potential for innovation activities.

4. The organization compares the value created from all kinds of innovative new products and services against that of similar organizations.

5. Leadership looks for areas of future failure and leverages these insights to create organizational energy (creative tension) to break current inertia and move the organization in new directions.

Exploring Innovation: Our organization and leadership explore and promote the exploration of innovative opportunities.

1. Relevant information is easily and widely accessible to support innovative activities.

2. The work environment supports the development of creative ideas and prevents barriers to innovation through breakthrough change.

3. Support is provided to staff for development of the necessary skills and competencies to be creative in a structured and repeatable way.

4. The organization collaborates with stakeholders and potential partners *within* and *outside* the industry sector to drive innovation.

5. Staff is encouraged to build and sustain relationships and external networks as part of their innovative activities.

6. Employees believe they possess the creative ability to make breakthrough innovations.

7. Employees see innovating new products, services, and business models as part of their job description.

Knowing: Understanding the Innovation Cycle

Enlisting Others in Innovation: Our organization and leadership enlist and enable others to enlist individuals in innovative activities.

1. Leadership sees individual passion around innovation as a key motivator for action and enables individuals to self-organize to create teams to pursue innovation activities.

2. The organization actively recruits and develops staff with necessary skills and competencies to support innovative activities.

3. Staff is empowered to get involved in the development and implementation of innovation activities.

4. Internal collaboration (e.g., multidisciplinary project teams) is used to drive innovation activities.

5. The organization actively rotates employees through different roles to both develop the employees' innovative capabilities and to ensure the success of innovation activities.

Strategizing Innovation: Our organization and leadership enable the creation of strategies that drive innovation.

1. Goals and objectives for innovation are defined as part of the organization's strategy.

2. The organization's strategy is regularly reviewed to take account of emerging opportunities for innovation.

3. The strategic goals and objectives for innovation are used to prioritize innovation activities and the development of new and improved products, services, and business models.

4. Innovation targets are set for all staff, and staff understands their individual roles, responsibilities, and requirements for achieving them.

5. Leadership understands the difference amoung strategy, operations, and innovation and the link between growth and innovation and sees these are moral imperatives for sustainability.

Capitalizing Innovation: Our organization and leadership enable multiple source of capital resources to promote innovation.

1. The organization has flexibility within the budgeting process to invest in innovation activities that emerge during the year and that were not part of the original budget.

2. Appropriate resources (i.e., people, time, finance, IT, etc.) are allocated at the right time to support innovative activities.

3. Resources for the development of new innovative products and services are allocated based on how closely they match the organization's strategic objectives.

4. The organization has multiple funding programs and mechanisms to invest in innovation actions to create proof of concept, proof of principle, prototypes, and pilots.

5. The organization compares the performance of its internal innovation process/system/structures against that of similar organizations.

Doing: Delivering Value-Creating Novelty

Incentivizing Innovation: Our organization and leadership provides the incentives necessary to drive and enable innovation.

1. Innovative behavior and activity are used as a key measure for rewarding leadership effectiveness in the organization.

2. Staff are respected, recognized, and rewarded for their contributions to innovation even though most innovative endeavors will fail.

3. The organization rewards and recognizes those who share knowledge and leverages social media technologies to facilitate knowledge sharing.

4. The organization has an innovation scorecard to measure the inputs, outputs, activities, and impact of innovation and rewards employees based on their level of engagement.

5. The organization measures the level of staff satisfaction and shares the results broadly throughout the organization.

Managing Innovation: Our organization and leadership enable the identification, quantification, measurement, and management of innovation risks.

1. Tools and techniques are used to develop innovative solutions to improve product and service offerings.

2. The organization has a range of financial indicators in place to measure innovation performance.

3. The organization has a range of non-financial indicators in place to measure innovation performance.

4. The organization measures the financial investment and return on its new and improved products and services.

5. The organization measures the brand and reputational benefits and impact from its innovative activities.

Exploiting Innovation Opportunities: Our organization and leadership enables the exploitation of innovative opportunities.

1. Intellectual property is actively considered, managed, and developed.

2. There are knowledge management systems in place to capture and share experiences, ideas, insights, and lessons learned.

3. The outcomes from innovation activities are used to enhance the organization's brand and reputation.

4. The outcomes from innovation activities are used to develop other opportunities, products, services, and business models.

5. The organization ensures it fully capitalizes on the outcomes (including increased brand awareness/reputation/recruitment and retention of skills) of its innovation activities and projects by involving appropriate stakeholders.

6. Innovative ideas in one area of the organization are routinely scaled and applied to the entire company.

After completing this assessment, most organizations will be surprised by what they find. Generally, you will see that those most interested in innovation tend to be the most senior and the most junior people in the organization. Why is that? What is wrong with middle management?

Through interviews within organizations where we have seen this phenomenon, we have asked people at all levels of the organization to explain these survey findings. What we have seen is that senior leadership imposes discipline on middle managers to efficiently run the business of today with virtually no focus or responsibility to create the business of tomorrow. What this means is that middle managers find innovation a distraction and counterproductive to their Lean Six Sigma discipline. For this reason, when their more junior team members excitedly share possible innovations in processes, products, services, technologies, or business models, middle managers provide no freedom or resources to further explore these opportunities. This is clearly a lack of ambidextrous leadership from the top.

This type of assessment has also revealed the difference in innovation capacity and capabilities among the various divisions, functions, and geographies of an organization. Understanding the root cause of these differences is important when trying to figure out how to design and implement your innovation operating model, where you should first start, and what type of progress can be made over different time frames.

Once you create your initial baseline and design and implement your innovation operating model, you will then need to provide a robust and regular measurement framework to identify, quantify, measure, and manage your efforts. Doing so will help you drive a more mindful discipline into the DNA of all your people and enable them to become creative geniuses.

There's No Simple Way to Measure Innovation

Leaders often want a simple measure for overall innovation similar to the one they use in their Lean Six Sigma operations. We don't think such a measure will ever exist.

Corporate finance theory, along with financial and managerial accounting, has developed many value measures of performance to assist in making decisions. Accountants focus on measures like return on investment, equity, or assets (ROI, ROE, or ROA) based on historic financial returns. The utility of this is that they can be a proxy for future expectations. The more sophisticated measures are based on corporate finance theory. They arise from conducting forecasts of future cash flows and discounting the value of these future cash flows. This is called discounted cash flows (DCF).

A variant on this approach is to net cash inflow from outflows to offer a net present value (NPV) on a forecasted and discounted basis. A related and similar method is to estimate the internal rate of return (IRR) that these future cash flows represent and then compare that to the organization's internal desired future risk adjusted rate of return to see if it meets or exceeds this target. These methods are useful when dealing with high degrees of certainty, but they fail when many different future scenarios are possible and any one is merely plausible.

So far, no one has come up with any measure for innovation as simple as ROI, DCF, NPV, or IRR. While we would love there to be a return on innovation investment (ROII), the very nature of innovation makes this impossible. Innovation should instead be seen as a meta-capability or an organizational capacity that is so intertwined in organizational DNA that it can't be attributed to a single department, much less cleanly weighed and measured. It therefore can become as difficult to measure as other meta-capabilities, such as good customer service or high employee engagement. With each of these, it would be almost impossible to determine what percentage of a dollar of profit was a result of great service, engaged employees, or the innovative DNA in the organizational culture. Innovation requires focus on providing a discipline that applies interaction, variation, and selection to accelerate and expand learning through failure. By contrast, typical mindless measures focus on eliminating variation, since you want the same outcome ever time. This cause them to also eliminate what could be considered as wasteful interactions. This then leads to measures that further constrain choice so that all decisions are controlled by standard operating procedures to delivery highly reliable, efficient and predicable outcomes

Creating an Innovation Scorecard Provides the Best Approach

For this reason, we have found that, when measuring innovation, it is best to use an innovation scorecard framework. It collects a number of measures that inform on whether or not the three rings—Becoming, Knowing, and Doing—that drive innovation are in practice and working. The innovation scorecard framework we developed is based on the following four pillars. These pillars mirror in many ways the approach around business model innovation outlined in the previous chapter and enable you to provide measures for each of four phases of the Innovation Lifecycle.

1. **Input:** This pillar looks at the structural elements (such as funding and human capital that support employees, inventors, and other stakeholders) across the Innovation Lifecycle.

2. **Activities:** This pillar looks at the scope of innovation services offered and practices performed to drive interaction, variation, and selection both within the organization (inreach) and with external stakeholders (outreach) to build a culture of innovation.

3. **Output:** This pillar looks at the efficiency and effectiveness of the organization in driving fast, frequent, frugal failure. This will include measures around MVPs, inventions, and commercialization along the entire Innovation Lifecycle.

Figure 21

INNOVATION SCORECARD TO MEASURE AND MANAGE INNOVATION

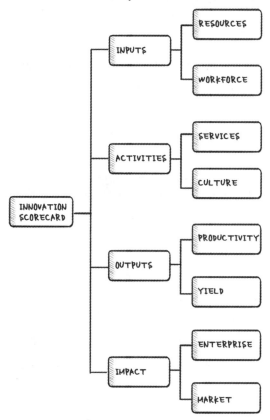

4. **Impact**: This pillar looks at the overall contribution of innovation to society, including the institution (internal) and the market (external). This can be measured in new revenues, lives saved, products delivered, industries transformed, etc.

Under each pillar are two varying dimensions of innovation that we measure, making a total of eight underlying dimensions that answer a set of key questions to reveal the success in enabling innovation across the enterprise and within the market.

Dimension	Key Questions Answered by Measures
Input	
Direct Resources	How do you provide adequate funding and access to other resources to enable innovation? What is the budget of the innovation support team? How do you provide separate funding sources and governance for each phase of the Innovation Lifecycle? What is the innovation budget for each business that goes beyond R&D?
Supporting Workforce	How do you provide everyone the option and free time to be creative and contribute to innovation? How do you support businesses by providing an innovation support team? How do you encourage and enable diverse groups of people to collaborate in creative problem solving? How many hours does leadership spend on innovation?
Activities	
Services Offered	What services does the innovation support team provide to the organization across the Innovation Lifecycle? What type and number of events are held within and without the organization to enable serendipitous interactions? How active are the social innovation and ideation programs? How do you leverage technology to better support and enable these efforts? How do you support incubating and accelerating?
Engagement Culture	How do you share and communicate the innovation goals, objectives, strategies, and performance? How do you celebrate and reward creativity, failure, and innovation? How many employees are trained in innovation? How many employees use innovation as a key performance objective and participate in innovation activities? How are employees' annual evaluations tied to completing innovation and improvement projects?
Output	
Productivity	How efficient is the process of turning ideas into innovations? How much time is required for failure and to move ideas from phase to phase in the Innovation Lifecycle? How many people are engaged in developing and advancing ideas across each phase of the Innovation Lifecycle?
Yield	How effective is the process of turning ideas into innovations? What is your failure rate by phase of the Innovation Lifecycle and your investment in failure (learning)? What is your conversion rate by phase of the Innovation Lifecycle and your investment in success?

Impact	
Enterprise	What are the internal benefits of innovation to the organization? What level of cost savings arise through innovative efforts? What is the employee satisfaction and engagement with the innovation programs?
Market	What are the external benefits to the organization of innovation? What is the customer perception of the organization regarding innovation? What proportion of annual revenues come from new innovative products introduced within the past five years? What proportion of revenues originated through open innovation and co-creative collaboration? What is the net present value (NVP) of the innovation portfolio across all phases of the lifecycle?

As we helped organizations apply this overall innovation scorecard framework to discipline their innovative efforts, we found that each organization develops their own unique version of the scorecard based on their priorities, goals, and approach to innovation. What we have also seen is that they will seek out and identify best practices associated with the implementation of an innovation operating model. Then they will generate measures to align with the best practices that they want to focus on and/or improve in.

For example, we developed an innovation scorecard for some leading academic institutions to help them compare their innovation operating model performance to their peers and to their historic performance. For each measure they identified a best innovation practice they both measured and tried to improve.

When this client compared themselves to fifteen peers across the pillars and dimensions, they found the same fro their peers. In fact, to their surprise, they found that even some organizations that were the worst overall performed well in one or two areas. From this exercise they realized they could learn best practices from many different kinds of organizations, not just from the best. From this exercise, they identified nearly 50 best practices from their peers, and selected a dozen to implement.

The outcome was that the client restructured their innovation program to adopt some best practices they found among their peers. This required some organizational and personnel changes to achieve the desired results, which, in retrospect, impacted very positively on their innovation performance.

The bottom line for this organization is that had they not developed their innovation scorecard, they would not have understood where and how to modify their innovation operating model by adopting different structures and practices to improve their performance.

Less Is More When Creating an Innovation Scorecard

To begin to form an innovation scorecard with our clients, we bring a long list of questions and things we would like to measure. Oftentimes, as you create your scorecard, it can be very helpful to ask and answer more questions than you would plan to put in a regularly produced scorecard. This may be because you don't know which measures would be the best to produce on a regular basis and you hope to refine this through the design process. Or it may be because there are many things you want to learn and benchmark through the process of gathering all these measures in a structured and organized effort.

As organizations look to produce a recurring innovation scorecard, they find they must simplify their measures and select only the most important and valuable in supporting their innovation operating model. A scorecard that has too many measures and that is difficult and cumbersome to generate will not last very long or be very useful.

The academic institution we referenced initially counted sixty measures to learn as much about themselves and their peer organizations as possible. But then they simplified this to less than twenty-four. Another client started with over thirty measures and then brought their final tally down to a little over a dozen.

The key to creating the right number of measures is to focus on the design, structure, and key practices of your innovation operating model and the disciplines you are focused on supporting.

Without Innovation Measures, You Don't Know How You Are Doing

Without an appropriate baseline, you don't know your current strengths and weaknesses when it comes to enabling and supporting innovation. You don't know where you need to provide better structural and practice supports to implement an appropriate innovation operating model. But an initial assessment is clearly not enough to ensure a more mindful discipline. You then must follow the implementation of the innovation operating model through an innovation scorecard to provide the measures necessary to apply the discipline needed. Without both an assessment and a scorecard, you can't ensure the mindful creativity necessary to create the company of tomorrow.

REMEMBER ——————————————————————————

- ✔ If it isn't measured, it isn't managed.

- ✔ Innovation can be measured, but not in a conventional way.

- ✔ We created a fifty-three-question survey instrument to assess an individual's or organization's overall BKD score along the spectrum between mindful and mindless (see www.innovationcycle.com).

- ✔ Additionally, we developed a scorecard framework that enables you to measure innovation based upon input, activities, output, and impact.

—————————— QUESTIONS ——————————

> ❭ How well do you measure innovation across the Innovation Lifecycle?

> ❭ How well do you understand your current capacity and capabilities to innovate as an organization?

> ❭ How well do you understand the gaps between your stated values and aspirations and your current state and approach to innovation?

Epilogue

Astory is told of two tribes that that were constantly at war. One tribe lived high in the mountains and was expert at rock climbing and hunting for food as a means of survival. The other tribe lived in a valley beneath the mountains and made its livelihood off agriculture. One day the mountain tribe realized they were running low on food, and in order to survive, they would need to raid the crops of the valley tribe. As the valley tribe saw the mountain tribe descending, preparations were made for all-out war. The war lasted for three days before the mountain tribe retreated with what few spoils they could carry.

As the chaos of the war died down and life in the valley got back to normal, it was discovered that a baby had been kidnapped. This infuriated the valley tribe, as this marked a new low in the brutality of their enemy. The chief of the valley tribe assembled his finest warriors and ordered them to retrieve the baby so as to make right this great wrong. The warriors prepared their provisions and began the journey up the mountain. The march up the mountainside was difficult, given they didn't know how to navigate the rocky rails and sheer cliffs of the mountain people. It seemed each tactic or alternate route they attempted ended in failure. And as their provisions ran out, the warriors became discouraged. Without the tools and knowledge to hunt mountain game, they had no choice but to turn back to the valley in failure.

As they began down the mountain, one of the warriors noticed in the distance a woman walking down the mountain. As the woman came closer, the warriors noticed she was carrying a baby in her arms. Soon the warriors recognized the woman as the mother of the kidnapped baby. The warriors ran to her in astonishment and asked, "How did you make the journey up the mountain and rescue your baby when the tribe's finest warriors weren't successful?"

The woman responded, "It's not your baby."

The mother's identity of "**I am** my baby's mother" proved to be the difference between success and failure in the challenge before her. She faced the same cliffs and trails and dealt with the same hunger as the warriors, yet her identity—her being—drove her forward. Assuming a powerful identity is the point at which *wants* become *musts* and *trying* is replaced with *doing*. The warriors likely had more *knowing* and *doing* experience, trying to climb the mountain and hunt for food. But what they lacked was *becoming*. The mother was more patient with her failures in climbing the mountain, less likely to feel like a failure when one tactic didn't work, and more willing to go hungry for longer periods of time because she didn't merely want to try to retrieve her baby. Rescuing the baby was a *must* driven by her *identity*.

You Can Climb That Mountain Too

Most failures in organizations are not the result of not knowing what to do (Knowing and Doing). As previously mentioned, there are over a thousand business books published every year, and the Internet has made knowledge so ubiquitous that most answers to your difficult organizational challenges can be easily found. The difference is that the intensity of your Knowing and Doing is greatly enhanced when you operate under a powerful identity. Like the valley mother, it is as though you open up more bandwidth for action than you ever thought possible. When you tap into that bandwidth, your creative genius can shine through.

The promising news is that the hardwiring required to become an innovative genius already resides in each of us. Your brain is already equipped to offer up innovative solutions—if you know how to mindfully use it. The identity of "I am an innovator" doesn't need to be managed as much as it needs to be unleashed. Most of us, by adulthood, have forgotten we are creative geniuses and require a reboot of our natural mental capabilities. We need to undergo the transformation from a being who believes "**I am** not the innovative type" to **becoming** a person who can honestly state, "**I am** a creative genius." Fortunately, shifting gears between the two identities can be easier than it looks, because the ability already exists.

There is a bridge between being and becoming that each of us must travel across. Yes, you might feel disingenuous purporting to be a creative genius when your ideas don't work or when your innovative mental hardware is a little rusty from lack of use. The mother and the warriors of the valley tribe each felt these feelings. Each of them likely thought, "**I am** not a mountain tribe person. I can't scale these cliffs!" Notice how identities grounded in failure are always phrased in the negative: "I am not" or "I can't." The difference between the mother and the warriors was that the mother channeled a higher and more powerful identity, which essentially said, "**I am** my baby's mother, and valley mothers can scale cliffs just as well as mountain warriors."

To make the shift from being to becoming often requires what the poet Robert Frost called "believing ahead of your evidence." To be successful, innovators must believe they are innovators during failures as well as successes. The reason is simple: failure is evidence that you are an innovator. Those who identify more with a fear of failure than with innovating begin, in essence, to walk down the mountain because they don't possess an identity that allows them to scale the cliffs. It certainty doesn't give them the courage to get on a mountain bike.

The identity of an innovator looks at failures and successes as two sides of the same coin. The failure is useful as it creates tension that the innovator can learn from. These failures provide clues as to whether you are getting hotter or colder in relation to your ultimate goal. They also signal whether you are on the wrong bike all together. Harnessing these tensions, as opposed to resisting tensions, implies that there is a useful energy in the tensions caused by failure. Unfortunately, the most common response in organizations is to resist the tensions of failure, thereby wasting the surplus energy contained in failure.

If failure is a concept that is not in your current definition of being an innovator, then you must mindfully reframe what it means to be an innovator. You must not just look at Steve Jobs and the launch of the iPhone; you must look at Steve Jobs being fired from Apple as well. You must not just look at Albert Einstein as the genius who discovered the theory of relativity, but also at his time in a lowly patent office. Failure or setbacks often provide the fuel, motivation, and new information that allow the true creative genius to emerge.

As You Get Ready to Go

We hope that this book contains not only the Knowing and Doing practices and structures to effectively discover, incubate, accelerate, and scale innovations, but that it also informs you how to address innovation with the brain in mind. In each of these phases of innovation, organizations tend to treat these steps as though they are activities that take place only in a reality outside of the human mind. We hope to have emphasized that all successful innovation starts with a powerful and immovable identity around innovation and that this identity can only be maintained if you resist the mindless and biologically based resistance caused by fear of failure. Only through mindful leadership can organizations unleash employees' identities as innovators. In addition to creating these identities, leaders must also sustain the identity of innovators by patiently and mindfully reframing failures as learning and fear as biological noise.

By joining the realms of Being, Knowing, and Doing, we hope to provide you with a comprehensive and holistic approach to innovation that is not only useful but also drives engagement and purpose of every employee within the organization. As leaders, employees, entrepreneurs, and innovators, we must free ourselves to hop off our stationary cycles and ride mountain bikes from time to time. It is then that we all can explore and discover exciting new ideas and opportunities and unleash the creative genius within.

> I thought of that while riding my bicycle.
> **—ALBERT EINSTEIN**
> ON COMING UP WITH THE
> THEORY OF RELATIVITY

Index